Showdown
in Virginia

Showdown in Virginia

The 1861 Convention and the Fate of the Union

Edited by William W. Freehling
and Craig M. Simpson

University of Virginia Press
Charlottesville and London

University of Virginia Press
© 2010 by William W. Freehling and Craig M. Simpson
All rights reserved
Printed in the United States of America on acid-free paper

First published 2010

9 8 7 6 5 4 3 2

LIBRARY OF CONGRESS CATALOGING-IN-PUBLICATION DATA

Showdown in Virginia : the 1861 convention and the fate of the Union / edited by
William W. Freehling and Craig M. Simpson.
    p.   cm.
Includes bibliographical references.
   ISBN 978-0-8139-2948-4 (cloth : alk. paper) — ISBN 978-0-8139-2964-4 (pbk. : alk. paper)
   1. Virginia—Politics and government—1861–1865—Sources. 2. Secession—Virginia—
Sources. 3. Taxation—Virginia—History—19th century—Sources. 4. Speeches, addresses,
etc., American—Virginia. 5. United States—Politics and government—1861–1865—Sources.
I. Freehling, William W., 1935– II. Simpson, Craig M., 1942–
   F230.S58 2010
   973.1309755—dc22   2009030984

Material from George Henkle Reese, *Proceedings of the Virginia State Convention of 1861,
February 13–May 1* (Volumes 1–4). © Virginia State Library, 1965. All rights reserved. Used
by permission of the Library of Virginia, 2009. Any further use, publication, or reproduc-
tion of this material must be approved by the Library of Virginia.

For
The Virginia Foundation
for the Humanities

And
In Memory of David M. Potter
and Don E. Fehrenbacher

Contents

Introduction

The Old South's 1860–61 disunion crisis transpired in dissimilar Lower South and Upper South phases. Each phase featured a searching debate in a key locale. The earlier verbal spectacle, in the Lower South, occurred in Georgia's antebellum state capital, Milledgeville, shortly after Abraham Lincoln's presidential election.[1] The subsequent oratorical showdown, in the Upper South, commenced in Virginia's capital, Richmond, shortly after the last Lower South state left the Union.

During the three months following Abraham Lincoln's November 6, 1860, popular election to the presidency, disunionists triumphed in the Lower South's seven states. They then faltered in the Upper South's eight states. South Carolina, Mississippi, Florida, Alabama, Georgia, Louisiana, and Texas all departed the Union between December 20, 1860, and February 1, 1861. In 1860 this most tropical tier of U.S. states, with 46.5 percent of its inhabitants enslaved, possessed 58.5 percent of the Old South's slaves. The area grew 85 percent of Dixie's cotton, 96 percent of its sugar, and 100 percent of its rice. In these deepest U.S. tropics, the short length of Georgia's debate over disunion typified the Lower South's rush toward revolution. The Georgia rhetorical showdown consumed only five mid-November evenings.

In contrast, both of the two tiers of Upper South states temporized for five months. The population of the Upper South's most northern tier, comprising the Border South states of Delaware, Maryland, Kentucky, and Missouri, consisted of only 12 percent slaves. None of these states left the Union, not even after war (and emancipation) came. The one prewar secession convention in the Border South, Missouri's, typified Unionists' borderland sway. Secessionists lost, 89-1.

1. William W. Freehling and Craig M. Simpson, eds., *Secession Debated: Georgia's Showdown in 1860* (New York, 1992). For extensive discussion and documentation of positions in this introduction, see William W. Freehling, *The Road to Disunion* (2 vols., New York, 1990–2007). For superb perspective on Virginia during the secession winter, see Daniel W. Crofts, *Reluctant Confederates: Upper South Unionists in the Secession Crisis* (Chapel Hill, NC, 1989).

The more southern tier of Upper South states, the appropriately named Middle South, cut between the Lower and Border South geographically and culturally. While only one in eight Border South inhabitants was a slave and almost half of the Lower South's residents suffered enslavement, three in ten Middle South inhabitants experienced that degradation. While the four Border South states never left the Union and the seven Lower South states seceded quickly, the four Middle South states—Virginia, North Carolina, Tennessee, and Arkansas—embraced disunion only after the Civil War commenced. While Georgia's prime rhetorical showdown over disunion lasted just a few days and the Border South never experienced such a phenomenon, the greatest Middle South secession debate, the Virginia convention's, dragged on through two months of indecisive mornings, afternoons, and evenings.

The protracted length of the Virginia convention's debate, filling four thick (and fine) modern volumes, has deterred everyone except specialists. This volume's condensed version of the deliberations widens access to Upper South secessionist and Unionist arguments. It highlights how violence drives procrastinators to decision. And it recovers the convention's almost forgotten oratorical climax, a brilliant exploration of the clash between constitutional and military necessities.

2   Virginia's national and Southern importance magnified the convention's significance. The Virginia Dynasty commanded the White House during twenty-four of the U.S. republic's first thirty-two years. Virginia's John Marshall presided over the U.S. Supreme Court still longer. Virginia's importance waned thereafter. But in 1860 the state remained first in the South in total population, first again in number of slaves, first yet again in acres under cultivation and farms' value.

This premier Southern state contained the divided South's every element. Two mountain chains—the Blue Ridge and the Alleghenies—threaded across the state, dividing Virginia into the Slave South's three essential zones. West of the Allegheny Mountains lay spottily enslaved western Virginia, exemplar of the Border South. Between the two mountain chains lay the Virginia Valley, with the moderate percentage of slaves typical of the Middle South. East of the Blue Ridge Mountains lay Virginia's oldest and most enslaved regions, the Piedmont and the Tidewater, with the heavy concentration of slaves that characterized most of the Lower South.

If divided Virginia could agree unanimously on an alternative to civil war, so could the whole South. If all seven other Upper South states followed Virginia out of the Union, Abraham Lincoln's truncated nation would have little chance of triumph (as Lincoln admitted). If Virginia and the entire Upper South stayed in the Union, Jefferson Davis's constricted Confederacy, containing but a third of the South's people, would have scant possibility of survival.

On February 4, 1861, Lower South rebels convened in Montgomery, Alabama, to form their new nation. On the same day, Virginia voters elected convention delegates, charged with recommending which nation the state should sustain. *Recommending* is the word. The Virginia legislature asked the voters to select convention delegates and to establish the delegates' mandate. Could a convention vote for secession suffice to withdraw Virginians' consent to the Union government? Or must the citizens subsequently ratify their representatives' disunion ordinance?

The state's voters answered on February 4, by a two-to-one margin, that a popular referendum must approve any convention ordinance. Virginians living east of the Blue Ridge, domain of most of the state's slaveholders, split evenly on the requirement. Voters residing west of the Blue Ridge, locale of far more slaveless areas, insisted on the referendum requirement five to one. Western Virginians' lopsided vote crafted a constitutional stop sign. Eastern slaveholders must not speed ahead with disunion unless and until both a convention majority and a popular majority withdrew their consent to the Union government.

The February 4 popular vote for convention delegates indicated that no majority for any action yet existed. On February 13 the badly split convention assembled in the Hall of the House of Delegates inside Richmond's State Capitol. The next day the 152 delegates moved to that city's Hall of the Mechanics' Institute. There they debated inconclusively for over seven weeks before moving back to the Hall of the House of Delegates on April 8, just as dread decisions could no longer be avoided.

Initially, around one-sixth of the representatives, almost all from the heavily enslaved east, sought immediate secession. Another approximately one-sixth of the delegates, almost all from lightly enslaved northwestern counties, sought permanent Union, even if their old nation waged war against the new Southern Confederacy. In the indeterminate middle of these determined warriors wavered two-thirds of the convention delegates, seeking Union-saving grounds that all Virginians—and all Americans—would accept peaceably.

Still another event, commencing on that historic February 4, indicated the difficulty of locating a middle ground. In January the Virginia legislature had invited all states to send delegates to a so-called Washington (DC) Peace Conference, to begin on February 4. The conference, meeting without a single Lower South representative, spent three weeks seeking a compromise that would reunite Northern Republicans and Southern rebels. These would-be peacemakers ultimately endorsed, with one important change, the program designed by Kentucky's venerable senator John J. Crittenden.

Having assumed Henry Clay's senatorial seat, Crittenden aspired to be the latest Great Compromiser. In December 1860 Senator Crittenden proposed that Congress make the 36°30′ geographic line, extending from the southern border of Missouri westward to the eastern edge of California, a perpetual boundary between the nation's enslaved and free labor territorial domains. North of the line, Crittenden proposed, territorial slavery should be barred. South of the line, territorial slavery should be protected, including—and here was the potential deal breaker—slavery in territories "hereafter acquired."

That wording would have required federal protection of territorial slavery in any subsequently acquired Caribbean lands. Especially for that reason, President-elect Lincoln rejected the clause. Republicans sustained their president-elect, but Lower South senators insisted on "hereafter acquired." So Crittenden's formula died in the crucial Senate committee before December expired.

The Washington Peace Conference revived the Crittenden Compromise but without "hereafter acquired." The conference instead proposed that before the United States could acquire new territories, majorities of both free labor states' and slave labor states' senators must approve the acquisition. This alternative to "hereafter acquired" attracted less congressional support than Crittenden's original proposal. The substitute attracted even less secessionist support. The disunionists' George Wythe Randolph (Thomas Jefferson's youngest grandson) ridiculed the alternative during one of the Virginia convention's most memorable moments.

Most Virginia Unionists thus fell back on "hereafter acquired" as the more plausible compromise. Some of them urged an ironclad ultimatum: the North must instantly accept "hereafter acquired," or Virginia would instantly secede. Because Lincoln and his party had dismissed that Crittenden proposal, this form of Virginia unionism made disunion inevitable.

But another centerpiece of the program favored by many Virginia Unionists—a border conference of all slave states remaining in the Union—would have less surely led to disunion. True, some border conference advocates would require the proposed Upper South assemblage to issue an ultimatum to the North: accept the Crittenden Compromise immediately or suffer immediate secession. That insistence would have paved another inescapable path out of the Union.

Other Virginia advocates of a border conference, however, favored formidable roadblocks to routes toward the Confederacy. Some delegates, deploring disruptive rush, would give Northern states many months to reconsider if Yankees initially rejected a "hereafter acquired" ultimatum. Others would not dictate "hereafter acquired" or any Virginia formula to a border conference. Others favored a third nation, a so-called Central Confederacy, if no formula could reunite Union and Confederate states.

Whatever their favorite method to avoid instant embrace of the Confederacy, few Virginia Unionists possessed complete confidence that their panacea would work. Between Unionists' divisions on the best alternative and their wariness about exposing any strategy to action's acid test, procrastination triumphed. Endless speeches comfortably avoided uncomfortable choice.

Secessionists piled on more talk, lest Unionists agree on an alternative to the Confederacy. Unlike their opponents, these delayers concurred on the best policy. They all demanded that Virginia instantly join the Lower South's new nation. But would-be Confederates lacked the numbers to prevail. On April 4, when they forced the convention's only prewar vote on secession, they lost 88-45.

These Virginia losers found defeat insufferable. Two perceived perils made Virginia secessionists as desperate for disunion as Lower South rebels. First of all, slaves' most promising route to freedom, running away, threatened the institution most in its northern locales, where Yankee aid loomed closest. Blacks, although without a voice in the Virginia convention, here exerted as much impact as if they had possessed delegates.

Second, faltering Upper South secessionists, in comparison with surging Lower South rebels, confronted not only a greater fugitive slave danger but also a bolstered Yankee menace. During the Lower South's earlier secession crisis, immediate disunion's opponents had correctly argued that Lincoln's Republican Party, lacking a majority in either house of Congress, could enact no antislavery legislation. But after the seven Lower South states departed the Union, along with their U.S. congressmen and senators, Republican majorities dominated both houses of Congress.

Lincoln's party quickly used its newly invincible numbers to enact previously unpassable laws. The Republican majority admitted Kansas as a free state and raised protective tariffs on imported goods to a level not approached since the 1820s. Whatever the minority South's vulnerability before the Lower South seceded, the remaining eight Southern states in the Union faced a permanent Northern majority. Between their outrage at greater Northern power and their apprehension of greater slave unrest, Virginia disunionists could not abide their powerlessness to join their Lower South brothers. As their encounter with Virginia Unionists wore on and on, exasperated revolutionaries grew ever more determined to strike, if circumstances beyond the convention offered an opportunity.

3 Until warfare outside the state shattered the delay inside, the Unionists' speeches featured the conceit that Virginia's decision would determine the Union's fate. These moderates seemed to presume that the Virginia Dynasty of Washington, Jefferson, Madison, Monroe, and Marshall still reigned. "The eyes of the Country are now resting on Virginia," soared one of the Valley's leading citizens. "What a dreadful responsibility." The "Old Mother . . . will be heard and heeded when she calls to her surrounding Family: Peace—Be Still!"[2]

Gunfire outside, however, could drown out Virginians' cries to be still. Except for northwestern Virginians, the state's Unionists usually assumed that if war erupted between the Union and the Confederacy, Virginia's would-be peacemakers must become rebel riflemen. War, as usual, would force those on the fence to decide only one question: whom they most wished to kill. Most Virginians preferred to slay insulting Yankee coercers rather than erring Southern brothers. And even if Lincoln could not threaten slavery in a peaceable Union, slaveholders' defeat in a civil war might savage the institution.

2. James Davidson to George Yerber, Feb. 3, 1861, to A. T. Caperton, Feb. 6, 1861, Davidson Papers, State Historical Society of Wisconsin, Madison.

The issue of black slaves aside, most white Virginians cherished a crucial supposed state's right: the right of the people of a state to withdraw their consent to be governed. If the federal government coercively sought to force citizens of a seceded state to be governed without their consent, the first principle of republicanism would be annihilated. Seceding citizens would confront the first principle of enslavement: coercion without consent.

Most of Virginia's whites who lived near slaves, whether secessionists or Unionists, whether slaveholders or nonslaveholders, would defy Northern "enslavement" of Southern citizens. This defiance helps to answer a perennial Civil War question: why slaveless whites in slaveholding neighborhoods matched slaveholders' rage against federal coercers. Any federal action that black belt Virginians perceived as enslaving whites could overwhelm Virginia Unionists' peacemaking illusions, if a civil war erupted outside the convention.

4 Contrary to popular myth, the outbreak of military hostilities at Charleston's Fort Sumter on April 12 did not itself turn most Virginia Unionists against the Union. So long as the war seemed confined to Fort Sumter, the Virginia convention's Unionist majority hoped that the gunfire in Charleston harbor would be a temporary setback and ultimately irrelevant to their calling: pacifying the Union. The moment that shattered the Unionists' self-importance (and the Unionists' majority) came instead when President Lincoln issued his April 15 proclamation. That deathblow to procrastination summoned 75,000 state troops, with a quota soon demanded from every state (including 3,500 from Virginia), to force Lower South rebels back into the Union.

At first, stricken Middle South Unionists could not believe that Lincoln had (in their terms) blundered so tyrannically. When shocking verification swiftly arrived, important convention Unionists split two ways. William Ballard Preston, lately a Unionist, introduced a secession ordinance, to be submitted to Virginia voters for ratification on May 23. Then Robert Scott presented a substitute ordinance, giving the May 23 voters a choice between secession and a border conference.

On April 17, in the key test of the convention's response to Lincoln's proclamation, Scott's alternative to Preston's secession motion narrowly lost, 77-64. The tally showed that 45 percent of Virginia delegates still preferred other paths to a road straight to disunion. A shift of only seven votes would have at least temporarily deflected secession once again. In the face of that continued resistance of so many would-be Virginia peacemakers, Virginia secessionists' patience snapped.

A so-called Spontaneous People's Convention furthered secessionist convention delegates' determination to act without delay. This hardly spontaneous assemblage met in another Richmond hall, except when its members spilled onto the streets to stage fiery demonstrations. The conclave of mainly younger Virginia hotheads had gathered to force older Virginia Unionists' reluctant hands.

In and out of the alternate assembly hall, revolutionaries boiled with threats to kidnap the (Unionist) governor, expel Unionist convention delegates from Richmond, seize federal military installations in Virginia, and provoke an extralegal revolution. This illegal movement threatened secessionists' legitimacy. A nonofficeholders' rebellion also threatened Virginia's political class, the seasoned pros who had long governed from above with the voters' approval.

One of the most seasoned professionals at the convention—and among the most exasperated secessionists—now deployed rebellious extremists to bypass constitutional stop signs. On April 16 former governor Henry Wise organized a preemptive strike of extralegal militia units, seeking to seize the federal government's Harpers Ferry Arsenal on the Potomac River and its Gosport Navy Yard at Norfolk. Wise worried that, otherwise, the federal government would remove the choice armaments in these installations, so useful to sustain a revolution. He also feared that without decisive action the indecisive Virginia convention would never, "for God's sake, quit talking."[3] On April 17, in a dramatic convention scene shortly after the narrow defeat of Robert Scott's alternative to secession, Wise intimated that his recruits at this moment marched toward civil war against federal troops.

What sort of a response to the Spontaneous People's Convention's threat of illegitimate revolution was this, a rebellion ordered by the former governor before the convention decreed anything and before the Virginia voters endorsed the decree? Immediately after Wise's April 17 announcement, the convention's approval of Preston's secession ordinance drew some sting out of the question. Delegates voted 88-55 to recommend dis-

---

3. George H. Reese, ed., *Proceedings of the Virginia State Convention of 1861* (4 vols., Richmond, 1965), 3:515.

union to the May 23 voters. Then before Wise's troops struck, the sitting governor, John Letcher, under heavy secessionist pressure, gave the state's imminently ambushing soldiers his reluctant official sanction.

But what about the voters' decision, back on February 4, that secession required popular approval in a postconvention referendum? So asked the Unionists' John Baldwin on April 17, after Wise's provocative announcement. The troops' extralegal strike, despaired the Valley moderate, would preclude the May 23 voters from deciding whether secession was wise. Instead, true-blue Southerners would have to decide whether to repudiate their brave sons who had risked their lives against federal tyranny.

The skewed results of Virginia's May 23 referendum vindicated Baldwin's fears. The voters' 85 percent landslide for secession swelled beyond the convention's 55 percent margin against Scott's resolution and its 62 percent margin for Preston's ordinance. The ballooning margin showed that Wise's illegal violence had helped change the very basis of legal decision.

In the Lower South, military ambushes had had a similar impact. In early January, secessionist governors had seized their states' federal military installations before disunion had been approved. These presecession military strikes, in the name of military necessity, had sometimes turned close contests over secession into landslides for disunion. A resulting question, everywhere in the secessionist South, was whether elections distorted by such illegal violence, and replete with other voter intimidations, yielded legitimate tests of whether majorities had willingly withdrawn their states' consent to be governed.

When John Baldwin posed this question, former governor Wise, like the Lower South governors, pleaded military necessity. The people's welfare required that the people's liberties be suspended. Otherwise, removal of federal military supplies would weaken an imminent people's revolution. Against Wise's argument, Baldwin pleaded the sacredness of civil liberties. The people's referendum must not proceed under the gun, mocking the people's natural right to decide whether to withdraw consent. With Wise responding by elaborating the claims for military necessity and Baldwin retorting by extending the claim for civil liberties, the two Virginians staged one of the first and most penetrating American explorations of a timeless democratic issue.

5 At the time-bound moment when Wise struck, western Virginia nonslaveholders especially relished Baldwin's insistence that voters, not militiamen, must decide first on withdrawing consent to be governed. Northwestern voters' support had pushed the popular referendum requirement over the top in the February 4 delegate elections. These intransigent Unionists would not now submit to a secession ordinance finalized by slaveholders' guns, at the expense of whites' rights to a prior referendum on whether guns should be deployed.

Northwestern nonslaveholding yeomen urged that slaveholders' firepower had now unconscionably expanded Virginia's victims of enslavement. These nonslaveholders rarely had objected to enslavement of blacks. They had objected often and furiously to slaveholders' antiegalitarian dominion over whites in the name of shoring up dominion over blacks.

Or as western Virginians more graphically exclaimed, Wise's gunmen must not enslave whites—must not enslave them. In yeomen's accusation of white enslavement, as in Confederates' charges against Lincoln's allegedly enslaving army, the definition of slavery shifted. Only black slaves suffered the plight of being permanently owned property, bought and sold like cattle. But in the Republic where the consent of white equals lent republicanism its legitimacy, unequal government, especially without the consent of the governed, chillingly resembled enslavement. A self-respecting white would not be lorded over as if he were black, and especially not if his presumptuous lord had never received legitimate consent to such dominion.

Western Virginians here echoed Northern Republicans' repugnance for the Slave Power (antebellum Americans' term for slaveholders who wielded undemocratic power over whites, to consolidate tyranny over blacks).[4] Republicans charged that slaveholding politicians had inflicted multiple sores on white men's democracy, including despotic gag rules on antislavery congressional speakers, draconian pressure on Northern citizens to return fugitive slaves, dictatorial governance on territorial Kansans, and tyrannical threats of minority secession unless majorities yielded. The more racist Republicans marched to the presidential polls

---

4. This important theme in Northern politics receives illuminating emphasis in Michael F. Holt, *The Political Crisis of the 1850s* (New York, 1978), and Leonard L. Richards, *The Slave Power: The Free North and Southern Domination, 1790–1860* (Baton Rouge, LA, 2000).

in 1860 less to emancipate supposedly unequal blacks from slaveholders than to liberate equal whites from the Slave Power.

So too, western Virginia's delegates descended on the 1861 convention especially to prevent one slaveholder threat to white egalitarianism and to dissolve another. Northwestern delegates meant to save their constituents' prize: white men's egalitarian Union. Mountain yeomen's champions also meant to demolish their constituents' bane: unequal tax breaks that benefited and bolstered the slavocracy.

The convention's taxation issue stemmed from Virginia's 1851 constitutional provision to limit taxation of slave property. Without such a constitutional safeguard, slaveholders feared that nonslaveholding majorities might enact high taxes on the peculiar property. Then hard-pressed slaveholders might be forced to sell slaves out of state. Nonslaveholders answered that in an egalitarian republic, all forms of property must be taxed equally.

This taxation issue periodically disrupted the Virginia convention's proceedings as convulsively as the disunion issue. After securing the convention's secession decree, however, eastern delegates surrendered their constitutional bar to equal taxes, in hopes that northwesterners would surrender opposition to disunion. But to western Virginians, Henry Wise's premature ambush of federal installations trumped eastern slaveholders' taxation concessions. How did equal taxation compare with slaveholders' demolition of the egalitarian Union, or with rebel soldiers' revolutionary fait accompli before the required referendum on whether the people consented to revolution? Self-respecting northwestern Virginians would secede from Virginia rather than bow their necks to secessionist swords, in the manner of the unequal and unconsenting black slave.

Thus did Virginia's most irreconcilable factions—eastern slaveholders and Trans-Allegheny nonslaveholders—ultimately fight irreconcilable battles for the same principle. Both demanded democracy's prerequisite: consent of the governed. Neither would subject whites to slavery's curse: coercion without consent. Virginia secessionists would not allow a president to coerce Lower South rebels, after those citizens had withdrawn their consent to federal governance. Rebels against secessionist Virginia would not allow a former governor to seize federal firepower, before voters' decision on whether to withdraw consent. Thus western Virginians' secession from Virginia followed on the heels of Virginia's secession from the Union.

During the convention's first two indecisive months, the issue had been Lincoln's menace to black slavery. During the April 15–17 days of decision, the issue partially shifted to Lincoln's (and the secessionists') menace to white liberty. As debates over black bondage broadened into considerations of all enslavements, the differences between unionism and secessionism became ever starker. And as confrontations touched on predicaments of civil libertarians everywhere when immersed in military crisis, this epic debate illuminated even more than the causes of one democracy's civil war.

Editorial Procedures

An editorial masterwork made this volume possible: George H. Reese, editor, *Proceedings of the Virginia State Convention of 1861* (4 volumes, Richmond, 1965). Reese based his almost 3,000 pages of text on both the convention's four published volumes[1] (supplying chronological order, communications, reports, and documents but no speeches) and the University of Virginia's files of the Richmond semiweekly *Enquirer* (supplying the official stenographic reports of almost all convention speeches). Reese reprinted all the semiweekly *Enquirer*'s initial texts of speeches with very minor editorial changes (correcting some misspellings and typos, replacing a few obsolete spellings with modern versions, and removing some extraneous dashes after colons and between sentences). He added a helpful synopsis of each day's speeches. He also included, in endnotes, delegates' occasional revisions of their speeches, as subsequently printed in the semiweekly *Enquirer*.[2] Like all scholars of this subject, we cherish George Reese's exhaustive achievement.

But the very completeness of the massive Reese volumes (and the absence of an index) makes them as inaccessible to nonspecialists as they are valuable to specialists. Because the convention's debates remain instructive to all who relish American history, we aspired to reduce the discrepancy. By carefully selecting what seemed to us the most important and oratorically successful speeches and equally carefully deleting what seemed to us those speeches' most repetitive and/or unimportant passages, we sought to compress a great American verbal encounter into its widely readable essence.

1. All published in Richmond and all available at the Library of Virginia (which published Reese's *Proceedings* and where he was Head, Historical Publications Division). These four 1861 publications include *Journal of the Acts and Proceedings of a General Convention of the State of Virginia* . . . (the most important of the quartet); *A Journalized Record of the [Convention's] Proceedings in [the] Committee of the Whole* . . . (helpful for the March 15–April 13 period); *Portions of [the] Journal of [the] Secret Session of the Convention* . . . (helpful for the April 16–May 1 period); and *Ordinances Adopted by the Convention* . . . (which includes more documents than the title suggests).

2. For further explanation of this Reese procedure and an account of our uses of it, see below, chapter 2, note 7, page 21, and chapter 14, source note, page 130.

To guide us toward the debates' essential moments, we valued the opinion of the debaters' contemporaries. We first selected speeches of the then-most admired delegates, including George Wythe Randolph, James Holcombe, Henry Wise, James Barbour, Waitman Willey, and George Summers. We then added more obscure delegates who we believed expressed Virginians' central attitudes as, or more, brilliantly, including George Brent, George Richardson, and especially John Baldwin. Because contemporaries accurately believed that moderates long controlled the convention, Unionists dominate early in Part I. Because Virginians correctly recognized that secessionists' relevance and confidence swelled toward the moment of decision, revolutionaries dominate later in Part I. Because the delegates' constituents accurately observed that the state (as well as the Union) might be severed, the disruptive state issue of taxation dominates Part II. Because Virginians correctly discerned that the tense hours immediately before and after secession brought arguments to peak insights, Part III highlights that culmination, and especially a pivotal confrontation that the very massiveness of the Reese volumes usually has obscured from even scholars.

To guide us in editorial methods, we followed Reese's precedents wherever possible. When Reese's endnotes provided alternate texts of our chosen speeches, we explain our choice between the alternatives in our footnotes. When we entered unimportant changes in punctuation, we followed Reese's practice of publishing the alterations without signals to the reader. Where Reese silently corrected misspellings, typos, and obsolete spellings (while also removing extraneous dashes), we silently corrected commas, periods, capital letters, question marks, and paragraphing, when our condensed version so required. Nowhere have Reese's or our slight punctuation changes altered meaning; and in every case, in his text and ours, the silent punctuation changes, without the clutter of editorial marks, ease the reader's way.

But where we subtracted or added words to Reese's scrupulous publication of every word, editorial marks are mandatory. At the many places where we deleted one or more words, ellipses signal the compression. On the far less frequent occasions when we added words to make the compressed text clearer and/or more seamless, square brackets signal the augmentation. Always we sought not only to make Reese's text more widely accessible but also to highlight (and never to dilute) the orators' central points.

We are grateful to the Library of Virginia for permission to use material from George Reese's four-volume *Proceedings of the Virginia State Convention of 1861* (Richmond, 1965). We are also grateful to our home institutions, the Virginia Foundation for the Humanities and the University of Western Ontario, for aid and encouragement; to the Virginia Center of Digital History at the University of Virginia (and especially the center's Kid Wongsrichanalai and Sean Nalty), for crafting our rough draft; to Erik Alexander, our superb research assistant, for fashioning our final version; to Bill Nelson, for his fine map; to Dan Crofts, for expert criticism; and to Alison Freehling and Hope Kamin, for brightening our way.

Chronology

1860

November 6	In the popular election for the presidency, Abraham Lincoln wins an Electoral College majority.
November 12–19	Georgians debate secession in Milledgeville.
December 20	South Carolina secedes.

1861

January 3	The Delaware legislature rejects secession.
January 7	The Virginia legislature convenes.
January 9– February 1	Mississippi, Florida, Alabama, Georgia, Louisiana, and Texas secede (in that order).
January 12	The Virginia legislature calls the Washington Peace Conference.
January 14	The Virginia legislature calls a Virginia convention to consider secession.
February 4	1. The Lower South states meet in Montgomery, Alabama, to form the Confederate States of America.
	2. The Washington Peace Conference begins.
	3. Virginia's voters elect convention delegates and require a popular referendum on convention ordinances.
February 9	Tennessee's voters reject a secession convention.
February 13	The Virginia convention begins.
February 27	The Washington Peace Conference sends its compromise proposal to Congress.
February 28	North Carolina's voters reject a secession convention.
March 1	Congress rejects the Washington Peace Conference's compromise proposal.
March 4	Lincoln inaugurated president.
March 18	The Arkansas convention rejects secession.
March 21	The Missouri convention rejects secession.

April 4	1. The Virginia convention rejects secession by a two-to-one margin.
	2. Unionist delegate John Baldwin unofficially and secretly meets with Lincoln at the White House. He learns that the president likely will provision the federal garrison at Fort Sumter in Charleston harbor.
April 8	The Virginia convention votes to send three official commissioners to meet with Lincoln.
April 13	The Virginia convention's three commissioners meet with Lincoln at the White House.
April 12–13	Confederates attack and capture Fort Sumter.
April 15	1. Lincoln, by proclamation, calls up 75,000 state troops to subdue the rebellion.
	2. Lincoln's secretary of war, Simon Cameron, calls on Virginia for 3,500 of the 75,000 soldiers.
April 16	Former governor Henry Wise begins secret extralegal organization of Virginia troops.
April 17	1. The Virginia convention rejects Robert Scott's substitute Unionist ordinance, then accepts William Ballard Preston's secession ordinance and schedules a May 23 popular referendum on the ordinance.
	2. Governor John Letcher sanctions Wise's extralegal troops.
	3. John Baldwin confronts Wise on the legitimacy of seizing federal installations before the people have voted to withdraw their consent to the federal government.
April 19–21	Virginia troops seize the federal government's military complexes at Harpers Ferry and at the Gosport Navy Yard in Norfolk.
April 22	A mass meeting of northwestern Virginians in Clarksburg calls for the first Wheeling Convention, to consider separate statehood for western Virginia.
April 26	The Virginia convention adopts an ordinance that mandates taxation on the full value of slaves and submits it to the voters for approval at the May 23 popular referendum.
May 1	The Virginia convention adjourns (to reconvene June 12).

May 6   Arkansas secedes.

May 13   The first Wheeling Convention stalls on West Virginia statehood.

May 20   1. North Carolina secedes.

                  2. The Kentucky legislature declares the state's neutrality.

May 23   Virginia's voters approve the convention's secession and taxation ordinances.

June 8   Tennessee secedes.

June 11   The second Wheeling Convention begins the process of making West Virginia a separate state.

June 13   Maryland's voters overwhelmingly elect Unionist congressmen.

June 20   Kentucky's voters overwhelmingly elect Unionist congressmen.

July 21   The Civil War begins in earnest at Virginia's Manassas (Bull Run) battlefield.

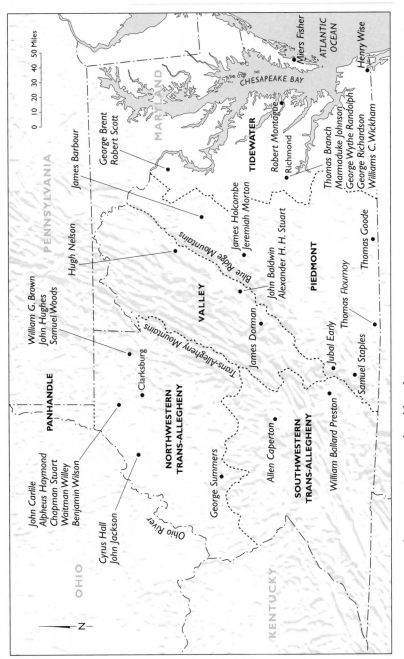

Virginia in 1861, with convention speakers' locales

Showdown
in Virginia

PART I

SECESSION DEBATED

Before Abraham Lincoln's April 15, 1861, presidential proclamation and the Virginia convention's ensuing rush toward secession and disaster, the convention spent two months averting decision. Yet this very procrastination helps give the best parts of the best pre–April 15 speeches lasting appeal.

The allure is partly emotional. Individuals seldom suffer a political crisis that may destroy their lives, their families, and their culture. At this crossroad, where recovery from a wrong turn could require a century, the high stakes generated a catch in the throat and a fright in the voice. Posterity can here empathize with the sense of frustration and fear of destruction that afflict those who dread decision.

The debates also present intriguing questions for detached analysis. What was the essential secessionist case? What was the essential Unionist alternative? Which orators best coped with their, Virginia's, and slave-holders' predicaments? And how well does this oratorical showdown measure up to epic American debates before and since?

1

Jeremiah Morton's Secessionist Speech, February 28

Jeremiah Morton, representing Orange and Greene counties in the western Piedmont (together 49.8 percent enslaved), was a convention exception in many ways. Most of Virginia's leading secessionists had been Democrats, and most Unionists had been Whigs. Morton was the anomalous former Whig who was a prominent disunionist. Most convention speakers were in their forties. Jeremiah Morton was sixty-one. Almost all the other speakers, lawyers by trade, owned only a few nonplantation slaves. Morton's several large plantations netted him a then-princely $30,000 per year. Few other speakers had held higher office than a seat in Virginia's lower house. Morton had been a U.S. congressman. This atypically aged, wealthy, and prominent squire, in short, exemplified the planter who supposedly led his class to ruin. But he actually was an oddity among those who guided the Virginia convention toward Armageddon. "The scourge of war," the fallen grandee would seven years later lament, "has swept all from me, and . . . I stand a blasted stump in the wilderness."[1]

Mr. President: I feel deeply impressed by . . . the vast importance of . . . this assembly. . . . [In] the history of the world, . . . [no] fanaticism, striking into the vitals of a proud nation, has progressed with the same rapidity as this abolition fanaticism has. . . . Our soil has been invaded; our rights have been violated; principles hostile to our institutions have been inculcated in the Northern mind and ingrained in the Northern heart, so that you may make any compromise you please, and still, until you can unlearn and unteach the people, we shall find no peace.

From Reese, *Proceedings* 1:251-71.

1. Quoted in Ann L. Miller, *Antebellum Orange* . . . (Orange, VA, 1988), 141. For biographical facts about Morton, as about most convention delegates, nothing surpasses William H. Gaines Jr., *Biographical Register of Members [of the] Virginia State Convention of 1861* . . . (Richmond, 1969), 60. Gaines published this collective biography four years after his colleague at what was then the Virginia State Library (now the Library of Virginia), George Reese, published the *Proceedings*.

Mr. President, suppose you were to take a boy of the size of that boy [pointing to one of the pages], and have him taught by a mother, and by a father, and by a preacher, and by every teacher, in the Catholic religion, in a Catholic country. . . . It would be a miracle, if, at the age of twenty-one, he would not be a Catholic—or a Protestant, if instructed in the doctrines of that church, by a similar process. When we find, therefore, that in the Northern States the youth are instructed in the nursery, in the school-house, in the church, by the press, to regard slavery as a sin and a crime, and those who cherish it as . . . unworthy of recognition upon a footing of social equality with the people of the North, and fit objects of the scorn and contempt of the world—I ask you what is the hope, what is the chance of effecting a change?

Mr. President, by the election of Mr. Lincoln, the popular sentiment of the North has placed in the Executive Chair, of this mighty nation a man who did not get an electoral vote South of Mason and Dixon's line, a man who was elected purely by a Northern fanatical sentiment hostile to the South. . . . The Government is no longer a Government of equal rights. Our enemies have now command of the Executive Department, they have command of both branches of Congress.[2] How long will it be before they will have command of the Judiciary Department? You may judge of that from the fact that a recent nomination to the Senate of the United States of a national man has been postponed—rejected, I believe—in order that that patronage may fall into the hands of the incoming administration. Who will a Black Republican President and a Black Republican Senate confer that appointment upon? I am led to believe that . . . the man of the most distinguished talents and the nearest approximation to the Black Republicans is the man upon whom that high station will be conferred.

They will administer the Government for the strengthening of the party; they will make capital out of every appointment; and, Mr. President, with a Government, every Department of which shall be in the hands of the Black Republicans, administered upon the principles upon which William H. Seward[3] and Abraham Lincoln will administer it, how long would our institutions be safe? . . . Whenever it comes to the administration of the spoils with the view to the advancement of party—and

2. When the Lower South's senators and representatives left Congress after their states' departure from the Union, the Republicans gained their first congressional majority.

3. William H. Seward, long a U.S. senator from New York, became Lincoln's secretary of state and remained one of the Republican Party's most influential leaders.

that for many years has been the general type of all administrations—what are the number that will be purchased up by the patronage of the Government? I do not mean to say, Mr. President, corruptly. But when there is a fat office which is tendered, and the aspirant for that office knows how important it may be that his opinions should be identical and should assimilate with the powers that be, how natural it is for a man under circumstances like these to satisfy himself that he once was a little wrong, and that the sober, second thought, is the best position. This is human nature. How often does it come to pass that a lawyer of distinguished talents and unquestioned integrity, receives a fee in a bad cause, and yet, in the hour of investigation, in endeavoring to induce the court and the jury to think that the wrong is the better side, he produces the very same effect upon his own mind?

And I tell you Mr. President, that Abraham Lincoln will seek to hold a power over all the Southern States. . . . If you stay . . . [in the Union] for the next twelve months there will be more beneficent showers of public patronage upon Virginia and Maryland and Tennessee—I think he would hardly go to North Carolina—but he will go to Kentucky and Missouri, sooner than to any other States. . . .

And, Mr. President, when a man gets a rich office, how many friends circle around him to congratulate him. . . . The donee of a fat office—be it a Judgeship, be it a Collectorship, be it a Postmaster of this city—has much power, and each one will form a nucleus of sympathizing friends with the powers that be. . . . Let us acquiesce, and I tell you that in the next Presidential canvass—if not in the next, in the second; certainly in the third—you will find Black Republicans upon every stump, and organizing in every county; and that is the peace that we shall have from this "glorious Union." . . .

My heart has been in this Union and my brightest hopes connected with its welfare. I have but one child, and her destiny is linked with a Northern man. But he is upon Virginia soil, and like many of the Northern men who are with us for a time, has become true, and even truer than her own native sons to the rights of the South. But his kindred are in the North, and his sympathies with parents and relatives and friends give me an interest in his behalf; so that I would do what I could to preserve the Union, if I could preserve it upon terms of honor and of safety.

But, Mr. President, it is as apparent to my mind as the sun at mid-day, that unless we can have security—and I am not speaking of such securities as this miserable abortion which the Peace Conference presents—unless we can have securities of political power, I say that this Union ought to be, and I trust in God will be dissolved. . . . We must have a settlement of this question, and a settlement forever. It has been an ulcer in our side for thirty years. . . . Men in every branch of the business of life do not know how to shape their contracts because of the agitation every four years of this never-dying question of African slavery—I say, I want to see this question put to rest, not where it will spring up to disturb my children and involve them in utter ruin twenty or thirty years hence; but I want to put it where it never will disturb my descendants—for if there is to be bloodshed, and this question cannot otherwise be settled, I would rather give the blood that runs in my veins, to preserve that which is in the veins of my helpless offspring. . . .

How can the question be settled? . . . If that National Convention had been held in time, we might, perhaps, have had some hope from such a source.[4] Who is to blame that there was not such a National Convention? Can it be said that that much-abused little State, South Carolina, . . . is to blame? No, that gallant little State cannot be complained of, for when you were invaded here[5] and your soil was bathed in Virginia blood, and you [turning to Governor WISE], like a true man, led the hosts of Virginia to repel the invader, however you may have received the censure of some, I do say every lady of Virginia paid you her meed of applause, and I tendered to you personally my thanks and my approbation.

When Virginia was invaded and you were in the Gubernatorial chair, South Carolina sent her Commissioner here to sympathize with Virginia, to make the grievance a common cause, and to invite co-operation in devising measures for future security.[6] Mississippi did the same. And how were they received and how were they treated? They were treated kindly, as gentlemen. You received them cordially as the Executive of the State. But the Legislature, after the most powerful and thrilling appeal, almost

4. Hoping to save the Union, many compromisers, North and South, unsuccessfully sought a constitutional convention, akin to the Philadelphia Convention of 1787, during the secession winter.

5. Morton here referred to the Connecticut radical abolitionist John Brown's 1859 raid on Harpers Ferry, Virginia, while Henry Wise was governor.

6. Morton here referred to the 1859 South Carolina initiative to call a Southern convention in the wake of John Brown's raid on Virginia. Christopher Memminger, commissioner from South Carolina to Virginia, appealed for his state's proposal in a dramatic address to the Virginia state legislature. But the Virginia legislators turned down the proposal.

that I think I ever heard, the Legislature of Virginia determined that she could take care of herself, and that each sovereign State could take care of itself. And after South Carolina had thus been turned away from the door of Virginia, and the time had come when she [South Carolina] felt that her honor and her safety were involved—because she took the responsibility of an independent sovereign State, she is denounced upon this floor for rashness, for indiscretion, for a want of deference, that she did not invite Virginia to a further council. . . .

Do not complain of gallant South Carolina and Mississippi, but complain of Virginia. If there is blame to rest anywhere, then denounce Virginia—denounce your legislature. . . . They were very adverse to going into a Southern council, because if they went into a Southern council they were fearful that the action of South Carolina and of other States would result in a dissolution of the Union. I believed then and I believe now, that if Virginia had taken her stand in that Southern Council she would have the same influence then that she did have in the times of the Revolution. Had Virginia, however much they might have differed from her, looking to her ancient fame, looking to her great material interest, looking to her position, had Virginia taken the stand which patriotism required of her, South Carolina would have yielded, and other Southern States would have yielded to the counsels of Virginia. But Virginia rejected the offer and the crisis came. . . .

The Union is already dissolved. If it is to be re-constructed, how can it be re-constructed with most safety to Virginia and to the South? Is it by Virginia standing, as she has been with the North and the South, in doubt, as to what her position is, whilst wrongs and insults have been heaped upon her continually? . . .

I would not have been in favor of an exclusive slaveholding Confederacy. No! Whilst I would have required all the guarantees necessary for our protection, I would have had those border States associated with us, whose interests in trade would have led them to the South—I mean New Jersey, Pennsylvania, Ohio, Indiana and Illinois. We would always have had the preponderance, and we would not let them in until they had purified themselves in some degree of Abolitionism, and I would have a provision to this effect: that, whenever they agitated this question of slavery again, and whenever they proclaimed that they were holier than ourselves and we were not worthy to sit at the communion table with them, we should say to them: "Leave us." . . .

Our friend tells us, that if we establish a Southern Confederacy, and bring a Canada to our borders, we shall lose all our slaves. I have no such apprehension; and I believe that our slaves will be as secure then, if not more so, than they are now. . . . Slavery is considered a festering sore by the fanatics of the North. They believe that they are responsible before God and the world, for the sin of African slavery, and that although it is within our borders, they must use all the means in their power to destroy it in the States, and never permit another slave State to be admitted into this Union. That is the platform upon which Abraham Lincoln was elected, and that is the platform upon which Wm. H. Seward has been standing for years, until at last he has become Premier of the President— a "power behind the throne, greater than the throne itself." . . .

If there is a man within the broad limit of this Union who will deserve and receive the curses of an indignant posterity for the breaking up of this glorious Union, that man is Wm. H. Seward; who in all his public acts has been governed by a desire to make political capital and to secure his political advancement. . . . I say, sir, for one, that I had rather perish, than say a kind word to that arch fiend who has destroyed his country. . . . I told him two years ago, that if this question were between him and myself, we would settle it in an hour, and settle it forever.

But, I say, Mr. President, that Virginia is not the Virginia of 1776. If Virginia has lowered herself so far as to receive such a compromise as has been tendered to us by the Peace Conference, it still leaves the question open. As mean and despicable as it is, to be scorned and spit upon, as it will be by every Virginian; there is not a man who believes that it can be adopted, and get a constitutional majority to make it an amendment to the Constitution. . . .

My friend from Bedford [Mr. WILLIAM GOGGIN] . . . speaks of a Middle Confederacy, and as an argument against the establishment of a Southern Confederacy, he tells you, as did the gentleman from Rockbridge [Mr. SAMUEL McDOWELL MOORE] that you would have a line of 1500 miles to be defended by a standing army; and yet, by the establishment of this Middle Confederacy, you would have two lines, one North and one South. So that the evil of a standing army, if an evil it would be, would in his Middle Confederacy be doubled.[7]

---

7. Samuel McDowell Moore, representing the Valley's Rockbridge County (23.1 percent enslaved), did urge a third, so-called Central Confederacy if Virginia's ultimatum to the

While upon that point, let me say a word here, in relation to runaway slaves: If we formed a Confederacy of the slave states, . . . we could have ample protection with proper securities. And what would be that protection? That protection would be a discriminating duty of five per cent against them, until they would give us a treaty stipulation that our fugitive slaves should be surrendered. I believe that would be effectual, because, although our Northern brethren love humanity, they love money more. That we should have fewer runaways, I am perfectly satisfied, from this fact, that when you cleanse the Northern mind of the sin of slavery and divest them of the idea that they are responsible for it, they would feel themselves as free from the sin of slavery here as they are from the sin of slavery in Cuba, Brazil and the rest of the world. . . .

But my friends from Rockbridge and Bedford, seem to be apprehensive that Virginia would act unwisely in going into a Southern Confederacy, because they might pass a law re-opening the African slave trade. . . . I have an extensive acquaintance in all the South, and I have had an ample opportunity to test this matter, and I state from my experience and knowledge of this subject, that there are very few persons there who advocate the re-opening of the African slave trade. Gentlemen need have no apprehension upon this subject. If Virginia and the border States should go into council with her sister States of the South, they could exercise, and would have a controlling power in regulating and keeping down, and suppressing this trade. It is, therefore, a very powerful reason why Virginia should unite her destinies with the Southern Confederacy. . . .

If you will go out, as I trust in God you will, you will not be deliberating with my friend from Rockbridge [Mr. MOORE] or my friend from Bedford [Mr. GOGGIN] in a Central Confederacy. If you go at all you will go with your Southern brethren. If they give us the post of danger, they will also give us the post of honor. They want our statesmen; they want our military; they want the material arm of Virginia to sustain ourselves and them in the great struggles. . . .

North failed. Secessionists scorned this Unionist option, which offered no path to the Southern Confederacy.

But Jeremiah Morton here mischaracterized the position of William Goggin, representing the Piedmont's Bedford County (40.6 percent enslaved). Goggin urged a border conference to decide on ultimatums to the North. But if peacemaking failed, he promised to embrace the Southern Confederacy. The important point is that secessionists, like historians since, homogenized the several varieties of unionism. For the difference between Moore and Goggin, see especially Reese, *Proceedings* 1:183, 230.

Where is the man who, speaking of the great interests of Virginia in connection with the Northern Confederacy, can forget that for thirty years they have been warring upon the fifteen States of the South; that they have been sending their emissaries into our families and our dwellings; that they have been poisoning our citizens and staining our own soil with the blood of our own citizens, when our wives and children, if they did not have the spirit of the matrons of 76, would have been alarmed—and some are alarmed—I say, with all of these transgressions committed by the North, I do not know, gentlemen, how you would feel in associating yourselves with them—I do not mean to make any reflections upon you; but I will speak the feelings of my own inmost heart, and say that I should feel that I was base enough to bend my knee to my oppressor, to take the yoke upon my neck, and to present my own hand for the shackles of slavery—were I to agree to associate myself with a people who have thus acted towards us. . . .

And is there a man who is a descendant of the patriots of 76, whose heart is chilled with fear in this hour of danger? They tell us of their nineteen millions and of our twelve millions. . . . Four millions of . . . [ours] are slaves. But I tell you, gentlemen, and you, Mr. President, if the tug of war ever comes, I would rather have the four millions of slaves and the eight millions of free men, than to have sixteen millions of free men and no slaves. . . . Give us four millions of slaves under the management and discipline of Southern planters and Southern men, and they will give you more sinews of war, than ten millions of free men, agitated with the cares of families and the harassments of military duties. So that if there is fear you cannot alarm the women—if you can alarm the men. . . .

It will be for the interest of Virginia—her material interests—to unite with the South and not with the North; that her agricultural, her manufacturing and her shipping interests will be promoted by it. I tell you if the folly of the North compels Virginia to take her stand with the South—and we shall be fifteen slave States—that the material prosperity of the city of Richmond in 10 years, will be beyond what it will be in 30 years in this Union. I tell you that in 50 years the city of Norfolk will be a larger city than the city of New York; so that if we were to look to the material interests of Virginia, they would be promoted by going with the South, and leaving the North by itself. But as surely as we pursue that course, the border States will come upon bended knees and ask permission for admission into the Southern Confederacy. . . .

2

Waitman Willey's Unionist Speech, March 4

On March 4, Abraham Lincoln's Inauguration Day, Waitman Thomas Willey delivered the first sustained answer to Jeremiah Morton. Willey, forty-nine years old in 1861, represented Monongalia County (in extreme northwestern Virginia, on the western edge of Pennsylvania, and 0.8 percent enslaved). He was born in a log cabin and educated at Madison College in Uniontown, Pennsylvania. Upon recrossing the North-South border, Willey soared in Virginia politics. A member of the state's lower house at age twenty-one, he advanced to the upper house at twenty-eight and vaulted to second place on the Oppositionist (former Whig) state ticket in 1859, losing the lieutenant governorship to an ultimate convention foe, Robert Montague. After his skillful defenses of the western borderlands' worldviews against the likes of Montague in the Virginia 1861 showdown, Waitman Willey would become the new state of West Virginia's most important early leader, one of its two initial U.S. senators, and the only one of the pair to win reelection.[1]

. . . We have indeed fallen upon evil times. . . . I have looked with fearful apprehension, not merely upon the magnitude of the great questions which brought this Convention together, but . . . [upon secessionists' intimidations in] this Convention, as destructive of the fundamental principles of a free people. . . . The right of free speech is a fundamental principle of republican liberty. Whenever that is destroyed the people's liberties are destroyed. And it matters not, sir, whether that destruction be the result of an imperial edict, or whether it be the result of popular violence and intimidation; in either case we are equally slaves. . . .

Does not history attest this great fact in all her pages? . . . [Witness] the classic pages of the historians of republican Greece . . . [and] of Roman history. . . . Whilst the Forum was free, whilst the Senate was free, whilst

From Reese, *Proceedings* 1:352–73, except the last paragraph, which is from ibid., 776.

1. Gaines, *Biographical Register*, 79–80; *Dictionary of American Biography* (hereafter *DAB*); *American National Biography* (hereafter *ANB*); Charles H. Ambler, *Waitman Thomas Willey: Orator, Churchman, Humanitarian* (Huntington, WV, 1954).

there was freedom of speech, Rome was free; and when Cicero, the last great defender of the Roman Senate and freedom of speech, perished, and his head was gibbeted on the Forum, where his eloquence had thundered against his country's oppressors, liberty fled from Rome, and the palsy of political dissolution settled forever upon that great empire.

Modern history has also furnished its example—an example abhorrent to every principle of humanity. Need I refer you to the reeking scaffold, smoking all day long with the best blood of France? Need I refer you to the deep dark dungeons of Paris, groaning with suffocating victims doomed to death, because of no other offence than having given utterance to their opinions? . . . Shall we have these scenes of Jacobin-violence renewed in our land? Shall we inaugurate a Reign of Terror here? . . .

I propose, sir, a cursory, running examination of some of the great evils brought to the notice of this Convention by the gentleman on the other side, demanding, as we are told here, the extreme remedy of breaking up this Government. . . . I admit the evils. . . . I am not here, sir, to apologize for them. I am here to acknowledge, I am here to denounce, I am here to repudiate these errors; but I am not here to consent to break up this Government. I am here for the purpose of endeavoring to correct those grievances, and to vindicate the honor of Virginia, not by abandoning her position in this great Confederacy, but by bringing her oppressors to acknowledge those errors and to redress her grievances. . . .

The remedy proposed by gentlemen on the other side is secession. . . . [But] there is no constitutional right of secession. . . . I never shall be made to believe that Washington, and Madison, and Franklin, and the other great sages who constructed the Union in the first place, and organized our Federal Government, brought . . . the States of the Federal Union together, . . . without any legal bond to bind the Union. . . .

I never could conceive that . . . the Federal Government . . . [purchased] the territory of Louisiana, and the freedom of the mouth of the Mississippi, and of the Gulf, for the purpose of protecting and encouraging the great trade of the interior empire of States, . . . at the expense of a great deal of money and of a great deal of trouble, upon the contingency that the little State of Louisiana might at her own pleasure foreclose these great advantages of commerce against all these interior States. Again, sir, I cannot suppose that the purchase of Florida—another little State—which cost us, in the first place, I believe some five millions, and a great many more millions in establishing forts and arsenals, and in driving the

Indians out of her marshes, until the sum that that little State has cost us will amount perhaps to fifty millions—I say I never can suppose that our government made that purchase, and expended all that money, under the contingency that this little State, after all these services had been rendered, after her territory had been made free, after the savages had been driven from her domain, might quietly walk out of the Union and leave us the bills to pay.

Again, sir, there is Texas, an empire in itself, which cost us some ten or fifteen millions to acquire, in the first place; which cost us, by the war brought upon this country, hundreds of millions. . . . The very effort to acquire this great State . . . well nigh dissolved the Union . . . —and we encountered all that for what? . . . [That Texas] may pass out of the Union, and leave us in this predicament? . . . Can it be possible that Washington, and Madison, and Franklin, and the other sages of the Revolution, have organized a Government upon such an absurd basis as this?

But, sir, when did this doctrine first find a lodgement in the public mind? I think, sir, it is rather a modern invention. . . . We are told we may find it in the celebrated resolutions and proceedings of the Virginia and Kentucky Legislatures in 1798-'99.[2] . . . [But] Mr. Madison, their author, . . . [wrote that] *"The Constitution requires an adoption in toto and forever. . . . The idea . . . of reserving the right to withdraw was started at Richmond, and . . . itself abandoned as worse than rejection."* . . .

Even in the States—our sister States that have seceded—this idea of secession is rather a modern idea. . . . We find, at least, as late as 1821, South Carolina herself . . . declaring . . . that she was opposed to "arraying, on questions of national policy, the States as distinct and independent sovereignties, in opposition to, or what is much the same thing, with a view to exercise control over the General Government." . . . And then, sir, . . . during the excitement which grew out of the compromise measures of 1850, . . . a Convention called in the State of Mississippi for the purpose of pass-

2. The resolutions written by Thomas Jefferson and James Madison and passed by the Virginia and Kentucky legislatures in 1798-99, in opposition to the federal government's recently enacted Alien and Sedition Acts, claimed each state's right to "interpose" itself against such allegedly unconstitutional federal laws. But neither state put "interposition" into action, explained how the remedy would work, or defined when interposition could be used thereafter. South Carolina's nullifiers in 1832 and secessionists in 1860 nevertheless claimed Jefferson and Madison's concept of interposition as justification for their latter-day remedies. Madison, still alive in the 1830s, denied that his precedent would justify South Carolina's nullification of the tariff.

ing an ordinance of secession . . . [instead resolved] "That in the opinion of this Convention, the asserted right of secession from the Union on the part of a State *is utterly unsanctioned by the Federal Constitution,* which was framed to establish, and not to destroy, the Union of the States." . . .

The first argument in favor of secession alleged, I believe, by the gentleman from Orange [Mr. MORTON], were the bitterness and acrimony with which Southern institutions are constantly assailed by the Northern press, Northern schools, and by the Northern pulpit. I would inquire of the gentleman from Orange and of this Convention . . . how the mere act of secession . . . will advance us one inch towards the silence of the Northern press, pulpit or school-house? It will only aggravate the evil; it will only add poison to the virulence and acrimony. . . .

Again—another argument in favor of secession, urged by these gentlemen, was to be found in the efforts made by the Northern Abolitionists to induce our slaves to abscond, in the operations of the Underground Railroad, in the Personal Liberty Bills[3] and the inefficiency of the Fugitive Slave Law for the recovery of fugitives. Now, sir, secession is proposed as a remedy to cure these evils. . . .

Let us look at this matter. You dissolve the Union. What then? The common national obligation is destroyed. Will not the negro find it out? The motives to flee across the line would be increased, because the negro would know that whenever he crosses that line, he will be free. There will be no fugitive slave law for his recovery, and he will know it. . . .

But then again, these gentlemen say: there are the Personal Liberty Bills of the North. In the first place I would ask, why should we condemn the General Government . . . because some of the States, members of this Confederacy, have seen proper to do wrong? We denounce those Bills . . . as not only an insult to Virginia and the whole South, but also to the people who ordained them. They are an insult to common sense. But . . . they have never been enforced. . . . Northern courts have uniformly declared them to be unconstitutional and to be null and void. . . . They have never interposed one jot or tittle of hindrance in the way of the recovery of a single fugitive slave.

But I pass to a third argument which gentlemen have urged in favor of secession, and that is, that the Republican party threaten to exclude

3. Laws were passed by many Northern states in the 1850s giving civil rights to alleged fugitive slaves and thus interfering with federal enforcement of the national Fugitive Slave Law of 1850.

the South from the common territory and to destroy the equality of the States. . . . As to the inequality in the territories, I have said that I will never submit to it. But . . . what danger is there of our rights being invaded? Are we not a law-abiding people, and has not the Supreme Judicial tribunal of the land decided to guarantee, to the full extent, the right of every slaveholder in the land to carry his property into all the territories of the United States?[4] . . . But suppose there were no such decision, and we had to redress our rights in any other way. I ask gentlemen to point out to me how . . . are we to acquire our equal rights in the territories of the United States, by seceding from the United States; by turning our backs upon those territories; by giving up all our right, claim and interest in those territories? Did ever the imagination of man conceive such an unsatisfactory way of redressing so great a wrong? . . .

I am not here, Mr. President to defend the election of Abraham Lincoln. I believe that his election was virtually a fraud, . . . nominated, as he was, by a sectional party, and upon a sectional platform, with no representation in the body which nominated him from the South; but he was nominated and elected according to the forms of law. As to the errors and wrongs of his administration I would meet them as I would meet all other errors and wrongs, by the force of reason, until reason has no force, and then I would resort to the *ultima ratio.*[5]

But, we are told that we are in a minority, and that the Black Republicans may swallow us up. Who placed us in the minority? . . . What would have been the complexion of the next Congress of the United States if our sister States, as they are called, had hearkened to our voice and entreaty? We implored them to wait, to pause, to deliberate and co-operate with us and see if there were no constitutional means, no peaceful means of preserving this Government and redressing our rights? But they would not wait. . . .

The next House of Representatives of the United States, if these States had been true to themselves and true to Virginia would have contained a majority of not less than thirty against Abraham Lincoln's policy. The

---

4. Although the U.S. Supreme Court's 1857 *Dred Scott* decision struck down the congressional right to abolish slavery in the nation's territories, Willey here erred in claiming that the Court declared that the federal government must intervene to protect slaveholders' property (that is, slaves) in the territories. That still-undecided issue provoked the breakup of the National Democratic Party at its 1860 conventions.

5. The final argument, that is, resort to arms.

Senate is so organized that if the Government had been preserved as it was on the 6th of November last, they would have had a majority in that body all through the Constitutional term of Mr. Lincoln as President. . . . Yet the bug-bear of being in a minority is paraded before our eyes, connected, at the same time, with most sympathetic demonstrations of affectionate regard for our Southern sisters. . . .

With all these protections against the policy of the Northern Republican party, what danger had the South to apprehend—what practical danger, I ask? None at all. Mr. Lincoln could not have appointed a member of his Cabinet without the consent of the South—he could not have appointed an officer in the whole Federal Government, whose salary amounted to a thousand dollars, without the consent and ratification of the South—and we never would have had a law objectionable to the South presented to him to be signed, and made final according to the provisions of the Constitution. Let us then hear no more about a minority. Let us hear no more about the tender sympathies of our seceding sisters, who have left us in this minority. . . .

It was alleged, Mr. President, by the honorable gentleman from Orange [Mr. MORTON], the other day, that the honor of Virginia required that we should secede. . . . I claim that honor and chivalry demand that we should stand fast, give not an inch to our foe, turn not our faces from him, but vindicate our rights to the letter and to the death, if need be. . . .

In his eloquent speech the other day, [Mr. MORTON] referred to another argument—I must say that it was an extraordinary argument to be addressed to Virginians— . . . that Lincoln would so employ the patronage of the Federal Government as to corrupt Virginia. It is an argument that I would not dare to make to my constituents—that I would not like to make in any section of Virginia; and I will say, that if Virginia is of such easy virtue as to be corrupted from her integrity by a little paltry pap from the Federal Treasury, her honor is not worth preserving.

Gentlemen have also referred to the John Brown raid. . . . [Yet] this raid . . . demonstrated the ample power of Virginia to vindicate her violated rights and her dishonored soil. She seized upon the traitors and the felons, and, without let or hindrance, hung every rascal of that marauding band. . . .

[But] dissolve this Union—take away the common obligation of a common government, how then will the case stand? Instead of one John Brown raid in 75 years of our history, we will have John Brown raids every month, and, perhaps, every week, all along our borders. Instead of frightening the women and children and exciting the alarm of the people at Harpers Ferry and vicinity, the peaceful valleys and blooming hills of 450 miles, close upon a hostile border in the section of the State where I live, will be subjected to these same John Brown raids; if, indeed, there is such hostility in the North as gentlemen assert there is. I believe there is not. I only mean to answer their argument.

But the argument that struck my mind with the greatest force was, that there is, in point of fact, an irrepressible conflict between the North and the South; that the social system, the system of civilization, of education and the interests of the people of the two sections are so diverse, that it will be impossible to construct a government that will harmonize them and enable them to live together in peace. . . .

Against this mere speculative opinion, I oppose stubborn facts. Against this mere prediction, I present actual history. I appeal to the record of the past operation and effect of the Federal Union. . . .

Whose heart does not throb, as an American citizen, in view of this experiment? Look around you, from the Pacific to the Atlantic, from the Gulf to the Lakes, from Texas to Maine. Three-quarters of a century ago we were only four or five millions of people in number, and but a few scattered and impoverished States. Now we are thirty-four States—for I will not admit that our sisters are finally gone—with cities rivaling in wealth, population, power and magnitude the oldest cities of the oldest Empire of the world; with a people unsurpassed for intelligence, for all the appliances and means of self subsistence, for happiness and prosperity, and the like of whom the sun of God has never before shone upon. . . .

I like to look upon the flag of my country; I like to contemplate its starry folds. . . . Originally there were but thirteen stars upon it, and . . . now there are thirty-four. . . . The starry field . . . shall still increase, until . . . the future shall reveal a galaxy of stars, representing States only bounded by the oceans which surround this hemisphere. . . .

Let us look, Mr. President, at the evils that must result from secession.

The first, in my opinion, would be that our country would not only be divided into a Northern Confederacy and into [a] Southern Confederacy, but, soon or later it would be divided into sundry petty Confederacies. We would have a Central Confederacy, a Confederacy of the States of the Mississippi Valley, a Pacific Confederacy, a Western Confederacy, an Eastern Confederacy, a Northern and a Southern Confederacy. . . . We would have between these several Confederacies a perpetual warfare, criminations and recriminations, inroads, strife and discord, until the energies and the wealth of this great people would be utterly destroyed and exhausted. . . .

Upon another subject. I say, sir, that a dissolution of the Union will be the commencement of the abolition of slavery, first in Virginia, then in the border States, and ultimately throughout the Union. Will it not, sir, make a hostile border for Virginia, and enable slaves to escape more rapidly because more securely? Will it not, virtually, bring Canada to our doors? The slave . . . will know that when he reaches the line he will be safe; and escape he will.

The owners of slaves, aware of this fact, will either themselves remove farther South, or they will sell their slaves to be sent farther South. Thus the area of soil divested of slave labor along the border, would be constantly widening, and rapidly widening, until ere long it would begin to encroach upon the States immediately South of Virginia, and banish slavery still further from the border, until finally it would sweep it from the country.

That is the idea of Charles Sumner, of [William] Lloyd Garrison, and of Wendell Phillips.[6] That is what they say; they want to surround the slave States, in the language of Sumner, "with a belt of fire." How is that to be done? We maintain that we have a right to carry our slaves into the territories. Let the Union be dissolved, and let the South yield those territories, and what then? . . . The slave States would be literally hemmed in by a cordon of hostile elements. . . .

Again! Whether rightfully or wrongfully, it must be acknowledged that the moral sense of the world is against the institution of slavery. The Northern States would of course declaim against it; all Northern influence will be directed towards its overthrow, and the influence of the world in its commercial policy, in its treaty stipulations, in its literature, in its social influence, and in all the power and patronage of its civilization, would be directly, or indirectly, modified and applied, so as to bear upon the institution of slavery. Especially would this be the case, when the South, severed from the Union, would become comparatively a weak and secondary power among the nations. . . .

6. These men were all Massachusetts antislavery agitators, Charles Sumner in the U.S. Senate, William Lloyd Garrison in his newspaper, the *Liberator,* and Wendell Phillips in his speeches and essays.

Let disunion take place—let this great nation be severed into several petty republics, and . . . England will seize on the Island of Cuba, the great gate to the Gulf and the mouth of the Mississippi, and . . . [soon] descend upon Mexican territory. . . . How will the South resist those encroachments? She has no navy, and no army. . . . The proverbial greed for power and territorial extension that has always characterized England . . . [warns] the South against a resort to any policy that involves division and weakness.

With such nations and such influences all around the Southern States— hemmed in by such adversaries without the power of expansion—how long can a Southern Confederacy endure? How long can slavery exist? . . .

But, sir, there are other perils to which this new Government would be exposed. . . . What sort of Government will we get? . . . Standing in the midst of a Convention like this, I . . . recognize the great principle that all power was derived from the people, . . . requiring us to send back to them for ratification or rejection, whatever action we take here. . . . [Our convention] recognizes the fact that our people were determined not to submit to any decision which should not have their full and undoubted sanction. How does the matter stand in the seceded States? Alabama went out of the Union with a popular majority against her action. The same may be said of Mississippi; and it is recently ascertained that Louisiana did the same thing. . . .

What had the people to do with the choice of the Congress at Montgomery? Nothing. . . . And yet it has ordained a government, and imposed it on the people without their sanction or authority. It has appointed a President and Vice President without any popular election or ratification. . . . [It] is imposing taxes, raising armies, and levying war, all without any direct authority or election of the people. . . . Gentlemen cry out against the tyranny of their own government, and yet denounce us because we hesitate to allow ourselves to be thrust into the embraces of such a military despotism. . . .

Secession necessarily implies the placing of this State upon a proper war footing. Sooner or later war is inevitable. If we enter into negotiations with the Federal Government, and separate peaceably, war may be avoided for a time, but we shall ultimately become engaged in war. Secession, therefore, implies a necessity of putting this State upon a war footing.

Now, gentlemen are acquainted with the geography of Eastern Virginia, and no doubt can well appreciate the difficulty of defending our long sea border. But . . . look at our Western border, . . . two hundred and fifty or perhaps three hundred miles of hostile border upon which lies one of the most powerful States of the Union—Ohio. And then [upon] . . . one hundred and fifty or two hundred miles more of hostile border . . . lies the most powerful State in the Union—the great State of Pennsylvania. Look how we are thus fixed—stuck in like a wedge between the enemy and the Red Sea—450 miles of hostile borders surrounding us. . . .

Look at our [western] position. Between us and you there is the almost impassable barrier of the Alleghany mountains; and you, gentlemen, of Eastern Virginia, have not seen proper to give us enough legislative aid to transpierce these mountains that we might have direct communication with you. We are cut off from the Eastern section of the State. How would we stand in a Southern Confederacy? Why, sir, we would be swept by the enemy from the face of the earth before the news of an attack could reach our Eastern friends.

Will you leave us in that condition? Will you drive us out of the State and leave us at the mercy of our enemies? . . . Will you expose our wives and children to the sword?—to the ravages of civil war? . . . Will you make North-Western Virginia the Flanders of America, and convert our smiling valleys into the slaughter pens of as brave and loyal a people as dwell in the "Old Dominion?" . . .

What, then, must you do—should you take the alternative of secession? The Legislature, I understand, are about appropriating a million of dollars for the defence of the State. A million of dollars! . . . The extent of hostile border . . . and other like considerations . . . would require not less than one hundred millions of dollars to put the State of Virginia in a proper state of defence. . . . What is our debt now? Forty millions of dollars or thereabouts. Will our people suffer any more taxation? . . . They cannot endure it. They have not the ability to endure it. . . .

In the Union Virginia is a central State; out of the Union, she would be a border State. Look at her position now. . . . Look at her immense seaboard. Look at Norfolk, which possesses the most magnificent harbor on the face of the earth, with the mighty arm of the Chesapeake stretching forth to grasp the trade of the North, and drawing it towards this great seaport. Look at the magnificent country, inviting the energies and wealth of the capitalist for the construction of railroads. Many of them are already built, and are in a fair way of commanding a monopoly of the Southern trade, and directing it to its great natural outlet at Norfolk. There are in my own section of the State, North-western Virginia, mineral resources extensive enough to furnish the basis of an empire's greatness. . . . If a great national line of railroad is built to the Pacific, and direct intercourse thus established between the Atlantic and the Pacific some Virginia city will be the terminus or depot; perhaps Richmond or Norfolk.

Let Virginia secede and all these bright prospects are forever dashed to pieces. . . . But it is said our Union is already dissolved; and there is no use in talking about these things.[7] I think not, sir. The Union is not dissolved in the true sense of the word. It still lives, and will live while Virginia stands firm. Let Virginia maintain her position; let her stand fast where she ever stood, and this Union can never be permanently dissolved. Some of the States may secede, as they have done, but they will be like asteroids flung off from the sun, hot, hissing through the trackless ether. But, sir, the sun still shines. The Union still remains while Virginia is steadfast. And I trust in God that such will be the centripetal influence of her moral power in the Union, as to bring back these wandering stars into their proper orbits in the great system of American States. . . .

7. Delegates' infrequent corrections of their speeches, printed in the Richmond semi-weekly *Enquirer* and reprinted (in endnotes) in Reese's *Proceedings,* occasionally offer subsequent editors a choice of texts. For the last paragraph of our condensation of Willey's speech, we have used the more eloquent revised version from Reese's endnote, *Proceedings* 1:776, rather than the more convoluted original version in his main text, ibid., 372.

John Carlile's Unionist Speech, March 7

Three days after Willey blasted secessionists, his western Virginia colleague John S. Carlile, representing the Trans-Allegheny's Harrison County (4.2 percent enslaved), raised similar alarms. Carlile, age forty-three and thus six years younger than Willey, had had an even more successful preconvention career: the same early service in the state senate but then elevation to the U.S. House of Representatives. Carlile, however, would have a less successful postconvention career: elected to the U.S. Senate from the new state of West Virginia with Willey but rejected for reelection.[1]

Mr. President, in this the hour of your country's greatest peril, . . . every movement that has been made in the State of Virginia, looking to secession, has been in exact conformity to the programme laid down by the Richmond "Enquirer." In October last, before the election, the editors of that paper advised the Cotton States immediately and separately to secede, and stated that they would inevitably drag Virginia after them. This is the sentiment of gentlemen who profess an ardent love for a mother Commonwealth—she who has been accustomed to give law to the States of this Confederacy— . . . to place her in a condition to be dragged at the heel of the Cotton States. . . .

Are we to be dragged into a committal of the people of Virginia, without their being consulted upon it, to a policy which unites our fortunes with those who contemn the laws of the country, and despise and set at nought its authority? The people I have the honor to represent upon the floor are a brave, and a gallant, and a law-abiding people, and you may travel where you will—North, South, East, or West—and a more honorable, or a more intelligent people is not to be found on the face of God's green earth; a more loyal people to the soil of their birth is nowhere to be found; a people devoted to the institution of slavery, not because of their

From Reese, *Proceedings* 1:449–77.
1. Gaines, *Biographical Register,* 25; *DAB.*

pecuniary interest in it, but because it is an institution of the State; and they have been educated to believe in the sentiment . . . which I cordially endorse, "that African slavery, as it exists in the Southern States, is essential to American Liberty."

The people that I have the honor in part to represent, have not been seized with this frenzied madness which has seized our friends in other parts of the Commonwealth, to induce them—brave and gallant though they may be—to adopt a cowardly—I use this language because I have no other, for I have never been inside a school house to learn since I was fourteen years of age—to adopt a cowardly course, to run away and give up all their inheritance in this great country. . . . Sir, we know we have the protection of our Common Constitution; we know that that flag is ours; we know that the army is ours; we know that the navy is ours; we know that in any battle in defence of our rights, fifteen hundred thousand gallant voters in the non-slaveholding States will rush to our assistance, and under the stars and stripes will hurl from power any and all who dare to take advantage of the position they have obtained to our injury or oppression. . . . We know, Mr. President—and no man upon this floor has denied it—that this Government we are called upon to destroy has never brought us anything but good. No injury has it ever inflicted upon us. No act has ever been put upon the statute book of our common country, interfering with the institution of slavery in any shape, manner or form, that was not put there by and with the consent of the slave-holding States of this Union. . . .

We are called upon to destroy—a Government which protects us even against our mistakes—a Government which has quadrupled the area of slave territory since it had an existence—a government in which we have to-day the right to make five more slave States, if we had either the whites or negroes to occupy them; but we have neither—and it is because we have neither that we do not have to-day 19 slave States in the Union.[2] We

2. In 1845, when Congress admitted Texas into the Union, the state received permission to divide itself into up to five states, at its permanent and sole discretion, with admission of the fragments to the Union guaranteed. Carlile correctly noted that if prewar Texas had sliced itself into five slaveholding states, nineteen slaveholding states would have been in the Union in 1860 (compared to eighteen free labor states). But Carlile oversimplified the reason why Texas legislators never dreamed of fragmenting their state. Oversized Texas pride as much as undersized Texas population deterred any gutting of the Lone Star State. Carlile also misspoke when he said "five more states," presumably in addition to Texas. If Texas had split itself into five states, the Union would have contained four more slave states.

have had the right to occupy them ever since 1845; and yet we . . . [seek territories] in northern latitudes, where all the legislation and stimulants on earth could not keep the negro for a week, even if we were to take him there. This question of African slavery is regulated by climate, by soil, by products, and by interest. . . .

But it is not because of any denial of right on the part of the Federal Government to allow us to carry our slaves into the Territories of this Union, that this Union is sought to be destroyed. S. Carolina scorns to place it upon any such ground. . . . [The territories are] only used here and reference is made to Personal Liberty Bills here, not because of the injury inflicted by these bills, but . . . to accomplish . . . disunion ends. If it were resistance to the Fugitive Slave Laws; if it were the passage of the Personal Liberty Bills that they considered as just cause for the dissolution of this Union, would South Carolina have inaugurated the movement of secession? . . .

This movement originated in South Carolina, where they never lost a slave, precisely as most of these Personal Liberty Bills are found in the statute books of such of the New England and Western States as never saw a runaway slave. Now, sir, South Carolina tells you boldly and frankly, as Mr. Preston,[3] her ambassador, told you in this Hall the other day, that it was not for that, but because of the irrepressible conflict that exists between free and slave labor.

Is it not strange, is it not remarkable that we get all our doctrines of secession, of irrepressible conflict from these Yankees, whom we love to abuse? Where did this doctrine of the right of a State to secede originate? In the hot-bed of all the *isms*—Massachusetts. In 1807, because of the embargo, citizens of Massachusetts and other New England States resolved that they had the right to secede. . . . Now, sir, how will you attempt, at this day and at this hour, to maintain . . . the rightfulness of secession? Astute, learned and great as you may be, you are not astute, learned and great enough for that . . . absurdity . . . ever to be maintained successfully before a Virginia people. . . .

I give you the true reason why South Carolina desired a separation from the Federal Government and the Federal Union. She tells you that she believes in this doctrine of the irrepressible conflict. Now that [Wil-

---

3. On February 19 John Preston, commissioner from South Carolina to Virginia, addressed the convention. The previous day, the convention heard from the Georgia and Mississippi commissioners. For the three speeches, see Reese, *Proceedings* 1:50–93.

liam H.] Seward has abandoned it and the Black Republican party is afraid to maintain it, the South takes it and we heard the Commissioner from the State of South Carolina proclaim it here in our midst the other day.

Mr. [Leonidas] Spratt sent from South Carolina as Commissioner to the State Convention of Florida, while the question of secession was pending before that body, and again in a letter which he addressed to a delegate from Louisiana to the Montgomery Congress, uses the following language [to describe South Carolina's irrepressible conflict dogma]:

> . . . The contest is not between the North and South as geographical sections, for between such sections merely there can be no contest; nor between the people of the North and the people of the South, for our relations have been pleasant; and on neutral grounds there is still nothing to estrange us. . . . But the real contest is between the two forms of society which have become established, the one at the North and the other at the South. . . . The one is a society composed of one race, the other of two races. . . . The one, embodying the principle that equality is the right of man, expands upon the horizontal plane of pure Democracy; the other . . . has taken to itself the rounded form of a social aristocracy. In the one there is hireling labor, in the other slave labor; . . . in the labor of the one there is the elective franchise, in the other there is not; . . . in the one the power of Government is only with the lower classes; in the other the upper. In the one, therefore, the reins of Government come from the heels, in the other from the head of the society; in the one it is guided by the worst, in the other by the best. . . . In the one, . . . the ship of State turns bottom upwards. In the other, . . . the ship of State has the ballast of a disfranchised class. . . .

That is it—that is the [aristocratic] feast to which the [common] people of Virginia are invited; that is the Government to be provided for the people I have the honor to represent here; for my children, for your children and the children of the people of this good old State. South Carolina initiated this movement; South Carolina will control this movement; South Carolina will give direction to this new cotton Government; . . . [and] it must of necessity . . . partake strongly . . . of the character of the present Government of South Carolina, where no man within her limits is eligible to a seat in the Lower House of her Legislature, unless he is the owner of ten negroes and 500 acres of land.

I have been a slaveholder from the time that I have been able to buy a slave. I have been a slaveholder, not by inheritance, but by purchase; and I believe that slavery is a social, political and religious blessing, and I so believed when . . . a boy, but seventeen years of age in the city of Philadelphia, I took the ground that slavery was right in itself. That day no man [in the] South took that ground in defence of the institution. The agitation of this question . . . has brought every man South of Mason and Dixon's line upon one common platform, and no man to-day denies the assertion I have made, that African slavery is right in itself. Believing that the institution of slavery is essential to the preservation of our liberties, I desire above all things to continue it.

How long, if you were to dissolve this Union—if you were to separate the slaveholding from the non-slaveholding States—would African slavery have a foothold in this portion of the land? I venture the assertion, that it would not exist in Virginia five years after the separation, and nowhere in the Southern States, twenty years after. How could it maintain itself, with the whole civilized world, backed by what they call their international law, arrayed for its ultimate extinction? —with this North that is now bound to stand by us, and to protect slavery, opposed to us, and united with England, France and Spain, so to control the destiny of the slaveholding Republic as to work out the ultimate extinction of the institution?

Think you that ever another square mile of territory can be acquired by a purely slaveholding Republic? You would have not only the North to prevent you, but England, France and Spain. I have looked forward to the day when Cuba, that gem of the ocean, would fall into our lap. I have never advocated any harsh or violent measure to procure it, but if we remain together, that island is destined to be ours. The commercial interests of the non-slaveholding States make them as anxious—more anxious—to procure it than we are; and nothing can prevent its addition to our Union but our own separation and dissolution.

Look at Virginia, to-day, standing in the centre of . . . by far the most powerful nation under the globe, with the most prosperous and the most happy government on earth. A government that has gone on in a career of greatness, of glory, of power, and of prosperity in a manner that is almost too much for the human mind to realize. This government that has conferred upon us blessings innumerable, and nothing but blessings, is to be destroyed, dissolved, not because of any act of its own, . . . not because of any intolerable oppression, for it has never oppressed us; but because a portion of its citizens, residing in a particular section of the Union, have so far forgotten their duty to their brethren of the same family, as to entertain hostile opinions of an institution belonging to the other section. . . .

I know that gentlemen, when they speak of coercion, cannot mean . . . a power to coerce a sovereign State, as such. There is no such power. No man in the land contends for such a power; and if no one contends for it, why level your anathemas against it? Why build up cob-houses that you may have the pleasure of knocking them down? Coercing a State, if it means anything—means making war upon it; war against a State affects the innocent as well as the guilty. This Government . . . preserves itself by the same means that the State Governments preserve themselves—that is by punishing the guilty and protecting the innocent. . . .

If every body would act as Christians should do, each rendering to the other what is his due, there would be no need for Government. The very fact that we have a Government and that it is necessary for the protection of society and individuals arises from the fact that all will not do right and that power must reside somewhere to punish the disobedient and enforce the laws. The Government, therefore, acts upon individuals, punishes the guilty, protects the innocent; and without this power you can have no Government. . . .

Sir, is there anything in this Inaugural Address to justify for a moment the assertions that have been made upon this floor, that it breathes a spirit of war? Read it again, gentlemen. . . . Mr. Lincoln . . . has told you, in effect, and told you in pleading, begging terms, that no war will be made upon you, that no force will be used against you—none whatever. . . . After that he tells you, that if States are so hostile to him that no one residing in them will accept the offices . . . [of] the Federal Government, he will not attempt to fill them by persons from other States who may be obnoxious to them.

But, these gentlemen say: "He says he intends to preserve and protect the forts and other public property of the United States." Well, sir, is he not right in doing so? . . . Did you not sustain Mr. [James] Buchanan in doing so to the extent that he did do so? Is it right that those gentlemen in Louisiana shall rob the mint of your money and of my money? That they shall rob you of your arms and munitions of war, and of your forts and arsenals and dock yards? Is it your duty as good citizens to stand by and thus connive at this act of bad faith, and to speak well of it, and to give it aid and support, and to say to the Federal Government: "If you do not give up these forts and arsenals and dock yards peaceably, willingly, why we will take them forcibly, we will make war upon you?" Sir, I, and the people I represent, do not read our duties in that way. Mr. Lincoln in his inaugural address virtually told you that he is not going to make any effort to retake forts which were taken before he came into power; it would be impolitic for him to do so. On the contrary . . . he will endeavor to preserve, sustain and hold the public property so that he may hand it over to his successor as it was handed to him by Mr. Buchanan; and that is all he does say.

Now, sir, . . . what would be expedient in the present condition of the country? I would say, not only let them go with what they have taken, but let them have what is still left to take, if they desire it. . . . I am satisfied, as much as I can be of any . . . future [occurrence], that one year will not roll round until the people of each and all of those States which have, in the estimation of some, withdrawn themselves from the Union, will rise in their majesty, assert their power, hurl those men from the places which they have obtained through their confidence, and raise again, high above the rattlesnake and the palmetto, the stars and stripes of our be-loved land. Believing this, I would let them alone. I would let them, to use the language of politicians, "stand out in the cold awhile," and, I warrant you, they will come shivering back, glad to get to a Union fire. . . .

Look at Virginia, her central position in the Confederacy, possessing within her broad limits the mineral wealth found anywhere and every-where in the United States; the products of the Union are hers with the exception of sugar and rice; wielding a power and an influence in this Government by virtue of her very position, her central position, that she could never wield if the Confederacy were dissolved. Look, when she recommended a Peace Conference; her recommendation is responded to by 21 States, as quick as the lightning can bear to them the resolutions requesting it. What other State could have accomplished so much in so short a time? Why is it that Virginia possesses the influence? Because of her position; because of her sacrifices made for the Union; because of her well known devotion to the Union; because she was the principal architect in its construction; because she has ever been governed by the impulse of a patriotic heart; because her material interests are such as make her interests equal between the sections.

But dissolve the Union, and hitch her on to the tail of a Southern Confederacy, to stand guard and play patrol for King Cotton, and where would she be? What son of Virginia can contemplate this picture without horror?

"O, but," our friends say, "if you don't unite in a Cotton Government, they will not buy our negroes." I say they cannot get them anywhere else. I have no fear of their ever re-opening the African slave trade. No, sir, no slaveholding Republic will ever be permitted to do it. England will not allow it, France will not allow it, Spain will not allow it, nor would a Northern Confederacy allow it. . . . [Therefore] they are bound to buy our negroes. They could never coerce me into any act . . . by threatening that they would not buy my negroes. . . .

"But, oh, our honor is at stake, our rights are denied," we are told by some. Pray, gentlemen, wherein has your honor suffered, or is likely to suffer? . . . What right has ever been denied? Haven't you equal rights in the Territories? Has not this very Government, that you are going to overthrow, declared that you have? . . . Has not the little State of Florida, with its forty-seven thousand white inhabitants, and its twenty-three millions of property, an equal share in this Government with the great State of New York, with its three millions of white inhabitants, and its thousands of millions of property? Has not the State of South Carolina, with a white population not half as large as the single city of Philadelphia, an equal voice in the control of this Government with the whole great State of Pennsylvania, with her two million five hundred thousand inhabitants? Then what has been denied you? . . .

Mr. President, with our extended frontier, with our defenceless sea coast, tell me the amount of money that would be required so to fortify the State, in case of a revolution, as to afford the slightest protection not only to our slave property, but against those John Brown forays upon a larger scale? . . . It was fourteen of the marines of this very Federal Government, which you want to destroy, that took John Brown and his . . . insurrectionary party out of the engine house, delivered them over to your civil authorities, who justly tried and hung them. . . .

Sir, can any man believe that in case of a dissolution of the Union, we would enjoy anything like the freedom and liberty and equality which we now enjoy under this General Government of ours? Could we maintain ourselves without a strong military force kept up at an enormous and exhausting expense? We are now, under the Union, and in the Union, the freest, the most independent, and the happiest people on earth. Dissolve the Union, and a military despotism, the licentiousness of the camp and ragged poverty will be substituted in its place.

And now, Mr. President, in the name of our own illustrious dead, in the name of all the living, in the name of millions yet unborn, I protest against this wicked effort to destroy the fairest and the freest government on the earth. And I denounce all attempts to involve Virginia to commit her to self murder as an insult to all reasonable living humanity, and a crime against God. With the dissolution of this Union, I hesitate not to say, the sun of our liberty will have set for ever.

4

George Brent's Unionist Speech, March 8

A day after Carlile echoed Willey's north-western themes, George William Brent demonstrated that an easterner could deliver an even more potent Unionist message. Brent, representing the Tide-water's Alexandria City (11 percent en-slaved), would never win office after the convention. Previously, he had been only an obscure state senator. But in a convention so often dominated by middle-class, middle-aged, previously uncelebrated men, this thirty-nine-year-old city lawyer and petty slave-holder was an oratorical force.[1]

Events . . . during the past twelve months in the politics of Europe and of our own country . . . awaken . . . the reflection whether permanent government, on any fixed principle, can be long maintained. . . . In Europe we behold political governments and institutions changing like the shifting scenes of a theatre; we see society upheaved, dynasties changed, constitutions re-modeled, and States extinguished.[2] . . . In our own country, . . . in the midst of a profound peace, when surrounded by all the elements of moral and material power and greatness, after a growth and progress unexampled in the history of nations, after exhibiting ourselves to the world as the great exemplar of Constitutional freedom and ideas, we behold inaugurated a revolution which has dissolved the Union of the States, and torn asunder those who have been long bound together. . . . The consequences, Mr. President, which are involved in this wonderful event are not only of great importance to ourselves and to our posterity, but to the cause of human liberty and of all future civilization. . . .

The secession of the cotton States from this Union, however sudden, has not come upon us by any sort of chance. It has been effected not

From Reese, *Proceedings* 1:493–518. The next day Brent promised to publish a corrected version of his remarks, but neither George Reese nor we could find a revised publication. See ibid., 528, 777.

1. Gaines, *Biographical Register,* 20.

2. Brent may have had in mind the crumbling of Russian serfdom and the creation of an Italian national state.

so much by the unsoundness of the system . . . as . . . by the conviction
. . . that the true interests of the Southern States consist in independence,
and this conviction has been fostered and strengthened, and has grown
in consequence of the mad agitation of the fanaticism in the Northern
States; and hence we have that studied attempt on the part of the Southern statesmen to transplant into the Southern mind the idea of an "irrepressible conflict" between the two sections of this Union.

Mr. President: Hostility to the Union of these States has existed for
more than thirty years. And the institution of slavery has been seized
upon at all times, by those who have been seeking the overthrow of this
Union, as the occasion or pretext for their motives and aims. Abolitionism in the North, trained in the school of Garrison and Phillips, and affecting to regard the Constitution as "a league with hell, and a covenant
with death," has, with a steady and untiring hate, sought a disruption of
this Union, as the best and surest means for the accomplishment of the
abolition of slavery in the Southern States. And hence, sir, the song of
triumph that went forth from the brazen throats of Garrison and Phillips,
when South Carolina passed her ordinance of secession. . . .

Mr. President, South Carolina, and those leading statesmen of the
South who have been educated in the philosophy of free trade, have like-
wise, with unwearied and constant assiduity pursued their schemes of
disunion. Conscious of their inability to effect their schemes within the
Union, they have sought a disruption of the States. Conscious of their
impotency, after the successful peaceful mediation made by Virginia in
1833,[3] against their disunion tendencies, to effect their object upon any
such political or economical policy, they have turned the Southern mind
to considerations of a sectional character upon which they well knew the
human mind was naturally sensitive and upon which there would be an
identity of interest and of sentiment. Hence the cry which went forth that
the institution of slavery was endangered.

The great excitement which was created in consequence of this cry,
was unquestionably strengthened, and gained power in consequence of
the lawless legislation upon the part of the North, by their attempt to
arrest the operation of the Constitution of the United States by their Per-

3. In 1832–33 John C. Calhoun's South Carolina declared the high federal tariffs of 1828
and 1832 null and void in the state. When President Andrew Jackson threatened to enforce
the nullified tariff in South Carolina, Virginia sought to mediate. The South Carolinians
eventually backed down.

sonal Liberty Bills, by their efforts to impede the right to capture and bring back fugitive negroes, by the attempt upon their part—unjust, unnecessary and wicked—to exclude the South, with their property, from a common participation in the public domain; and the cry that went forth, that the equilibrium between the two sections had been destroyed, that the independence, the freedom and the institutions of the South were in imminent peril, increased the excitement; and they were still further excited when they were told that the position of the South in this Government was not unlike that which is described by Spenser in his Fairy Queen, of two brothers. One . . . saw the soil of his inheritance daily wasting away and added to that of his rival, without the power of maintaining or restoring the original equality. . . .

South Carolina has never concealed the cause of her grievances, whether fancied or real. She has always boldly avowed it. Believing, on her part, that the system of protective tariffs had been adopted as the fixed and settled policy of this Government, she has regarded that system as the source of all her decadence in commerce and trade and has pertinaciously sought to secede from this Union, as her sole and only remedy. It has been more a desire to relieve herself of this system of protective tariffs than for protection of the institution of slavery, which has animated her in her political course.

The causes [relating to slavery], Mr. President, which have been most generally assigned for the secession of Virginia, are, in my humble judgment, more specious and plausible, than sound or real. . . . We are told that the South has been excluded from the Territories, that Southern planters have been prevented emigrating there with their property. I acknowledge that the South has equal rights in the Territories, . . . sanctioned by the highest judicial tribunal in the land. The constitutional right is valuable and ought to be maintained, but I would ask how far is it available as a question of practical statesmanship? The absolute right is one thing, but the practicability of its exercise is another. In that view I take the ground that it has little real practical value.

We have in the first place no territory belonging to the United States into which slave labor can profitably go. It will never go into any Territory where it is not profitable. This is the great economical law by which slave labor is governed, and this would present an insuperable barrier to its introduction into the Territories. . . .

But it is not the nature of territorial soil, climate, productions and different modes of thought, that presents a barrier to the introduction of slavery into the Territories. The truth is, that the South has no slaves to go there. The South has yet vast and valuable cotton lands unoccupied, and the demand upon the slave labor of the South is so great that it is inadequate to meet it. Cotton has become, as we are told here, the great necessity of the world, and wherever civilization has gone, cotton has followed in its track. The only limitation on the production of cotton is the want of labor, and hence every available hand that can be found, is turned upon the cotton fields, for the purpose of increasing the production of that staple; yet the South is still unable to meet the demands which are made upon her. . . .

The transfer of slave labor from the cotton fields of the South, where it is valuable, can never take place to the territories of the United States, where it is not valuable, where it would be worthless; nor is there any probability that territorial expansion for the blacks will be shortly needed. Not more than one-fourth of the cotton lands of the South are now in actual cultivation, and the number of slaves necessary to till those uncultivated lands would require three times the present number, and it would require the lapse of 100 years before that number could be supplied by natural increase. . . .

Another cause which gentlemen have assigned as a reason for secession is that our fugitive slaves have escaped to the North, and the Northern people, faithless to their constitutional obligations and duties, have not surrendered them but have prohibited their re-capture and reclamation by their personal liberty bills. Have South Carolina and the Cotton States suffered from any such cause? The evils resulting from the escape of fugitive negroes are borne principally by the States along the border, by Virginia, Maryland, Kentucky and Missouri. The extreme Southern States, having two tiers of slaveholding States between them, have had little to complain of in regard to run-away negroes. And for these reasons, for these wrongs, for these grievances, not endured by the Cotton States, but endured by the Border States, Virginia has been invited by these Cotton States into an immediate secession, and to link her destinies with the Cotton Confederacy. I will endeavor to show that Virginia is not invited to a banquet of peace, harmony, union, prosperity and power, but she is invited to a carnival of death. . . . The Southern Confederacy, we are told, will remedy all the wrongs and evils which we upon the border endure. . . . [Instead,] secession will only aggravate and increase them.

We are told . . . that if Virginia seceded from the Union, we would have the privilege of emigrating into the territories of the United States with our slave population. This argument assumes . . . that there will be a peaceable secession, . . . a peaceable partition of the public domain, and that the South will get her just and proper share. [But] how is it, if the South can obtain her portion of the public domain by means of a peaceable partition, that we have here been daily told . . . that it is the policy of the dominant party to make war upon the South? How can we effect this peaceable partition when we are told that in his Inaugural, the President of the United States threatens war, coercion and subjugation of the States which have seceded from the Union? . . .

If there is a probability, or even a possibility, . . . [of] a peaceable separation of these States, [and] if . . . the North and the South cannot agree upon . . . guarantees which the South shall deem adequate, . . . would it not be much better for the border States to remain in this Union . . . to effect this peaceable partition of the public domain? Will not the border States . . . carry a more potential weight in effecting this peaceable settlement and averting the horrors of civil war by remaining than by instant secession, thereby increasing the irritation, bitterness and strife which already exist between the two sections of the country? . . .

But we are told that secession will remedy the escape of our slaves. In what manner? What is the remedy proposed? We have been told . . . that we could establish along the border, a cordon of military posts to intercept the fugitive. Mr. President, the remedy is worse than the disease. You would establish in the midst of the border States, within their very heart a standing army dangerous to the liberties and freedom of the people, and which would entail upon us for its support and maintenance a cost far greater than the value of the slaves lost. Such a policy would invite the establishment of corresponding military posts along the line of the free border States, and strifes and collisions would inevitably ensue.

And, finally, Mr. President, the remedy would be ineffectual, for experience has demonstrated that in all countries where no natural barriers intervene, large standing armies have proved ineffectual to resist the escape of fugitives from justice, or the operations of the smuggler. But what would be the effect of secession upon the escape of fugitive slaves? Secession would relieve the Northern States from all constitutional obligations of duty to return our fugitive slaves. It would relieve the negro-stealer from all legal and constitutional restraints, and it would give a secure and safe asylum upon our borders for the escape of the fugitive. As has been well said by some member upon this floor, it would bring Canada down to our very doors. . . . I think, then, that the evil in the matter of escaped fugitive negroes will be aggravated by secession rather than diminished.

But, apart from this, Mr. President, I regard secession as the doom of slavery within the border States. Secession, in the first place, will have the tendency to promote increased facilities for escape on the part of our negroes. The insecurity of the tenure by which your property will be held in the border States will render the emigration of slaves from these States more frequent and numerous. The owner, conscious of the insecurity of his property, will be anxious to put it in a place of safety and security.

Apart from this, Mr. President, the increased price of cotton and the negro will cause the removal of slaves from the border States, and the vacuum thus created will be supplied by persons from the North or from foreign emigration—thus introducing into the State persons who are hostile to the institution of slavery. All these causes, co-operating together, will, in a very short period of time, cause an entire exodus of slaves from the border States of this Union. But who can tell whether disunion will come in peace or in the storm of war? I, for one, believe that a peaceful separation of these States cannot be effected. The interests are too great and too pervading to be snapped suddenly asunder without causing irritation, bitterness, strife and civil war.

What shall become of the public domain? What shall become of our army and navy? What shall be done in regard to the free navigation of the great rivers of the Ohio, Mississippi and the Missouri? Will the Northwestern States, whose territory is bounded by those great streams, in view of the greatness and magnitude of their commercial interests upon those rivers, tolerate or suffer, for one moment, the mouth of the Mississippi to fall into the hands of a foreign republic or hostile State? . . .

If this Union is to be involved in war, the institution of slavery will vanish from our midst. The perpetuity of that institution depends upon peace and upon repose. Let civil war once sound its horrid tocsin in this land, and slavery is at once ended. In those countries where there have been alternate scenes of anarchy and military despotism, as for instance in Mexico, and the South American States, slavery has disappeared from their midst—leaving the institution alone remaining in Brazil and Cuba, which have been free from civil war and intestine commotions. . . .

What guarantee have we that the Southern Confederacy, which we are invited to join, will be maintained for any great length of time? Will not the causes which have operated in the present Union to disintegrate and overthrow one of the most beautiful fabrics that the ingenuity of man has ever contrived, press with equal power, force, and effect in overthrowing the new Republic? Will they not have the same ever recurring question of taxation? . . . Will not the same question of political equilibrium between the different sections still operate in a Southern Confederacy? . . . And . . . will . . . [not the] question of re-opening the African slave trade . . . have a powerful effect in producing dissent and strife in their midst? . . .

Mr. [William Lowndes] Yancey, at the Montgomery Convention, in Alabama, . . . conclusively shows that the re-opening of the African slave trade is a necessity upon the part of the Southern people. . . . He complained that in the Southern States there was a scarcity of labor, and he denounced that policy which compelled the Southern people to procure their negroes within the border States. He asked the question, why was it that the people of the South were forced to go to Virginia and purchase negroes for $1,500, when the same could be procured on the coasts of Congo and Guinea for $200? We know the fact that there are many eminent, powerful and influential men at the South, who are combined together for the re-opening of the African slave trade. If it be the interest of the South to re-open the African slave trade, will they not repeal all those laws which inhibit it? . . .

But, Mr. President, it is said that the Southern States will not encourage the African slave trade, because it would be destructive of their interests. We are told that by an additional supply of African labor the value of slaves would be depreciated. What does the Southern planter care about a depreciation in the value of his negroes? He does not own the negro necessarily for the purposes of sale, or as a vendable commodity. The chief value of the negro to him is for the production of cotton. Cheap negroes to him are desirable. . . .

But, Mr. President, we are told that if we do not enter into this Confederacy, if we do not link our destinies with the Gulf States, that the Gulf states will inhibit the States on the border from sending their slaves for sale into the cotton States.

Mr. President, can they do it? Dare they do it? Their own power, their own interest depends entirely upon the production of cotton. In order to compete successfully with the other cotton growing countries of the world, the price of cotton must be kept down to a certain minimum price.

When it goes beyond that, the production of cotton is stimulated in the other cotton growing regions of the world. They, therefore, cannot dispense with our labor—they are forced to have it. If they are cut off from the supply of labor from the border slave States, the production of cotton, which is the source of their prosperity and wealth, must necessarily decline, or else they come into competition with Algeria and other cotton growing countries.

They boast, Mr. President, that Cotton is King, they tell us that his supremacy is so firmly established that it cannot be borne: that his sway is so omnipotent that England, with all her antipathy to slavery, with all her instincts in behalf of freedom, must bow in submission before his power. . . . Is this boast justified by the facts? . . . Why, sir, India produces already more cotton than the Southern States. . . .

It has [also] been demonstrated that in Central America, in the Valley of the Magdalena, and in the Valley of the Amazon, there are rich cotton lands yet untouched; and if the cotton Confederacy should interpose a law inhibiting the sale of negroes from the border States, the result would be that labor would be enhanced in value in the cotton States, and cotton would necessarily cost more, and that India, Algeria, Central America and South America would come into competition with the cotton States in the production of cotton.

But, Mr. President, what are we to gain by immediate secession and by linking our destinies with the Southern States? We are told if we join the Cotton Confederacy we will become a great manufacturing interest within the Confederacy—that Virginia and the border States will occupy the same relations to the Southern States which now exist between the States of New England and the States of the South. Why, Mr. President, how does this invitation to join the Southern Confederacy and these promises comport with the idea that France and England are ready to enter into treaties of alliance and commercial reciprocity with these Southern States? If they enter into these alliances with England, as has been intimated by Southern papers, in the interests of the new Confederacy, what will become of the promised manufacturing industry and enterprise of Virginia and the other border States of which we hear so much?
. . .

Educated, as I have ever been, in that school of political philosophy contained in the resolutions of '98–'99, and the report on their vindication by Mr. Madison, and regarding them as the true source of all sound political teaching, I cannot for one moment sanction all the doctrines contained in the Inaugural of the President of the United States. . . . We, sir, who recognize the right of a State to secede, deny that he has any power within these States. We deny that he can, by virtue of any Federal authority, execute the laws of the United States within the seceded States, and therefore we advocate the propriety and the policy upon the part of the Administration to surrender to the seceded States the property within their limits, and to abandon the idea of enforcing the revenue laws. . . .

If Mr. Lincoln should assume the power, without authority of law, and in violation of the Constitution, and should attempt to collect tribute of the Southern States, would that be of itself a sufficient ground to justify the State of Virginia to resort to immediate secession from this Union? I say not. If the President of the United States were to make an illegal, un-authorized and unconstitutional attempt to collect tribute in the seceded States, it would be promptly resisted and met by the Southern President, and by the confederated arms of the Southern States. They have power sufficient to protect and defend themselves against any such attempt. But suppose that the Executive of the United States is sustained and sup-ported by the Congress of the United States, or by the Northern people, in furnishing supplies, and aiding and co-operating with the President of the United States in any movement which he may set on foot for the enforcement of what I regard as tribute upon the part of the Southern States? I would say, then, that every man within the limits of the slave States, whether they be the cotton or the border States, would be united in resisting such an unconstitutional and oppressive exercise of the power upon the part of the President of the United States. . . .

Let us test Lincoln by what he has said. He says he will only enforce the laws as far as practicable, unless his masters, the people, shall otherwise direct. What have the people, his masters, directed? Have they given him authority to enforce these laws within the limits of the seceded States? On the contrary, when the Congress of the United States was asked to . . . [empower] the President of the United States to call out the militia to aid in the execution of these laws, Congress, although the Black Republicans were then in a majority, gained by the withdrawal of the representatives of the six or seven seceded States, refused to confer upon the President any such authority.

The lower branch of Congress has gone still further. Although the Republicans were in a majority, they passed the resolutions which were reported by the Committee of Thirty-Three in regard to the Personal Liberty bills. These resolutions declared that these bills, passed by Northern State Legislatures, were, in their spirit and tendency, unconstitutional, and requested other States to repeal them.

Congress went even a step farther. We have been frequently told that slavery is in danger within the States. We find that Congress passed a resolution recommending an amendment to the Constitution of the United States, declaring it beyond the power of Congress to interfere with the institution of slavery within any of the States of the Union, and then declaring that this amendment shall not be altered unless by unanimous consent of the slaveholding States.[4] . . .

This . . . Republican Congress, pledged to carry out all the principles of the Chicago platform, and having . . . a majority, yet did not attempt, in pursuance of their pledge, to repeal the laws in New Mexico, establishing the status of slavery within its limits; nor did they, in the bill organizing the territories of Colorado, Nevada and Dacotah, incorporate the proviso inhibiting slavery north of 36 deg. 30 min., which was incorporated in other territorial bills, and which was so offensive to the South. Therefore, . . . you may well infer that the President did not mean that he intended to march an army into the Gulf States, or in any other way to coerce and subjugate them. . . . If such acts of Mr. Lincoln shall be sustained by the Northern people, if they shall be sustained by the Congress of the United States, the representatives of the people, then Virginia, with all the border States, will present one united and determined front against the exercise of any such power. . . .

Virginia has no sympathy with that doctrine, whether it comes from the North or from the South, that there exists an irrepressible conflict of opposing and enduring forces between the two sections, growing out of the diversities of soil, of climate, or productions, and of domestic institutions. On the contrary, she regards these diversities as links in the great chain of Union, binding the States more closely together. But in order to form a perfect Union, each link must be preserved in all its original

4. Brent slightly misinterpreted the wording of this amendment, which Congress did pass and send to the states for ratification in early March 1861. The amendment declared that Congress could never abolish slavery in a state and that this prohibition could never be amended. The Civil War ended most states' consideration of ratifying this proposed Thirteenth Amendment (which was the exact opposite of the emancipating amendment ratified in 1865).

integrity. Under such circumstances, Virginia is called upon to discharge the duties of her ancient office. Her position is truly grand and sublime. The country looks on for some grand and magnanimous experiment which will rescue it from strife and civil war. Let, then, Virginia, Mr. President, strive vigorously to remove all causes of discontent between the two sections of the country. Let her strive vigorously and earnestly to bring back the seceded States of this Union and re-construct it anew—to re-construct and bind together a Union in fact, in feeling and in interest. It should be her duty to impress upon the people of the different States that noble lesson, that

> No matter that at different shrines,
> They prayed unto one God;
> No matter that at different times
> Their fathers won the sod.
> In fortune and in fame they're bound
> In stronger links than steel,
> And neither can be safe or sound
> But in each other's weal.

What then, Mr. President, should Virginia do? The duty of Virginia is to act in the present emergency with decision. Let her speak out. Let her demand a settlement of the issues pending between the two sections of the country, now and forever. . . . Let her . . . call a conference of the border States. Let them determine upon such amendments to the Constitution as may be deemed necessary for the protection of the South. I care not whether they are the Crittenden amendments, or any other amendments equivalent to them. Let her propose them as the ultimatum upon which the settlement of the questions at issue between the two sections is to be adjusted.

It is due to the border States that we all should meet in convention. I would not rashly and precipitately rush out of this Union, or first undertake this settlement without the counsel of these border States. We have condemned the cotton States for their action. We should not imitate the same action on our part, but we should call them into council.

But, Mr. President, if all this shall fail, if the propositions thus tendered for a settlement of the pending issues, shall be rejected, what, then, will be the duty of this State? The duty of this State will be, to unite with the States of the South and such of the non-slaveholding States as shall agree with them. Not, however, to withdraw from this Union, but with the intention of re-constructing it afresh; supersede the Government at Washington, take possession of the National Capitol, of the archives of Government, of the public domain, and of the ancient flag—the stars and stripes of the nation.

But, Mr. President, in the mean time Virginia should demand that the arm of Federal authority should be stayed, that no attempt should be made, on the part of the Federal Government, to coerce and subjugate the States that have seceded from the Union. Recognizing, as I have always done, the right of a State to secede, to judge of the violation of its rights, and to appeal to its own mode for redress, I could not uphold the Federal Government in any attempt to coerce the seceded States to bring them back into the Union.

If then, Mr. President, these efforts on the part of Virginia for conciliation and harmony shall fail, if the Northern States shall reject the overtures of peace thus tendered, and shall attempt to inaugurate the policy indicated by the Chicago platform, if then, in the battle's wreck and midnight of storms which shall follow, this Union, the Rome of our hearts and affections, with all the storied memories of its pictured past

> Shall in Tiber melt,
> And the vast range of its wide Empire fall,

we shall be cheered by the consoling reflection, that we, at least, are innocent.

Mr. President, one word more, in conclusion. My lot is cast with that of Virginia; come weal, come woe. Beneath her soil repose the remains of those who gave me existence, and of my children, and when my own journey of life shall have been run, my prayer will be that I too may rest in her bosom.

5

George Summers's Unionist Speech, March 12

George William Summers represented Kanawha County, one of the more enslaved Trans-Allegheny counties, despite its modest 13.5 slave percentage. Older than most delegates at age fifty-seven, he was also more politically experienced than most. He had served as a state legislator, a U.S. congressman, a state judge, and a member of the recent Washington Peace Conference. He was widely expected, in and out of Virginia, to be the convention's pivotal Unionist. Secessionists such as Henry Wise thus picked him out as the target for angry tirades. But Summers was a fading star, speaking less successfully at the convention than the young western Virginia comers John Carlile and Waitman Willey. Thereafter, Summers would play no public role in the Civil War or in West Virginia's separate statehood movement.[1]

. . . Mr. President, it has been urged that neither the Peace Conference adjustment, the Crittenden project, or anything that we were likely to obtain in the way of guarantees, will induce our sister States of the South to return to the Union, and that Virginia ought to be content with nothing short of what will satisfy and restore them. . . . My own ardent personal desire [is] for the restoration of those States to their former place in the Union. But . . . [any] settlement . . . satisfactory to the slave States still remaining in the Union . . . ought, *a fortiori,* to be acceptable to the seceded sister States of the South. Sir, we have infinitely more interest in all the perplexing questions . . . connected with slavery, than they . . . can possibly have.

In regard to the fugitive slave law, . . . they lose exceedingly few slaves by escape, none in comparison with the number lost by the border States. They are hedged and surrounded by slave States, interposed between

From the March 12 portion of Summers's speech reported in Reese, *Proceedings* 1:614–29. For the earlier portions of the speech, which commenced on March 11, see ibid., 549–78, 590–614.

1. Gaines, *Biographical Register,* 73–74; *DAB.*

them and the free States, so that their slaves cannot escape, except in rare instances by vessels.

Again: What interest, compared with ours, have the Cotton States in the territorial question? . . . Is there a man from South Carolina, Georgia, Louisiana, Mississippi, or Alabama, who would leave the fertile fields of the South, to migrate with his negroes into Arizona or New Mexico . . . [or] any of the Territories now owned by the United States? . . . The slave migration to Territories, so far as there is any, will be from the border States, and not from the cotton States.

In all these questions, we have the larger interest. Nor am I prepared to admit that in their settlement they have any right to claim a higher standard of honor, or nicer appreciation of right, than ourselves. . . .

Should, these States refuse to return upon a proper settlement of our difficulties, . . . satisfactory to Virginia and the other slave States yet remaining in the Union, such refusal would furnish strong evidence that they left us, not on the ground of the slavery issue and difficulties, but for other causes, and upon a foregone conclusion. I delight, as much as any one, to anticipate the hour when these States shall come back to us. . . . And they will come. We belong to the same race. We cannot long be separated. . . .

What are we to gain by secession . . . on the territorial question? The entire abandonment of all connection with and control over them! . . . On the question of our absconding slave population, what do you gain? You exchange the constitutional provision which requires the rendition of fugitives from service, the laws of Congress to enforce it, and the amendment now proposed for the payment in full of unreclaimed and lost slaves—you exchange all these provisions and guarantees securing you in your rights, . . . for . . . a border attitude along the line of States, no longer connected with you, not participating in that institution, but becoming possibly, by your own act, more hostile to it than ever. . . .

Mr. President, I remarked awhile ago that it was better to protect slavery in Western Virginia than in New Mexico; better to legislate for the encouragement of that institution upon your own borders than elsewhere. If you do not afford such protection, what is the condition of Western Virginia in regard to the institution of slavery? Do you not perceive that the institution at once becomes worthless to us? In my region of the State, bordering upon the Ohio river, can you hold slaves at all after separation? . . .

Look at the region represented in part by my friend from Monongalia [Mr. WILLEY], watered by streams running to Pittsburg—the head
springs of the Ohio—his Pennsylvania neighbors within 12 miles of his
own residence, in the charming village of Morgantown. What, I ask you,
is to be the condition of this great portion of the State, . . . [with] about
400 miles of free State border? . . .

These remarks . . . are applicable to the whole State in greater or lesser
degree. Here is our northern border—the Potomac line—separated from
the free States only by the narrow interposition of Maryland. Your whole
sea-coast is all to be opened up, and we are to become, to use a homely
phrase, the outside row in the corn field. We are to protect slave property
in States south of us, but to lose our own. So far from secession rendering the institution of slavery more secure in Virginia, it will be the potent
cause of insecurity.

Slave property cannot be retained in that position of affairs; it will di-
minish instead of increase. We shall find this diminution encroaching
first upon the counties of the northwest, then on the central west, compelling us to sell our slaves or permit them gratuitously to run away, dis-
abling us from holding them and rendering them worthless; that border
widening and encroaching upon you in the centre, stretching to the East,
until at last, in all human probability, by such separation, Virginia herself
in the course of time, perhaps not far distant, will be placed in the attitude, if not of a non-slaveholding State, at least slaveholding so partially
as not to be regarded by her sister States of the South as any better than a
Yankee appendage. I believe that the sundering and dismembering of the
Union is the signal not only of vast injury to the slave institutions of the
country, but possibly of its extinction in Virginia. God forbid that such
results should follow. . . .

Will you go out without consulting Maryland, North Carolina, Tennessee, Kentucky—all concerned with us, bound up in our fate, affected
necessarily by our act of secession? Do you mean to take a jump outside the magic circle which now encloses us, without taking counsel with
those whose fate is intimately connected with yours, and whose destiny
for good or evil would probably be consummated by your act?

Why, sir, we hear the argument advanced continually, that whatever
Virginia does, the other States will do. Mr. President, have we come to
this? Are we to assume before the world, and put forth as our justification
the idea that Virginia can properly go out of the Union in her present po-

sition, without arrangement or consultation with her surrounding sisters, upon the theory that so commanding is her attitude and her influence, that these other States will be compelled to follow where she leads? This is not an argument upon which Virginia can stand. It is not worthy [of] her ancient fame, or her yet unsullied justice and magnanimity.

Sir, we are constantly expressing ourselves and in strong terms against ... the policy of coercion. Yes, sir, and rightly; and yet, in the same breath, shall we ourselves coerce? You will not let President Lincoln or the Federal Government coerce any of the Southern States. You announce yourselves as utterly determined to resist this policy, and yet you take a course towards your sister States ... which will inevitably coerce them into a system which they would not willingly adopt. . . .

We are asked if we are willing to submit to Mr. Lincoln. . . . But Mr. Lincoln is the submissionist, not us. He is at this moment submitting to the noble position of the border States. He is submitting to the exigencies of his own position. . . .

My course cannot be governed by ... newspaper paragraphs or telegraph dispatches, those swift-winged messengers of sensation and alarm. I think we should act cooly and calmly, and only upon full information of the facts. . . . We are [told] to be alarmed by the declaration of the President that it is his duty to hold, possess, and occupy the forts. . . . [But] I think we ought to judge of every one by rule of common sense. . . . There is no motive to impel the administration to resort to force which will bring on a conflict between those seceded States and the General Government.

Then, again, he has no means of retaking them even if he desired. He can only retake them by a force which he has not the power to raise. He has only the little standing army belonging to the country, that is scattered over your entire frontier, West and Southwest, and utterly incapable of taking these fortified places or any of them out of the hands of the seceded States. . . .

I do not propose to discuss the question of the right of secession, about which we all have opinions of our own. I will not go into that argument now; it is not necessary, it is not opportune. I think that, in whatever aspect that right may be regarded, we are bound to accept secession as an existing fact. . . . It has come upon us and we must meet the event as best we may.

And what is the best? I say, Mr. President, just to let them alone. I would use no force. Force now is civil war, and with civil war, the bonds of our Union can never be renewed. I am happy to say that the news of this morning leaves no reasonable ground of doubt that a pacific policy has been wisely determined on at Washington, and that the troops in Fort Sumter are now or will soon be withdrawn. These States must be left to time, to their experiment, to negotiation, to entreaty, to sisterly kindness. That is my mode of treatment. Under its operation all may be well. The old affection will return—the memories of the past will incline us to each other—our joint struggles and joint triumphs, . . . our great experiment of free government and enlightened civilization, and . . . more than all, a sense of common interest and common safety, will bring us together again, and our Union be more strongly cemented than ever.

Virginia is master of her own position and of her own movement. . . . What then is her duty? Is she to plunge into an unknown future? Is she to rush into the arms of a Southern Confederacy? . . .

No, Mr. President. No! no! The duty of Virginia lies in another direction. It is hers to be faithful when all others shall prove faithless; it is her duty, when all others shall forget duty, to stand by it to the last, and only to give up its performance when performance shall become impossible. It is hers, Mr. President, not to fly from, but to stand by these monuments of her glory—the Constitution and the Union—constructed by herself more than by all others. If these monuments need repair, if they need retouching even, in their inscriptions, who has so much right as Virginia to lead the way in this remodeling and amendment?

Let her call . . . a Conference at Frankfort, [Kentucky] . . . [of] all the slave States remaining in the Union. Let her there consult, devise, express her own opinion, consult the opinions and wishes of others—her daughters and her sisters—she will go there their equal, and no more—not to dictate, but to commune. She will have her full share of influence—she should ask no more. . . .

The brave and powerful man is always a generous man. The position of Virginia is power—her voice when uttered, is decisive. She will not exert that power or speak the word to carry her out of the Union and involve the fate of her sisters. She will consult those sisters on every point of common interest, and on every scheme of common deliverance. . . .

The Frankfort Conference will, upon full consultation, agree upon the guaranties which will be satisfactory to the slave States now remaining in the Union, and will devise the plan of bringing them to the consideration of the other States. Let an appeal be made, not to the politicians, but to the people of the nation. What shall be agreed on there, will be accepted by the whole nation. . . .

What more can you do? . . . I would have you to say by your action that all is not lost. I would have you, by your action, remove this fear and trepidation from the minds and hearts of our people. Say to them distinctly that the State is not to be precipitated; that she is doing her duty under the Constitution which our fathers made; that she is in the Union which they constructed, and expects to remain there. . . .

Say to the people in the city and in the country that Virginia knows her duty and will perform it; that she will perform it in her own time and in her own way. She is neither to be forced by outside or inside pressure to do wrong. If she is ever to leave this Union, she will leave it with no stain upon her justice, and with no remorse for duty unperformed. But she will not leave it.

Let that announcement go forth. . . . Make it known that you intend to keep the peace and restore the Union—and that you are taking your own time and your own mode to accomplish it. Do it, Mr. President, and send a thrill of gladness throughout this State and over this broad land to animate every heart. Let it be known that however dark and lowering have been the clouds upon us, that they are breaking away, and that soon the bow of promise and peace will span the whole heavens again.

6

George Wythe Randolph's Secessionist Speech, March 16

George Wythe Randolph was as close as they came at the Virginia convention to possessing royal blood. This representative of the Tidewater's Richmond City (30.9 percent enslaved) was born and would be buried at Thomas Jefferson's Monticello, as befit the former president's youngest grandson. Forty-two years old in 1860, Randolph, a prominent Richmond attorney, would briefly become Jefferson Davis's Confederate secretary of war.

His eldest brother, Thomas Jefferson Randolph, had ruined a promising career by proposing gradual emancipation at the Virginia legislature's famous antislavery debate in 1832. He thereby publicly risked some of Thomas Jefferson's private heresies. The younger Randolph brother, perhaps careful to avoid the familial ideological snares, had never publicly expressed qualms about the peculiar institution. But in a memorable line in this speech, he winced that some Virginians still echoed his grandfather's apologetics about slavery.

In the bulk of his address, Randolph more comfortably dwelled on the supposed modern economic virtues of slavery and secession. Thomas Jefferson had called Randolph's adopted Richmond locale, like all cities, sores on the body of an agrarian republic. But armed with Richmond compatriots' statistics and the census of 1850, the urban grandson reversed his agrarian grandfather's judgments. Yankee capitalists inflicted the only sores on Southern cities. Northern exploiters also alone impoverished Southern white free laborers. The solution, for both the South's slaveless and slaveholding whites: sever Mr. Jefferson's Union.[1]

. . . On the 6th of November last the Government passed, in strict accordance with Constitutional forms, into the hands of a sectional party,

From Reese, *Proceedings* 1:729–59.

1. Gaines, *Biographical Register* 1:65–66; *DAB; ANB;* Freehling, *Road to Disunion* 1:123–30, 155–57, 181–90, 2:508; George Green Shackelford, *George Wythe Randolph and the Confederate Elite* (Athens, GA, 1988).

organized upon principles hostile to our institutions, social, political and industrial. In the opinions of some, the observance of Constitutional forms in that election robs it of all wrong. In my judgment, it is that very observance of form which renders the election so dangerous to our liberties. Had revolution been attempted, we . . . should have opposed with the strong arm of force the seizure of the government. But the fact that our enemies found it unnecessary to violate the forms of the Constitution proves the insufficiency of that instrument for our protection. . . .

The Government, then, if I may so express it, is constitutionally revolutionized, and requires a counter revolution to restore it. We know that while the South and its friends were in possession of the Executive, the Judiciary and one branch of the Legislature, we were assailed in the territories, we were robbed of our slaves, our soil was invaded, our citizens murdered, our right of transit with slaves from one Southern State to another was obstructed, our right of property in slaves was denied, our slaves themselves were incited to rebellion, we were threatened with Abolition in all places of exclusive Federal Jurisdiction, and our character was systematically traduced through all Christendom. These things, and many more, were effected by our enemies out of power, and while fifteen slave States were in the Union. Now that our adversaries possess the Government in all its branches—for the Judiciary will soon be theirs—and that our number is reduced to eight [States], what may we not expect? . . .

The Peace Conference plan is much eulogized . . . because it confers upon the South equality *of power in the acquisition of territory,* instead of *equality . . . in the territory when acquired,* as provided in the Crittenden plan.[2] In my judgment, Mr. Chairman, the [Peace Conference's] proposed equality of power [in acquiring territories] will be a fertile source of agitation, intrigue, bargain and corruption, and a most unreliable safeguard.

By the [Crittenden plan's] equal partition of territory [once acquired], we should have gained at least one thing. We should have withdrawn the question from Congress, and escaped all further agitation on the subject.

---

2. To repeat the point made in the introduction, the distinction here is between sectional equality *in already acquired territory* (per the Crittenden Compromise proposal for dividing the slave labor and free labor territorial areas at the 36°30′ line) and sectional equality *in the process of acquiring territory* (per the Washington Peace Conference's proposal that majorities of both Northern and Southern U.S. senators be required for acquisition of new federal territory).

But this [Peace Conference] proposition, which requires the majorities of the Senators of each section to concur in the acquisition of territory, exposes us again to all the annoyances of controversy; and, much worse than that, to the dangers of intrigue and infidelity.

We have now but seven slave States [in the Union], for Arkansas is trembling on the verge of secession and cannot be relied on. By this [Peace Conference] proposed partition of power, it will only be necessary [for the North] to gain eight Southern Senators [from four states] to admit all the Canadas; while we shall have to win twenty Northern Senators to acquire slave territory. All the Northern States are equally interested against us, while four of the Southern States, sufficient to control us, have less than a third of the [Union's remaining] slave population, and are but little interested in our behalf.

Of the 1,550,000 slaves in the [Union's remaining] seven slave States, the States of Delaware, Maryland, Kentucky and Missouri have only 428,000—less than 28 per cent of the whole. The North will wield all the patronage of the government, and we shall be powerless. Have we not just cause to fear that as the white population of the four States before mentioned gains rapidly on the blacks, and their interest in the institution of slavery sinks to almost zero, they may yield to temptation, and suffer the acquisition of free territory, without requiring an equal addition of slave territory? The odds against us in the struggle will be tremendous; it will be all the world to nothing. To such a partition of power [to acquire territory] as this [Peace Conference] plan proposes, I much prefer the [Crittenden plan's] partition of [already acquired] territory. . . .

I shall now proceed to consider the subject in its other and more interesting aspect—as a commercial question. . . . Will the material interests of Virginia be promoted by adhering to the North or by joining the Southern Confederacy? . . .

In the North the [tariff] system is, and always will be, highly protective.[3] . . . Observe the haste they made to adopt a tariff higher than any

3. A tariff imposes taxes on foreign imports at the time of importation. A protective tariff seeks not only to raise revenue but also to protect American manufacturers from foreign competition by making importation ruinously expensive. An effectively protective tariff allows American industrialists to raise prices for their protected products. Southern agrarians resented the resulting higher prices for goods they consumed. Southern cotton producers added that their best customers, English cotton manufacturers, would pay less for raw cotton from America or go elsewhere to buy it if they were inhibited from sending finished cotton goods to America.

before known, so soon as they were relieved from the presence of some fourteen Southern Senators and thirty-odd Southern Representatives.[4] In the South, as we see from their provisional [Confederate] Constitution, their provisional tariff and the debates of their Congress, a tariff for revenue will be adopted, . . . averaging not less than 15 or 20 per cent as the settled policy. . . . Such being the case, I shall now proceed to consider the staples of our agricultural and mining industry and to enquire in reference to each, where lies the market? where the competition? and how the revenue system affects the price? . . .

WHEAT—The latest reliable statistics in reference to the production of wheat, . . . those of the census of 1850, . . . [show that] Virginia had a surplus, after deducting seed, foreign export and her own consumption, of 5,036,595 bushels. The North had a surplus, after similar deductions, of 3,049,141 bushels. The border slave States, exclusive of Virginia, were deficient 3,130,159 bushels, and the cotton States were deficient 4,955,577 bushels. It thus appears that . . . [Virginia's] competition was at the North and . . . [her] market at the South. Let us now enquire what comparative effects may be expected from the high tariff of the North and the low tariff of the South upon the prices of wheat. . . .

The tariffs of 1828 and 1842 . . . constituted a protective era; those of 1832 and 1846 . . . gave us an era of comparative free trade. . . . The average price of superfine flour in New York . . . during the period of excessive protection . . . was $5.88⅞ per bbl.; during the . . . years of comparative free trade it was $6.93¾ per bbl. . . . In view of these facts it is astonishing that gentlemen on this floor, in maintaining that our material interests were connected with the North and had no connection with the South, have selected wheat as illustrating and proving their proposition. . . .

TOBACCO— . . . The prices of leaf tobacco have [also] responded . . . accurately to the changes of the tariff. . . . Under the [low] tariff of 1816 leaf tobacco averaged $71.27 per hogshead; under the higher tariff of 1824 it fell . . . [to] $71.09; under the still higher tariff of 1828 it fell . . . [to] $62.57; under the lower tariff of 1832 it rose . . . [to] $82.03; under the higher tariff of 1842 it fell . . . [to] $51.94; and under the lower tariff of 1846 it rose . . . [to] $69.40. If these changes of tariff and price stand not to each other in

4. During the secession winter, shortly after Lower South congressmen departed Congress, Republicans used their new majority to pass the so-called Morrill Tariff, the highest protective tariff since the 1828 Tariff of Abominations.

the relation of cause and effect, they present an accidental coincidence perfectly marvellous.

If asked where the competition was I should say that it was at the North, and that the home market was at the South. In 1849 the North produced in round numbers about seven millions of pounds, and the Cotton States about half million of pounds of tobacco. . . . [Furthermore], the fine tobacco manufactured south of James River, I am told, is exclusively consumed at the South, being merely shipped to New York, if shipped at all, as a point of distribution. . . .

Virginia exports nine millions of dollars worth of manufactured tobacco per annum, of which the Southern States consume about six millions, and the remainder is exported to Europe. Richmond, alone, exported in 1858, manufactured tobacco worth $6,228,496. It is the leading export of the State. . . . I fear much that a separation from the South and union with the North will . . . cut us off from our customers, . . . transfer to the South the manufacture of all the tobacco consumed in the Southern market, and strip us of our leading industrial interest.

LIVE STOCK—The third and last agricultural staple is live stock, the product chiefly of Western Virginia. . . . The competition is at the North, . . . in this, as in all the other productions of the State, . . . [and] the market for live stock must be in the South. From the want of grass, . . . [the Cotton States] find it cheaper to buy the matured animal than to raise it . . . [and] are incapacitated, by their climate, from curing meat. . . . Notwithstanding the fact, therefore, that the great packing points are at the North, the greater comparative consumption must be at the South, and if Virginia live stock find their way to Cincinnati to be packed, they probably go thence, in the shape of salt meat, to a Southern market. . . .

SALT—I find, from the census of 1850, that the domestic production of salt for the preceding year was $2,222,745, of which amount $1,452,554 was produced at the North, $700,466 in Virginia, and $69,725 at the South. This clearly shows where the domestic competition lies. From the larger [Southern] consumption of salt meat, and the greater proportionate number of live stock at the South than at the North, and from the further fact that . . . our salt region is in South-western Virginia, in juxtaposition with the South and separated from the North, and . . . in the valley of the Kanawha, which possesses water communication with the South and Southwest, . . . I infer that our market also lies at the South. Nor would it at all affect this conclusion to show, if such be the fact, that most of the Kanawha salt goes to Cincinnati. . . . Cincinnati is . . . a point for the distribution of salt or salt meat to the South. . . .

IRON— . . . In the iron interest, . . . the trade of Richmond . . . may fairly be considered as representing that of the State. . . . An annual average decrease of 379 tons in the Virginia iron brought to Richmond since the 1st of July, 1857, and an annual average increase of 3,867 tons in the Northern iron brought to that city during the same period . . . [show that] the Northern iron masters . . . were absolutely exterminating the production of iron in Virginia. . . . [Our] union with the North . . . [surrenders] our miners and manufacturers to the overwhelming competition of their Northern adversaries.

COAL—[We see] . . . the same state of things with regard to the coal trade: the gain of Northern production . . . and the gradual extinction of our own production. The anthracite coal sent eastward from Pennsylvania in 1846 was worth $13,337,314. . . . In 1856 the Pennsylvania coal had trebled in value, having increased to $39,834,098. . . . While this enormous increase of Northern production was progressing, the coal trade of Virginia was steadily declining. From the 1st of July, 1856, to the end of 1859 the amount of coal brought to Richmond from the interior diminished at an average rate of 2,307 tons, while the importation of Northern coal increased annually on an average 4,033 tons. . . .

MANUFACTURES— . . . [In] the production of manufactures and the mechanic arts . . . in 1850, there was a surplus at the North of $264,637,000, and a deficiency in the cotton growing States of $139,401,000. If we wish to become a manufacturing State, it will be an extraordinary policy for us to unite ourselves with a people who produce vastly more than they consume, and to decline a union with States who will take everything we produce. . . .

We have now large manufactories of iron which have their entire market at the South. . . . If we be separated from the Southern Confederacy, [their] . . . duty . . . on manufactured iron, proposed in their provisional tariff, . . . will destroy our iron manufacturers. . . . The magnitude of this interest may be conceived when I inform the Convention that the production of one establishment alone had risen to $100,000 per month before the present troubles began. Its owners fear that they may be compelled to follow their customers in the South, should this State adhere to the North.

I have thus reviewed . . . our industrial products, and, as I humbly conceive, have proved that the market for them is at the South or abroad; that the competition is at the North, that prices are better under the Southern than under the Northern revenue system; and that what we require is moderate protection against the North. . . . In order that we may import, we must export. . . . By separating from the South, we impair our export trade. . . . If we sell our exports well, . . . we shall be in the best possible condition to develop our manufactures. . . .

An intelligent friend . . . [estimates that] of manufactured goods sold in Richmond, . . . one-half . . . were imported from the North, and that the imports were chiefly such things as in his youth had been the product of household and neighborhood manufacture in Virginia. Every member on this floor recollects this state of things, when the spinning wheel and the loom were in every house, and the estimate was that a sheep would clothe each member of the family.

This extensive branch of industry has been transferred to the North, where accumulated capital, machinery and skill enable them to make and bring into our market most of the articles formerly made at home. . . . In 1858 the ready-made clothing sold in Richmond amounted to $1,221,000; of which $762,000 was imported from the North—more than two-thirds of the whole amount. The amount of shoes sold was $1,151,350; of which $898,350—nearly four-fifths—was imported from the North. The sales of hats amounted to $315,000; of which $250,000—about four-fifths—was imported from the North. Thus in these necessary manufactures, formerly made at home, and which, with a very slight protection, could be again made at home, we find Northern competition nearly exterminating our domestic production. . . .

Mr. Chairman, it is in vain that we struggle to make ourselves a manufacturing State, while we have adversaries so powerful, so sagacious, and with such easy access to our markets, as the manufacturers of the Northern States. They fully appreciate the value of the Southern market, they know us better than we know ourselves, . . . and they never will permit manufacturing industry to raise its head at the South so long as they have the power to suppress it.

Their mode of operation is familiar enough to us in Richmond. So soon as a branch of manufactures is attempted here, it immediately draws upon itself the most powerful and concentrated competition from the North. A few years ago a glass factory went into operation in this city, and began to sell profitably wares equally good and quite as cheap as those imported from the North. Immediately the market was flooded with Northern glass ware at reduced prices. The Virginia manufacturer not having the capital to endure long continued competition succumbed, and in the course of time glass resumed its former price.

By means of their vast accumulations of capital, Northern manufactures can bear heavy losses, expecting in the end to regain them with interest. And, sir, they are sagacious enough and bold enough not to fear losses when contending for such a prize as the Southern market. . . . While we were tilling the soil, the North was growing great in commerce and manufactures. Thus they have got the start of us, and it must be confessed that they have made good of it.

It would be an imperfect view, however, to confine ourselves to a consideration of the mere staples of our industry, without considering the relative effects of a union with the North or a junction with the South upon our system of labor, the basis of our industrial fabric.

That system is mixed, partly slave and partly free, and is admirably adapted to our soil, our climate and our physical geography in general. We have pontine[5] districts highly productive, but unhealthy for the white man, where the negro is impervious to the local diseases and cultivates the soil with impunity. We have the manipulations of agriculture, and some of the coarser processes of mining, where the small intelligence and power of endurance of the negro, come into play, but where the white man would be misplaced, and would be withdrawn from occupations more suited to his superior intellect. We have the higher processes of mining, manufactures, navigation and the mechanic arts, for our white laborers, in which they may do themselves and their race justice, and quicken their intellect, while they develop the wealth and power of the State. This mixed system of labor, if left to the law of supply and demand, works not only without conflict, but in harmonious conjunction. The slave produces food for the white laborer and raw material for him to manufacture and transport, while the white laborer furnishes a market for slave products and imparts to them additional value.

It is not true that there is an irrepressible conflict between white and slave labor. That notion is the coinage of men who deserve to be degraded from the rank of statesmen for their sacrifice of truth to the base purposes of sectional strife. . . . It is not the negro laboring at his humble voca-

5. Marshy.

tion in the cotton and tobacco fields of the South, or deep under ground in the coal shaft, or in menial employments, who makes himself felt by the white man as his competitor. The true competitors of our laboring whites are the gigantic manufacturing corporations of the North which flood our market with everything that white labor can produce. When our manufactures are discharging their operatives, or working on half time, it is not because we have negroes making wheat or tobacco, mining coal, and occasionally cobbling a shoe or doing a rough job of work as carpenters or blacksmiths; but because the Northern manufacturer, by his capital, machinery, and skill, is enabled to capture our market. . . .

In the Eastern part of the State where slave labor preponderates, we do not feel Northern competition to such an extent as Western Virginia. In that regard, possessing as it does, great capacities for mining and manufacturing, where the climate is healthy, the people energetic and intelligent, the earth filled with minerals and the country abounding with water power, we find the population restricted in the main to agriculture, and to an agriculture not very productive.

Why is this? Why are the unrivalled advantages of this fine region unavailing, the industry of this most intelligent and active people dwarfed and undeveloped? It is because their labor is exposed to the overwhelming competition of the North; because their iron and coal are driven out of their own market by the iron and coal of the North; and because they cannot accumulate the capital necessary to wage this most unequal war.

Let them go with us into a Southern Confederacy, and receive protection from Northern industry, and they will be what they ought to be—the manufacturers and miners of a great nation. Their country will resound with the hum of industry, and their mountain streams, instead of purling idly over their stony beds, will make their glens musical with the chatter of machinery.

Let not Western Virginia suppose that she has no interest in the slavery question, because she owns but few slaves. She has a vast interest in maintaining the equilibrium of our system of labor. . . . What she needs is capital, . . . and if . . . [eastern Virginia] flourishes, its capital will seek investments in the West. . . .

We must bear in mind that we are not assembled to consider whether we will remain as we were, but whether we shall rest in the new and perilous [Union] . . . in which we now find ourselves. . . . Three courses are proposed to us. . . . First, that we shall demand guarantees (most insufficient in my opinion), and give the North their own time to answer. Second, that we shall demand much more satisfactory guarantees, and fix a time for the response; and, third, that we shall make no further demands, but shall dissolve our connection with the North.

My objections to the first and second plans proposed are very great, to the first they are insurmountable.

I believe that no application for adequate guarantees to the Northern people will be successful. It is an appeal to the constituent body from the public functionaries who have denied such guarantees. It is, in effect, to stigmatize the leading public men of the North, to charge them with misrepresenting their people, and to challenge them to a trial of the charge before that people as judges. We, with no means of access to the Northern people, with all their prejudices, sectional, social and political against us, expect to prevail over their tried and trusted leaders, connected with them by ties of blood, of party, of social intercourse, sharing their sympathies and prejudices, wielding the power of State and Federal Government, and forced by our charges into a position where victory or political death are the only alternatives. To expect success in such a contest, seems to me chimerical in the last degree.

But, this plan not only proposes to take us again, cap in hand, through the weary round of supplication, but fixes no limit to this disastrous if not degrading experiment. How long shall it last? It is to be one, two, or three years, as Mr. Seward suggests? Are we to stand for an indefinite period, with our industry paralyzed, our people feverish and impatient, our manufacturers ready to emigrate in search of their customers? Such delay will be ruinous, it will bankrupt our mercantile community. Already they have endured agonies and have shown extraordinary powers of endurance. But these powers ought not to be taxed beyond all reason.

And while we are thus dallying by the wayside the imperial throne of Southern commerce, now vacant for our occupancy, will be seized by some more enterprising rival, and, when at the end of our unwise delay, we find ourselves compelled to quit the North, and turn with a people exhausted and impoverished by the dreadful process to which they have been subjected, to grasp the advantages of the Southern trade, we shall find it occupied in all its branches and be forced to contend with rivals where we could have entered as friends. But suppose we obtain a favorable answer from the North, and the South, in the meantime having consolidated its Confederacy and resting in quiet from the assaults of abolition, decline to live again under Northern rule—what then will be our situation—separated from our friends, connected with our enemies, cut off from our customers, delivered over to our competitors. . . . Mr. Chairman, far better will it be for us to risk a rupture with the North than separation from the South. One will not injure us permanently—the other will undo us quite. . . .

The greatest of all wrongs, one which in my judgment would require separation from the North if they had never otherwise injured us, is the translation of anti-slaveryism to power, the change from passive sentiment to energetic action. While the anti-slavery sentiment was merely speculative we had no right to complain; but now that it has become an efficient agent in the government, it is no longer safe for a slave State to remain under that government.

Take the history of abolitionized Governments and it is a history of abolitionized people. Look at England, France, Denmark, and at their magnificent Colonies; the pearls of the Antilles, sacrificed without remorse. Look at Russia. Abolition mounts the throne and serfdom disappears. What right have we to expect better things from our Government? Will the Constitution restrain it? Abolition will soon have the power to make that what it pleases, and as the gentleman from Augusta [Mr. ALEXANDER H. H. STUART], well said, in his excellent report on the Harpers Ferry raid, "The whole argument against the *extension* of slavery is soon by a very slight deflection, made to bear against the *existence* of slavery, and thus the anti-extension idea is merged in that of abolition. Accordingly we find, notwithstanding the denial by the Republican party of any purpose to interfere with slavery where it exists, that the tendency of its policy is to its extermination every where."

This disposes most satisfactorily of the denial of our Chief Magistrate in his inaugural . . . of any intention to interfere with slavery in the States. This . . . head of the army and navy . . . has informed us that . . . *"he who would be no slave must consent to have no slave. Those who deny freedom to others, deserve it not for themselves; and, under a just God, cannot long retain it."* . . . With such views held by the chief Executive, the dispenser of honors and fortune, must we wait for an overt act—must we stand until the bayonet is at our throats?

But we are told that we should give the Northern people time to change—that they will come right after a while. Sir, they are much more likely to make us wrong than we are to bring them right. Their anti-slavery sentiment is old as slavery itself—it is backed by Christendom—it is taught in their schools, their pulpits, their press, and pervades their literature—it is crowned with the laurels of repeated triumphs—it has all the signs of a great mental movement. The opposite sentiment with us is recent—it is comparatively a thing of yesterday—it has not been inculcated in early life—it is not backed by sympathy abroad—it has hardly yet had time to be understood and appreciated by our own people. To dash it now against the iron-bound fanaticism of the North, would be the height of folly; at a future day it may be otherwise. The most friendly portion of the Northern people look on slavery as an unmitigated evil, and would reject any defense of it as an assault upon religion and morality. . . . Toleration of what they consider a nuisance is all we can expect from them. . . .

Abolitionism has been sown on a most fertile soil. The North and the South were originally different and have diverged from each other farther still. . . . One became Commercial, the other Agricultural, one held slaves, the other comparatively none; their climates differed, their pursuits differed and they themselves became unlike in every thing except their common tongue. . . .

Twenty years before the Revolution, Dr. [Benjamin] Franklin pronounced it impossible to unite the Colonies. Common danger forced them together, and common weakness for a time made the Union practicable. But that period passed away. The necessity for union . . . ceased. Abolition came and widened the differences until the Common Government has become a mere anarchy, a nuisance, a reproach to civilized man. . . .

Let us go, but to no Border State Confederacy. That is a commercial absurdity, and politically objectionable. The border slave States have the same products, are competitors, present no market for each other's productions, and would have no inter-State trade, no union except a political one. A majority of those States have a small and a decreasing interest in the institution of slavery, and are not such protectors as we should select for that institution, in preference to other States having a greater stake in it.

Let us go to the Southern Confederacy—with the border States, if they will; if not, without them. If we encounter the evils of disunion, let us reap its advantages. We are told that North Carolina will intervene and cut us off. . . . [But] the same causes impelling us operate as strongly upon her. If we go first, our example will influence her; if she go first, her example will unquestionably influence us. We shall soon come together . . . in a Union where we may rest from the discord so destructive of our peace and prosperity in the existing Confederacy.

We are told that it will bring war. On the contrary, it will tend to avert war. Virginia, united with the Southern Confederacy, will present small inducement for war upon that Confederacy. If we stay where we are, and war ensues, we must either fight our friends or fight our own Government. Neutrality is impossible and would be dishonorable.

View the questions before us as you will, and a withdrawal from the present Union seems to be the safest and best course for us to pursue. Let us not hesitate to take it and to submit our action to the people for their approbation. . . .

7

James Holcombe's Secessionist Speech, March 20

Professor James Philemon Holcombe, representing the western Piedmont's Albemarle County (52.3 percent enslaved), reversed George Wythe Randolph's relationship with that celebrated county, site of Monticello, Charlottesville, and the University of Virginia. Randolph, born at Monticello, perhaps had imbibed Grandfather Jefferson's misgivings about slavery and had moved outside, to Richmond. Holcombe, educated outside (at Yale College), had repudiated his emancipating parents' antislavery convictions and had moved inside to Charlottesville, to teach law at the University of Virginia. Although only forty years old in 1861, the prolific Holcombe had already written many legal textbooks. His professorial fame and his secessionist zeal made him the idol of the inflamed students who marched on Richmond in mid-April demanding an end to the older generation's procrastinations.[1]

. . . The institution of slavery is so indissolubly interwoven with the whole framework of society in a large portion of our State, and constitutes so immense an element of material wealth and political power to the whole Commonwealth, that its subversion through the operation of any unfriendly [federal government] policy . . . would, of necessity, dry up the very fountains of the public strength, change the whole frame of our civilization, and inflict a mortal wound upon our liberties. . . . I believe that this danger is impending; that it is of overshadowing magnitude; and that there is no rational hope of escaping from it, but in the prompt severance of the relations of this Commonwealth through the Federal Government, with the free States of the North. . . .

Prior to . . . 1820, slavery in theory was condemned universally, at home and abroad; but the condemnation was a mere passive sentiment, . . . a sleeping abstraction, as inoperative for any practical purpose of mis-

From Reese, *Proceedings* 2:75–111.
1. Gaines, *Biographical Register,* 44–45; Freehling, *Road to Disunion* 2:507–10; *DAB; ANB.*

chief as if it had been a dream. . . . It hardly embarrassed the reclamation of the fugitive; it scarcely offered an obstruction to the transit . . . of slaves through free territory; it suggested no offensive discrimination in private or public life. . . . We lived together in peace and in friendship, as members of a great family of freedom. . . .

[But now] that sleeping, harmless abstraction has been awakened and converted into a principle of active and dangerous aggression. The public conscience of the Northern people has been aroused, and pervaded with a conviction that it is within their power to suppress this institution, and that it is their duty to assail such an embodiment of moral, social and political evil, by the exercise of the public authority in every Constitutional form, and by the rebuking pressure of public opinion at every accessible point. Antagonistic forces have been working during the same period upon the hearts and minds of the Southern people, producing a revolution as complete but in another direction. It has become their universal conviction, that African slavery constitutes the wisest and most beneficent adjustment possible of the relations between the two races, and that it is to be cherished and defended to the last extremity.

Now, whatever other elements of dissatisfaction may have contributed to bring upon the country this fearful strife, . . . the convulsive throes . . . spring mainly from an irrepressible conflict of opposing opinions and sympathies on the subject of slavery. . . . Between the people of the North and the people of the South there lies to day a moral gulf of angry and jealous passions, wider and more impassable than . . . [the] feuds of a thousand years [that] have divided the people of France from the people of England. The Northern people, . . . by the repeated obstructions they have offered to . . . the fugitive slave law, . . . [display] a standing infidelity to the most sacred compact of the Constitution. They have cherished in the bosom of their society, associations extensive in number and wealth, openly avowing their purpose to incite and aid the escape of our slaves, and not infrequently expressing sympathy with insurrection, rapine and murder. . . . This same people . . . have avowed the fixed and deliberate policy of excluding us from our fair and legitimate portion of the public domain. . . . Finally, sir, . . . they have . . . taken possession of that Federal agency, . . . established for the equal maintenance of the rights and honor of all, to execute this systematic injustice; thus converting the . . . Constitution into an instrument for the destruction of the great ends it was ordained to accomplish. It is . . . a revolution as fatal to the independence and honor of the Southern people, as if their liberties had been lost in a disastrous battle with a foreign enemy. . . .

The first wish of the people of Virginia [is] to preserve this Union, . . . upon terms of equality, of honor, of friendship, and of justice to all. . . . What elements should enter into such a scheme of adjustment? . . . Our English forefathers . . . [and] our American ancestors, whenever questions of liberty came up for consideration and decision, . . . [demanded] guaranties of power; power in their own hands, to protect their own rights. . . . [We now need] guarantees of . . . the power of expansion and the power of protection from . . . anti-slavery agitation and from the humiliation and injustice of sectional ascendancy.

And, first, unless we have positive power . . . in our own hands for the expansion of . . . slavery, . . . and its protection as it goes, its extinction . . . in a comparatively short period of time will be . . . inevitable. . . . [In one clause of the Peace Conference proposal], I am glad to see . . . a guarantee of power. . . . The concurrent vote of [both] Southern and Northern Senators . . . is made necessary for the acquisition of territory. But . . . except in the barely possible . . . chance to obtain Canada and Cuba at the same time, I can see no contingency . . . [to] make a bargain with the North. The acquisition of free territory is of slight importance to the North. . . . No expansion is necessary to its safety. For hundreds of years, with the largest emigration from Europe, there will be ample room in . . . our present free territory. . . .

Expansion with us, [however], is a question of existence. The races cannot be amalgamated; they cannot be severed; their diffusion, under such circumstances, over an area which will prevent a dangerous superiority, in any section, or at any point, of the black race, is a necessity of our position, and essential to the preservation of our civilization itself. Now, if there is any obstruction by which the natural and legitimate channels, for the overflowing of a redundant black population, are closed, the emigration of the white, or the emancipation or destruction of the black race, at some future period, are rendered certain. This policy of ultimate extinction, by contraction, "compelling slavery, like a scorpion girdled with fire, to sting itself to death," . . . [is] uniformly avowed by the leaders of the Republican party in this country, and . . . its truth . . . must be acknowledged. There are now four millions of slaves in the United States. . . . They will, in the short space of fifty years, amount to sixteen millions—one-third more than the entire population, black and white, of all the Southern States, at this time.

There are laws now in operation, and which will not fail, impelling the black race in mighty currents, towards the warm latitudes of the South— the pressure of the free States upon the North, and the greater productive value of black labor in the South. Whilst the slave population is thus constantly gravitating towards the tropics, their presence discourages white emigration to that region, and the character of the climate and soil render exposure to the sun in the culture of cotton and rice, unendurable by the white man. I might add that the statistics of the census illustrate and confirm these statements. They exhibit the fact that the white is gaining upon the black population in Delaware, Maryland, Kentucky, Missouri, and, to a slight extent, in Virginia, whilst the black is gaining on the white in all of the Gulf States and in some of them very rapidly. . . .

Diffusion is therefore an element of safety. Notwithstanding the immense superiority of the white over the black man, . . . a numerical equilibrium . . . is essential to preserve in peace, the requisite subordination and control. To adopt any policy by which slavery would be hemmed in, within its present limits, does appear to me, when we look at the growing disparity of numbers between the races, the perpetual stimulus to dissatisfaction which will be held out to the negro, and his enlarging capacity and increasing facilities for mischief, to be providing for a renewal upon our own soil of the scenes of St. Domingo, and the destruction of the race or the relation, amid national and social convulsion.

The Southern States, especially those to the South of Virginia, are deeply interested in this policy of expansion. To them it is of more vital importance than to us. The destruction of slavery would bring upon Virginia a blight and ruin . . . for centuries; yet it is possible that the lands of Virginia may be cultivated by the white man. But the question of cultivating cotton and rice with white labor does not admit of debate; in the cotton and rice States the existence of African slavery becomes a question of civilization. They could not acquiesce in any principle or policy . . . by which the expansion of their institutions . . . should be prevented, without betraying . . . the guardianship of an inferior race, . . . committed to their keeping by God himself, and purchasing an ignominious . . . security . . . during their own lives, at the price of . . . the lives of their children, amid the probable horrors of servile war. No Southern statesman under such circumstances, could, with reason, anticipate any other result . . . than one of two alternatives—either that his countrymen would be prepared in a debasing school of political degradation for civil and social equality with their emancipated slaves, or that from its darkness would burst

> Some dread Nemesis, crowned with fire,
> To tread them out forever.

. . . This great necessity . . . to diffuse and to protect slavery as it goes . . . [will be] a rock upon which all schemes of reconstruction will be wrecked. But there are other reasons why we should require guarantees of power. We want power to put an end to this irritating strife because it is fatal to our peace, dangerous to the security of our property, and through the sectional ascendancy which it has established, irreconcilable with every principle of liberty.

How are we to control the further agitation of this subject? If the concurrence of a majority of the Southern members of the Electoral College was rendered necessary to the appointment of the Executive, . . . and the assent of a majority of the Southern as well as Northern members of the Senate, required whenever either of such majorities should call for a sectional vote, . . . you would go far towards rendering it impossible, to use the agency of the Federal Government in any form whatever to the prejudice of slavery, and thus strike at the very root of this political agitation. . . .

Without security against the continuance of this agitation, not only will all useful legislation be obstructed; not only will the irritated passions, that now inflame the sections, be perpetuated, but a danger, already formidable to the very security of our fire-sides, will continue to increase in magnitude. . . . Look at the experience of the past, and take a lesson from it. The struggle between the races in St. Domingo commenced long before the enactment of the French Assembly, decreeing liberty to the blacks. It began with the public discussion of the question, out of, as well as in that body. The tragedy at Southampton, in our own State, has been traced to the influence of agitation. The John Brown raid was its offspring. . . .

The slave is a man as well as his master. He is an ignorant man, and liable, therefore, like all ignorant men, to be misled by extravagant expectations—by false hopes held out to him; and with the noise of a mighty movement for his emancipation sounding always in his ears, can you expect aught else, . . . from time to time, . . . [than] outbursts of violence in your society, which will fill the master with continual apprehensions, and render it necessary for him to provide safeguards so costly and so burdensome, as that the institution itself will become intolerable? . . .

This Republican party has not been founded upon a question of expediency . . . but upon convictions of right and wrong, convictions of duty which . . . commit men . . . until they have achieved their purpose. The sentiment of hostility to slavery is more generally diffused, and is as strong in the minds of the Northern people, as any passion with which a nation has ever been animated. It . . . is the irrepressible out-birth of the conscience of the North, expressing its highest intelligence and purest virtue. . . . That policy has achieved its first great triumph—and that policy is invincible, unless you can bring about some re-adjustment of the Constitution, which will repress and control this fanaticism, by rendering it utterly impossible, to employ the Federal Government in any way in its service.

Shall we rely upon the good faith, the good feeling or justice of the Northern people for security against the wrong and the degradation of a sectional ascendancy? . . . Will not the Executive patronage be prostituted in the North, to reward the active enemies of slavery; in the South, to reward those who, at least, are willing to sprinkle incense on the altars of fanaticism? In regard to the Legislative department, is there any security against the most partial and unjust laws? Prudence or fear may withhold, for a time, the heavy hand of oppression, but where the impulse, the power and the opportunity coincide, sooner or later wrong must come. . . .

Sectional domination . . . transfers the decision of all questions . . . to the forum of the North alone. Look at the last election! . . . The exclusion of slavery from the territories . . . was discussed in the North, but in the North only. It will be the same hereafter in reference to all other great questions, so long as that ascendency continues. Unless some divisions should occur in the ranks of the Republican party, before the next Presidential election takes place, the North, being able to control the election, and that party having the ascendency in the North, would it not be the merest mockery to open a poll for an electoral vote in the South? . . .

Another feature in this sectional ascendency . . . [embittered] the oppression of the Jew by the Christian, of the Moor by the Spaniard, of the

Saxon by the Norman: the element of humiliation; not only the iron hand of oppression, but the insolent spurn of contempt. . . . The peculiar feature of this despotism [is] not only to rule but to ruin, not only to ruin but to degrade. . . . Are we so recreant to the exalted strain of our great fathers, as to be willing to endure the humiliation and ruin of a sectional ascendency, worse than colonial vassalage? . . . When any people lose that self-respect which is the spring of public virtue and private honor, the public spirit and public conscience, which constitute the most valuable possession of a nation, must become extinct. . . . Sooner or later, ruin overtakes every people who surrender their rights to their fears, and prefer their ease to their duty. . . .

Tell me not, sir, what our ancestors have said in their day, . . . just and appropriate in their own time. . . . No doubt they desired this Union to endure forever. . . . But there is an inspiration in their . . . higher sentiment, . . . embodied in that glorious scene commemorated by the genius of painting, now so fitly gracing this Hall.[2] . . . Issues of liberty are . . . revealed in the majesty of that form, in the serenity of that brow, in the luster of that eye, as amid the wintry torrents of the Delaware, the Father of his Country pours into a dismayed and desponding patriotism, in its hour of darkest trial, his own unfailing heart of hope. . . . From every memorial tomb of the mighty dead, through all our borders [his sentiment] bursts into speech—"Whenever this Union and your liberties cannot exist together, throw the Union to the winds, and clasp the Liberty of your country to your heart." . . .

We are standing amidst the ruins of the Union; the Union has been shattered, and there is no human architect that can rear the temple again. A number of our sister States—seven, soon in all human probability, to become eight—have not only left the Union, but have actually organized a new Union, and have established a permanent Constitution. They are frequently accused of hot haste, in not having shown proper deference to your opinions, and your feelings in changing their Federal Relations, without appeal to you. . . .

Let us bear in mind, [however], that it is hardly twelve months since Mississippi and South Carolina sent a mission to Virginia, and that Alabama would have taken the same course, had there been any indication

2. Probably a copy or a print or another version of Emanuel Leutze's *Washington Crossing the Delaware* (1851).

that it would be acceptably received. The object of this mission was to obtain a conference of all the slave States; a conference, by whose decision it was expressly declared that South Carolina, as well as Mississippi, would be bound, however opposite it might be to their own views of the policy to be pursued. They had previously, by Legislative resolutions, expressed their own conviction that, in the precise contingency which has since arisen, and which was then imminent, the Southern States should withdraw from the Union. That the responsibility of acting upon their own judgment in this grave crisis might not be forced upon them, they [futilely] appealed to Virginia to meet them in general council. . . .

Mr. Chairman, anterior to the election of Lincoln, there was not the slightest indication . . . that another proposition for conference would have been received with more favor. No alternative was left to . . . [the Gulf States] but to acquiesce in our decision, or to take such course as, in their own judgment, might be requisite for the protection of their rights. . . .

It is stated . . . that Virginia has more interest in this controversy, than any other State. . . . [But] I maintain that the cotton States are more deeply interested than Virginia. So far as the number of fugitive slaves is concerned, . . . the actual number of slaves lost this way, is about as great in those States, in proportion to white population, as in Virginia or Kentucky. . . . The degradation of enduring a sectional ascendency, will as deeply wound their honor and liberty, as it would wound our honor and our liberty.

On the great issue of expansion and future protection to slavery, [however], they are more vitally concerned than we are. They want future acquisition of Territory, that the normal relation of the races may be preserved for all time, and that there may be no great struggle for existence or supremacy between them at any remote day. We are in no danger of such a contest in Virginia. The Southern States will receive all our slaves, but the Southern Territory, with the slaves of Virginia emptied into it, will not be adequate to the peaceful accommodation of the black race. . . .

Agriculture may revive from the depression consequent upon a loss of your slave labor, but if you confine the slaves to the cotton States within their present limits, you will compel the white population of that region either to abandon it to the black, or to endure the debasing consequences of an admixture of races. Thus they have to decide a question both of existence and civilization, as well as of liberty; with us it is equally a question of liberty, so long as we remain a slaveholding community, but it is not a question of existence or civilization.

From the position of the border States, they may have more to fear from the dissolution of this Union; but the cotton States, from their position on the Gulf, have infinitely more to fear, from its duration. Delaware is nominally only, a slave State. Maryland will soon be a free State; and so it is with Missouri, and Kentucky. Is it to be expected that States, which by natural and political laws are compelled to be slave States forever, will surrender the keeping of their destiny to States, which may at no distant day, give up this institution? . . . It was a solemn duty resting upon the people of the cotton States, to . . . place their vast interests beyond the reach of peril. Their Confederation has become a fixed and irreversible fact of history, and . . . the sooner we realize [that fact], the better.

Upon what do you ground the hope of a reconstruction of the Union? Do you think it will be voluntary on the part of the Southern people? . . . They have been living for the last three months in anticipation of . . . desolating invasion by a Northern army. During this time all the deadly and all the noble passions of human nature, have been aroused and inflamed. Do you think that the men who have been sleeping upon the sand banks of Charleston, expecting nightly and hourly to be brought into deadly collision with the Northern people, are ready to come back and mingle with them on terms of friendship in the administration of a common government? No, sir; . . . the men who have organized this government, and the great popular body that has sustained it so far, can be brought back into this Union, and induced to submit to Black Republican rule . . . [only] by bloody revolution at home or subjugation from abroad.

Are they not able to maintain themselves, in their independent condition? . . . These States contain a white population larger than that of the thirteen colonies when our independence was achieved, a territory more compact and defensible, vastly superior resources in money, trained soldiers and all the muniments of war, and a great staple, which makes it almost a necessity, for every civilized nation to preserve with them relations of peace and commerce. . . . The prosperity of these States has never been greater than at this day. . . .

Will the Government at Washington . . . close the Southern ports as ports of entry, by an act of Congress, when . . . [the closure] would be regarded by every Government in Europe, as equivalent to a paper blockade and . . . a violation of the rules of public law? Can an army be collected and supported, sufficiently numerous to establish the Federal authority? . . . No, sir; the Federal Government can neither tempt these States to return, nor can it force them to return. Without some change in its own policy, according to the reliable statement of the New York "Evening Post"—the most conservative and ablest Republican journal in the country— . . . the Government will be bankrupt, before the next crop of corn is ripe. . . .

Now, Mr. President, every material interest of this Commonwealth is going to wreck under the uncertainty as to what is to be her future policy. Whilst we ought to exercise all the deliberation requisite for an intelligent and well considered decision of this momentous issue—yet deliberation protracted one moment beyond that period, would not only be a weakness, but a crime.

Whilst we are making a movement, [to save the Union], hopeless in all human appearance from indications North as well as South, . . . we are exposing the cause of peace. . . . The most violent and ultra organs of the Black Republican party have acknowledged, that if Virginia acceded to this Southern Confederacy; if her voice of strength and influence, called for negotiation, and recognition of independence, this fact alone, would make peace a necessity. . . . Uncertainty as to our course . . . alone puts the peace of the country in jeopardy, and . . . may, and probably will, precipitate upon Virginia, Maryland, Kentucky and all the border States, the horrors of civil war.

If this Border conference will not contribute to [peace], . . . for what do you ask it? Is it that you may commit the destiny of Virginia to the decision of a majority of the Border States? It must be borne in mind that Delaware is really a free State. Maryland has little upwards of eighty thousand slaves. . . . Missouri has only one hundred thousand slaves, and in five or ten years, is likely to become a free State. Kentucky, . . . separated by the river only from Ohio, with an almost virgin soil, equally adapted to the growth of the staples of Ohio, with a large proportion of white population, and with a strong anti-slavery feeling in existence, is destined at a later day to lose her slaves. Are we prepared to commit the fortunes of Virginia into the keeping of States so unequally interested in the preservation of this institution? . . .

But, sir, the only real issue for this Convention to determine is shall she remain in a Confederacy with the North, or associate with the States of the South? Our efforts to reconstruct the Union, will prove abortive.

. . . Sooner or later, you must decide with which of these Confederacies, you will link your destiny. . . .

Suppose the government pursues a pacific policy towards the Southern States, resulting in the recognition of their independence. . . . If Virginia remains with the North, the uncertainty as to the security of slave property, the repugnance, moral and political, in the minds and hearts of a large portion of her people to such a connection, must be speedily followed by an immense emigration of slaves and their masters, from the Commonwealth. What effect will be produced upon all our great interests, by this loss of capital, and population? . . . Private ruin and public bankruptcy, social anarchy and civil convulsion will overwhelm the Commonwealth.

Look at it, in its political aspect. [We now have] . . . association, without power or influence, [as] . . . one of seven slave States, in a Union with twenty free States. Virginia has been accustomed to lay down the rule for the construction of the Constitution, and to fix the principles of public policy. . . . I wholly mistake the temper of her people if she is ever willing to follow, a spiritless and degraded captive, in the train of the victor.

There are moral, as well as industrial and political considerations, which unmistakably point us to the South. There is to be found our own form of society; they are our nearest kindred; there are the habits and institutions of our own people; there we may wield the noblest form of power—a moral and intellectual dominion; there we may improve and perpetuate our own peculiar type of civilization; there we may build up a splendid Confederacy, homogenous in its feelings and its interests—a Confederacy that will change the moral sentiment of the world in reference to slavery, . . . —a Confederacy that will march in unity, in power, in glory and in liberty, upon . . . nearly half a continent. . . .

Why should we not form this association? . . . The most serious difficulty that disturbs gentlemen, seems to be uneasiness as to the condition of the border, which Virginia, Maryland and Kentucky would then constitute. . . . As to the escape of fugitives, it is said the Canada line will be brought down to the Ohio. My own impression, is, that the Canada line, for a long period, has been very near the Ohio, and that the security of our slaves is rather the result of our ability to keep them home than our ability to recover them, when they reach the free States upon the border.

But if the Southern Confederacy is established on a permanent footing, the Northern people will soon recognize the necessity and advantage of favorable commercial treaties with it. They will then learn that one of the terms of good neighborhood between contiguous nations is that neither should permit its citizens to disturb their neighbors, in the enjoyment of their property; and a refusal on the part of the Southern Confederacy to receive Northern manufactures . . . would lead to a treaty, in which they would stipulate to pay for fugitive slaves, not delivered, their entire value. . . .

Apprehension has been expressed, lest we should have the European system of standing armies, introduced upon our continent. This seems to me a phantom. . . . Peace is being recognised more and more, as the standing interest and policy of all civilized nations. . . . England within the last fifteen years would, on more than one occasion, have declared war against the United States, but for the strength and political power of the manufacturing and commercial classes which it would have prostrated.

Will not these considerations apply with equal force, between the Northern and the Southern Confederacies? What will induce the Northern people to maintain large armies on their side of the border, . . . [causing] a similar force upon our side? . . . Be assured, sir, the agricultural, manufacturing and commercial people of the North will never court the burthen of sustaining upon their frontier an immense army, to repel an invasion they have no reason to anticipate or fear, or to prosecute a war of aggression they have no motive to undertake, and no means of rendering successful.

We have, at this moment, a standing and conclusive answer to this apprehension. We have an immense border on the North—the Canada border. . . . No standing armies [are] collected upon either side of that border. On neither side do the people live in constant apprehension of war. They rely for security not only upon their courage and their arms but upon those great economical and commercial reasons, which make peace the interest and therefore the policy of their governments. . . .

Again, sir, the Southern people along that border are eminently military in their spirit and habits. They are the descendants of men who reclaimed that land from the ruthless savage; men who went serenely to their couches at night, when there was constant danger that they might be roused from their slumbers by an Indian war whoop or a blazing roof; the descendants of the men who fought, at Point Pleasant, and of the men of West Augusta, to whom Washington looked in the darkest hours of the revolution. If their border was ever invaded, these proud historic memories would lend an inspiration of courage to its defence which . . . would strike terror into the heart of every foe. . . .

I ask our friends from the West to consider this whole question . . . in the light in which we view it. The North-western district of Trans-Allegheny has, according to the statistics of the last census, about 8,000 slaves, while there are more than 400,000 in Piedmont and Tide-Water. . . . Your people can never, therefore, be disturbed by any apprehension of present or future servile wars. The destruction of slave property would only affect you by the re-action of our ruin. We, as a great slaveholding people, whose whole civilization is interwoven with this institution, may naturally be more sensitive to all which threatens its disgrace or its destruction. By all the hallowed associations of our common ancestry and common glory, I invoke you, gentlemen of the West, to let us march, keeping step together, through all the future, as our fathers have done in all the past. Let us ever be as ready, as they were in their generation, to cover with interlocked arms, the rights, the institutions, and the honor of whole State. . . .

But, sir, suppose the policy of the Federal Government is not pacific, but coercion is attempted, where will Virginia go then? I am glad to know that the voice which says Virginia will go nowhere, is very faint and low. . . . Every material interest we possess would be destroyed by the subjugation of the Gulf States; all the principles of Constitutional liberty we have cherished, would be trampled in the dust; but there are stronger considerations yet, which would never permit us to stand by, and witness such a consummation. . . . Sir, for nations as well as individuals, there is something worse than death. Sooner than behold this glorious Commonwealth stoop to the abasement and degradation of this course, I would . . . rather see her fall in a glorious struggle for her own rights, and the rights of her sister States, and leave to future history the memorable response in her behalf, "dead upon the field of honor." . . .

8

John Baldwin's
Unionist Speech,
March 21–23

These pages may lift John Brown Baldwin from obscurity. The Staunton resident, aged forty in 1861, represented the Valley's Augusta County (20.2 percent enslaved). Baldwin never achieved higher office than a seat in the Virginia lower house (although he briefly became Speaker after the war). He never rose above the respectability of a middle-class attorney (although he owned ten slaves in 1861, a relatively high number in this convention and evidence that personal slaveholdings were no prediction of a delegate's preference). Baldwin was not even the most important Whiggish politician in his immediate family; Alexander H. H. Stuart, his wealthier cousin, brother-in-law, and fellow convention delegate, held that honor. History books have rarely noted Baldwin for more than his hapless secret interview with Abraham Lincoln at the White House on April 4, when his effort to persuade the president to abandon Fort Sumter became an exercise in exasperated futility.

If Baldwin was equally exasperated at his failure to win fame in the Virginia convention, the fault was partly his own. His interminable speech, consuming three days, buried his superb points under a snarl of poorly organized words. No convention speaker, however, benefits more from editorial intervention. When the verbal flab is removed, the muscularity of Baldwin's mentality arguably surpasses that of any other Unionist, in or out of Virginia, and matches the best secessionist logic anywhere. Moreover, later in the convention, when imminent secession left no time for excess words, Baldwin's terse warnings need scant editorial help. The positions of this forgotten Unionist show that when history books overly dwell on a debate's winners, the losers' insight becomes tragically lost.[1]

. . . I claim for the [Valley] county I have the honor to represent, . . . Augusta, a position . . . at the centre of the State, connected with both East and West by the great lines of travel and improvement. . . . She is identi-

From Reese, *Proceedings* 2:138–46, 165–201, 210–37.

1. Gaines, *Biographical Register*, 14–15; *DAB*; John R. Hildebrand, *The Life and Times of John Brown Baldwin* . . . (Roanoke, VA, 2009).

fied with every interest and every institution . . . of value in Virginia; and in regard to them all occupies what I might call a great central, conservative position. If anywhere in Virginia there are extremes of opinion, . . . Augusta county and her people know nothing of them. . . .

The great cause of complaint now is the slavery agitation. . . . There seems to be an impression entertained in some quarters, and industriously disseminated, that upon this great question . . . some of the people of Virginia, in some portions of the State, and some of their representatives upon this floor . . . are, for some reason or other, not to be trusted. . . . For years past I have seen this thing industriously resorted to for the baser ends of . . . all parties in this Commonwealth. . . . This insinuation seems to be . . . a species of terrorism, . . . brought to bear . . . in the vain hope that it will repress, if not freedom of thought, at least, freedom of speech. Sir, this terrorism . . . is exceedingly ridiculous and contemptible. I hope, when I proceed to define my position in regard to this great interest, that I shall not in any quarter be deemed to defer, in any respect, to a clamor which I despise.

Sir, in regard to the question of slavery, . . . I have always entertained the opinion that African slavery, as it exists in Virginia, is a right and a good thing—on every ground, moral, social, religious, political and economical—a blessing alike to the master and the slave—a blessing to the non-slaveholder and the slaveholder. . . . I am not one of those who look forward with expectation or desire, to its extinction . . . or to restrict it to any particular locality. . . . If it can be done by fair, legitimate and honest expansion and extension, I have no objection that this mild, beneficent and patriarchal institution may cover the whole earth as the waters cover the great deep. . . . [Wherever] my views of what concerns the interest and the honor of Virginia may differ from the views of other gentlemen in other parts of the State, . . . I take them from the stand-point of a pro-slavery man, representing a slaveholding constituency. . . .

Virginia . . . has been upon all subjects of administration, including this great question of slavery, the directing spirit of this government, from its foundation down to the election of Abraham Lincoln. . . . Who has ever had a better right than Virginia to the celebration *"L'etat, c'est moi"*?[2] . . . Her past has been one march of glory. But . . . look at her now! . . . She holds the destiny of this Republic in her own hands. . . . Let us join

2. *I* am the state.

hands with one another here and swear, before high Heaven, that as . . . Constitutional Liberty has been committed to us, we . . . will, with God's help, lift up our bleeding country from the dust and set her free. . . .

The election of Lincoln . . . has been spoken of by both the distinguished gentlemen who have preceded me [Messrs. RANDOLPH and HOLCOMBE], as an overthrow, or a subversion of the Constitution, by the use of its own forms. . . . I regard this assumption, that the election of any man to the Presidency can justify disunion, as a direct assault upon the fundamental principles of American liberty. . . .

The powers conferred upon our government which the Constitution limits, defines and restricts, are . . . divided among coordinate departments of the government to operate as checks upon one another. . . . Our fathers . . . have built . . . up one, two, three, four, five distinct barriers. One may fail, two, three, four may fail, and yet the fifth may remain and be sufficient to protect the Constitution from overthrow. . . .

Our forefathers . . . anticipated that the time might come, aye, in all probability would come, . . . when the House of Representatives, fresh from the people by short tenures, might yield to the popular clamor of the moment, . . . overstep the bounds of constitutional limitation, and encroach upon the liberties of the minority of the people or upon the rights of the States. And, sir, to avoid that, they erected another barrier, the United States Senate, removed farther from the turmoils and excitements and passions of the multitude. As another barrier against this encroachment they armed the President of the United States with the great conservative veto. And yet another in the Supreme Court of the United States. Then they reserved to the people themselves, at the polls, . . . the great safeguard. . . . The administrators of this entire government must come back at last to the people for judgment in regard to their public conduct. . . .

Now, sir, these barriers were erected as an injunction . . . to us, if we are . . . beaten in the popular branch of the National Legislature, to appeal to the Senate. If beaten in the Senate, to appeal to the Constitutional Executive veto. If that fail, to appeal to the Supreme Court. . . . And, if . . . all these means of protection have failed, not to give up the ship, but to appeal from the false agents of the people . . . to their masters at the polls. . . .

At the time of the election of Lincoln, . . . it will not be pretended here that the enemies of the South had ever been in a majority in either branch of the Legislative department. . . . It will not be pretended that the Supreme Court had ever failed . . . to expound the Constitutional rights of the South. Then in the Senate of the United States, on the day of Lincoln's election, the south and the friends of the South were in a majority. In the House of Representatives on that day, the South and the friends of the South had control. In the Supreme Court the South and the friends of the South were in the ascendant. In this condition of things, the Presidential office was gained by the Republicans. . . .

What then? Immediately the cry was that the government had been seized. The government, the government, Mr. Chairman. I fear very much that we have gotten into the habit of exaggerating, grossly exaggerating the importance of the Executive office. . . . The Republican party, in the election of Abraham Lincoln, obtained possession of the weakest department of the government. . . .

If our adversaries, our enemies, our oppressors, or whatever you choose to call them, are in the ascendant now, who is responsible? Who has withdrawn fourteen Senators from the Senate of the United States, and left us in the lamentable condition of being in a hopeless and helpless minority in that body? Who, but the seceding states of the South, that have also withdrawn more than thirty members of Congress from the House of Representatives, and left us in a minority not only in the Congress just closed, but in the Congress that is to assemble next fall? . . .

Was there any necessity for our leaving the Union? None, sir; none whatever. The Constitution itself provided sufficient guarantees and sufficient protection. While we had the Legislative department we had the guarantees of power spoken of by the gentleman from Albemarle [Mr. HOLCOMBE]. . . . We had the power of withholding the supplies of Government until we compelled them to yield justice, and protection and safety to the South. . . . We had that power, we had that right, and . . . my impulses were not to fly from the Constitution and seek refuge in other resorts, but . . . to rally, with all my might and heart and soul, to the defence of this last hope—as I verily believe, of the permanent success of civil and religious liberty in the world. . . .

But, sir, . . . seven States have withdrawn, *de facto,* whether *de jure* or not. . . . It becomes necessary for us to consider the new relations which devolve upon us. In the first place let me consider our relations to these cotton States.

I deny the assertion that we are in any sense dependent for our policy upon them. I deny that it is either a physical, moral, or commercial necessity, that we shall follow their fortunes. I deny that we are so "hitched on" to them as to be "dragged after" their destiny. I hope, and I will not abandon the hope, that some day or other, sooner or later, the people of these States will see . . . [that] with all the talk about the glory of a Southern Confederacy, with all the talk about the splendors of a Confederacy, . . . it is after all but a *Southern* Confederacy, which is to have but *half* a continent; and those of us who have lived under the glorious Confederation of these United States, embracing a whole continent, may well refuse to go into ecstasies of admiration over the proposition to become members of a dismembered half, aye, less than half, of a continent. . . .

What are our relations to the border States? . . . North Carolina . . . has refused even to call a Convention to consider the question of secession or disunion. . . . Tennessee . . . has done the same thing. And so in regard to Kentucky. In Maryland no meeting of the Legislature or Convention has been had. How, then, are we situated? Why, sir, I asked a boy in the street, the other day, how Virginia would go out of the Union? and the reply was: "I suppose she will have to go by water, in a dugout." [Laughter.] . . .

Our earnest and rapid friends . . . tell us . . . that North Carolina, in deference to the voice of Virginia, will reverse her matured and deliberate opinion, and will go South with us. Do you not think, to say the least, that it would be a little respectful in us, to ask her whether she will? . . . The border States have all the claims upon us that the Cotton States have, and some additional. They have the claim, that the Cotton States have, of past association, and they have in addition the claim of present association. The Cotton States have the claim of similar institutions; so have the border States, and, in addition to that, they have the claim of similar dangers, and similar wrongs. . . . I think we would be derelict in duty to ourselves, would act in disregard of our common prudence of the rights, feelings and interests of those States, if we were to undertake to move one step without a conference with them. . . .

It becomes the Border Slave States to stand firm together, and to demand from the people of the North guarantees and securities, ample and complete, and overflowing in their abundance, against the new dangers to which we are to be exposed, and against the recurrence of this miserable, abominable agitation which has brought us into this serious difficulty. It is the duty of the North to . . . hasten to give to us . . . such guarantees as will afford us safety for the future and as will, or ought to, bring back our sister States of the South. If they refuse, . . . I for one will not submit, . . . Virginia will not submit, . . . and . . . the Border Slave States now remaining in the Union will not submit. . . .

We must have the most thorough and complete guarantees for all our rights, without exception, or we must separate—one or the other. I hope the conference of the border States will be called, and I hope when it meets, it will agree upon some proposition of guaranty that will satisfy the South. I hope they will lay it down distinctly as their *ultimatum,* and that they will present to the people of the free States, in one hand this *ultimatum* of protection and guaranty, and in the other, the alternative of a peaceful dissolution of this government. That is the plan which I advocate, and upon which I propose to act.

But, sir, we are told, there is no use of making a bargain with these people; that there is such a hatred between the people of the two sections; that there has grown up such an anti-slavery fanaticism among the people of the North as to render it unsafe to live with them any longer; that . . . there is an irrepressible conflict that has grown up between the people of the North and the South, and . . . that either the North must succeed in overturning the institution of slavery, or the South must take the institution of slavery into its own keeping. . . .

[But] is this irrepressible conflict a living thing? . . . We have in the last Congress this remarkable fact, that will not be controverted, that by a vote of two thirds of both Houses, they have, with a Republican majority, in each passed and propounded for ratification by the States of the Union, a constitutional amendment . . . by which it is provided that the Constitution never shall be amended so as to give the right to the General Government to interfere with slavery in the States, in any respect whatever.

But, sir, what about this . . . great increase of danger to the South from the increase of the abolition sentiment? I deny the fact at the onset. . . . There are more pro-slavery men in the North than there were in the whole earth when I can first recollect. We have not only revolutionized the mind of the South and presented her redeemed, regenerated and disenthralled from this oppressive weight that bore her down in times past, but we have invaded the mind of the North. We have gone with them into the school of philosophy and theology, and we have grappled with them there, with success. . . .

It is true there has been developed in the North an active principle of abolitionism. It began there; it first took possession of the harebrained

men and the old maids of the North—the materials of fanaticism everywhere. [Laughter.] There it stopped, with an occasional lift from some
weak member of the clergy, until after a while the clergy found favor
among the fair sex; and abolition, putting on the garb of religion, came
through the country in a white cravat, singing "psalms and *hymns,* and
spiritual songs." [Laughter.] Its race was short, and was soon run; the institution of slavery, against which it was directed, existed at that time only
in the States and the District of Columbia, and all the efforts of fanaticism to make an anti-slavery party had to come directly over the ram-
parts and bulwarks of the Constitution. . . . The institution of slavery is so
entrenched within the inner citadel of the Constitution that no man but
a madman has ever yet undertaken to hazard the opinion that Congress
had anything to do with it, and while it was confined to the States the
party of abolitionists were such as I have described, fanatical, ridiculous,
harmless. . . .

Black Republicanism has only gotten a respectable number of supporters by backing down from all the fierce claims of the Abolition party.
In old times the political Abolitionists always claimed to repeal the fugitive slave law—to abolish slavery in the District of Columbia, and in the
United States dock yards, &c—to interfere with the slave trade between
the States, and ultimately to extinguish slavery in the States by amendments to the Constitution of the United States. Black Republicanism had
to give up all of them and to take its stand upon the naked isolated question of restricting slavery from going into the Territories of the United
States, and until it took that comparatively abstract position it never
could succeed in getting the support of the Northern people. . . .

But we are told that this fanatical feeling is so strong and that it is so
blind that, . . . [according to] the gentleman from Albemarle [Mr. HOL-
COMBE], . . . there can be no contract between us and the people of the
North. . . . Sir, I cannot and I will not believe that we cannot bargain with
these people. On the contrary, I am strongly convinced that in the North
and the South, the great masses of the people, leaving out the politicians
and fanatics of both sections, have this day an earnest yearning for each
other, and for peace and union with each other. . . .

But we are told that if we make any bargain with them, it must be a
kind of contract new to this country; it must be a bargain in which, by
some mysterious process, we are to correct a great mistake. . . . The South
has come to be in a minority; and now we are to undergo some curious

transformation under what is called a contract or guaranty of power by which this minority is to be converted into a working majority of this Government. . . .

I protest that . . . our system of government has but one foundation on which it can rest safely, and that is the virtue and intelligence of the people; that it has but one administrative body that it can trust with safety, and that is the body of the majority of the people. . . . It is founded upon confidence that our people have sense enough to make a bargain, and integrity enough to keep a bargain. The Constitution recognizes the propriety of a distribution of power among various departments of administration, for the purpose of securing the matured and deliberate judgment of the people. But, sir, it has never been, and never will be, admitted to be sound, that the governmental administration of this country should be confided to the hands of a minority of the people. . . .

The opinion of Virginia has been declared upon this subject very recently and very distinctly. By her General Assembly and by the votes of her people in the recent election it has been declared beyond dispute that the Crittenden propositions, as amended by the General Assembly, would be satisfactory to the people of Virginia. Here we have a declaration, not only that Virginia is willing to bargain with the people of the North, but that she does not regard as essential . . . the extraordinary . . . guaranties of power . . . suggested by the gentleman from Albemarle [Mr. HOLCOMBE]. . . .

In her effort to rise above the passions and the excitement of the moment, and to address herself, in a spirit of calm, patriotic statesmanship, to the work of pacification, and the re-construction of this government, . . . Virginia desired a conference of States by commissioners, to meet in the city of Washington. . . . These representatives . . . were in session for a fortnight or three weeks; they gave us the result of their labors and suggested a plan of constitutional amendments. . . .

It has been assailed in several ways. In the first place it is said . . . to have failed because the Congress of the United States refused to refer it to the action of the States. Ah, is that the failure? . . . With but three days in which to consider the subject and act upon it, what could you expect? Sir, I never expected them to give a two-thirds vote in favor of any plan of pacification, especially in so short a time. . . . It has never yet had a fair chance; and . . . if this Convention of Virginia had accepted the recommendation of the "Peace Conference," and sent it to the country with our endorsement upon it as a satisfactory adjustment—before this time you would have had the Union men of the country, North and South, East and West, rallying with one voice in favor of it. . . .

Let us now look at this Peace Conference proposition. . . . The first section of the Crittenden proposition and the first section of the Peace Conference plan refer altogether to the Territorial question. . . . I have not been able to see . . . [why] the people of this mighty nation . . . have been wrought up to the extreme of passion, sectional strife, bitterness and hate about this Territorial question. . . . Is it not a matter perfectly familiar to every member of this Convention, that in regard to the present Territories of the United States, we have not one foot of Territory that is fit for the employment of slave labor? . . .

It is true that in the Territory of New Mexico the officers of the army stationed there have carried along with them as members of their families their body servants and their house servants; . . . yet there have never been found more than twenty-five slaves there. . . . In a country where Mexican peons are to be had almost for the asking, it will hardly pay to transport negroes worth a thousand or fifteen hundred dollars for the purpose of working their silver or quicksilver mines. That is not the sort of labor for which slaves are adapted; and I believe it is the unanimous judgment of the country, so far as New Mexico is concerned, slavery can never go there. . . .

That is partly owing to the fact, there is an unsuitableness in the Territory for that sort of labor; but it is also owing to the other important fact, . . . that there is a deficiency of slave labor in the South; that their great, pressing necessity at this day, is the want of slaves enough to cultivate their great staple crops. . . . The drain made upon us . . . [from] the great demand for slaves . . . is constantly going on; and it is owing to the fact, more than to any other, I presume, that the distinguished gentleman from Albemarle [Mr. HOLCOMBE] anticipates that Missouri, Maryland and Kentucky will eventually become free States.

I take it that these two propositions are incontrovertible, that we have not the territory to take the slaves into; and, if we had, that we have not the negroes to take there. If that is true, what are we to think of . . . the infatuation, madness and fanaticism that are seeking to overthrow such a Government as this, and to imperil and destroy the rights and interests of millions of freemen, North and South, upon an issue like this? I suppose if the question had never been raised, . . . if we never had locked arms, as it were, upon the argument of the right, I suppose everybody would say . . . that this miserable, poor territory should be settled by whoever choose to go and live in that remote region.

But the point has been made; and what is it? It is that the South has a right to go into all the territories with her property, and have protection for that property. What is the other side? It is that the North has a right to prohibit them from going there with their property. . . . The South claims them all for her civilization and her institutions; the North claims them all for her civilization and her institutions, and thus we have, what seems to me, to be a very absurd quarrel. . . .

The [Peace Conference's first assumption is that the] only practical and feasible way is . . . to divide the territory and say to one kind of civilization, "Here, this is suitable for you and yours, settle here," and to another kind of civilization, "This is suitable for you and yours, settle here, and let there be no strife." Is not that the suggestion of common sense? Is not that the suggestion of common prudence? of common right?

Our fathers in 1820 . . . undertook to divide the Territory by the line of 36 deg. 30 min. [in the Missouri Compromise], and I think they did right. . . . I take it as a happy omen, that all the plans which have been proposed on this subject, look to the restoration of this same great line of peace, 36 deg. 30 min. If we go back to it, . . . we may yet be able to retrace the forty years that we have been wandering—the forty years of strife and bickering, the forty years of sectional jarring and discord, and that we may go back to the days of Monroe, to the era of good feeling, and take up anew, not merely the language of compromise and adjustment, but take in the ancient Virginia school, the spirit of compromise, the spirit of settlement, the spirit . . . in which the Constitution was formed. . . .

It seems to weigh upon the minds of the members here, and the minds of others discussing the subject elsewhere, that we are in danger of having the South converted into a St. Domingo; that we are in danger of being overrun by the increase in the number of slaves, driving the white man from the South, and converting it into one vast community of slaves, or, what is more, of free negroes. . . . The gentleman from Albemarle [Mr. HOLCOMBE], the other day . . . told us he apprehended that in fifty years, . . . there would be sixteen millions of slaves in the slave-holding country now owned by the United States; and . . . we would have this expulsion of the white man, and a necessary surrendering of the fair fields of the South to the African race. Sir, I [see] . . . no danger, within hundreds of years, of any such number of slaves as to render it at all impracticable to hold them all in slavery, and to apply their labor, as slaves, to the cultivation of the great staple crops of the South. . . . I am sustained upon this point by . . . Governor Hammond, of South Carolina, . . . who has contributed more than all others to the spread of sound opinions in regard to this vital interest of the South. . . . In the Senate of the United States, within the last year, . . . he states . . . [that] "the South is capable, within its present limits, of sustaining a slave population of two hundred millions.". . .

Now, sir, if this be true, or if it approximates to the truth, what becomes of this apprehension of the Africanization of the South, within fifty years? . . . If we can manage, in the mean time, to sustain the great vital interest of the country, only having to apprehend danger upon this question of slavery in that far distant future, if we can do this without dishonor, without any sacrifice of vital right and interest, . . . it would be wise for us to leave that question when it arises in the distant future, to the disposal of an Allwise Ruler, who doubtless has preparation to meet that as he has to meet all other great issues and questions of human life. . . .

Sir, how is it in regard to future territory? . . . It happens that we have settled our last territory in the wilderness. Our hardy pioneers . . . have exhausted all the wilderness around us, and from this time forward, if the United States acquire territory, they must acquire countries already settled. . . .

Look at the countries that infringe upon our borders; at the North, the British possessions; at the South, Mexico—old settled countries with large populations; Cuba, just over the way, settled already with a crowded population. In all these countries they have systems of laws recognizing and establishing their domestic, social and proprietary relations, and in all of them, except Cuba, slavery is prohibited. . . . [If] you acquire Mexico and cut out of it a slice large enough to make a State, . . . you would have in it already a population large enough for a member of Congress. . . . You say that the territorial judiciary, territorial Legislature, and territorial Government, are all bound to give it [slavery] protection during the territorial condition; but it would have no territorial condition. It would come in like Texas, full grown, and as such entitled to admission as a State. . . .

[The Peace Conference's second] principle is, that hereafter, no new territory shall be acquired, either by joint resolution or by treaty, except by the concurrent vote of a majority of the Senators from the slave States and the non slaveholding States. There is a complete protection in regard to future acquisitions. No new territory, either slave or free, can be introduced without our consent, without the consent of the South, without the consent of a majority of Southern Senators. If it should ever happen in the progress of future ages, that we should dwindle down to but one single State, it would require the consent of that State to acquire any territory whatever. . . .

Something has been said about this section being a check and a clog upon the acquisition of territory hereafter. . . . It is no objection with me that it will operate as a restriction upon the fierce spirit of territorial aggrandisement, upon the wild lust for the lands of our neighbors. . . . Unless some case arises of sufficient public necessity and public benefit to command a concurrent vote, I take it that the true interests of the nation require that we shall have no more Territory. . . .

The [Peace Conference's] third section . . . covers the irrepressible conflict all over like a blanket. . . . We have been told that the Abolitionists and the Black Republicans intended to abolish slavery in the District of Columbia. This report prohibits them from doing it except by the consent of Virginia, Maryland and the people of the District. Will you trust that? Will you trust Virginia, Maryland and the people of the District with the guardianship of slavery in the District?

We have been told too that this Black Republican party intends to interfere with the slave trade between the States and to abolish slavery at all the dock-yards, &c., belonging to the United States, within the slave States. . . . We have been told that these Black Republicans will keep on adding free State after free State, and after a while when they get strong enough they are going to amend the constitution so as to authorize them to legislate upon the subject of slavery and abolish it in the States; and this is to be the outcome of the irrepressible conflict in its legal and constitutional aspects. This section provides that they never shall have a right to abolish, or even to legislate upon slavery in the States under any circumstances; and then there is another section which provides that they shall not only not have a right to interfere with slavery in the District of Columbia, or with the interstate slave trade, or with slavery in the United States dock-yards, &c., or to touch slavery in the States; but that they shall not even have a chance to grow strong enough to do it: because they are prohibited in the last section from ever amending the Constitution of the United States so as to do any one of these things, or to affect the Fugitive Slave Law, or to affect any provision touching the institution of slavery except by the unanimous consent of all the States. . . . If that amendment to the Constitution becomes . . . part of the fundamental laws of the United States, it may be regarded as driving the last nail into the coffin of the Irrepressible Conflict. . . .

That is the plan which we propose of amendments to the Constitution. We propose to refer that plan to a conference of the border States, to be held at the city of Frankfort. We do not propose to declare an ultimatum bill, because we do not conceive that it would be respectful to our sister States whom we invite into the conference, to declare here in advance what is our ultimatum. . . .

But we are told that we are to go into this proposed conference and give up our opinion to the will of the majority. No body has proposed that. For one I say, that while Virginia ought not to act finally in this matter without regarding the wishes, the feelings and interests of her sister States, yet I will never consent to commit her honor to any conference whatever. . . . I will never consent that any body else shall determine for Virginia what is to make for her best interests, her highest honor and her greatest safety. . . .

But if we get this plan, if it answers the purpose I have suggested, if it secures us against what we have apprehended in the past, against what we apprehend in the future, if it covers up completely the whole subject of this unfortunate controversy to the satisfaction of the slave States now remaining in this Union, will it not give satisfaction to those which have gone out? Will it not bring them back? . . . I shall be exceedingly slow to believe that when we have settled to our own satisfaction and to the satisfaction of the border States, when we have declared that our honor is satisfied, that our rights are safe, that our interests are protected, when the seceded States come to look the future sternly in the face, when they come to consider their relative positions toward us and toward the outer world, when they think of the glorious past in connexion with this mighty Union, . . . I will not believe that they will consent to remain outside of it.

But, suppose they will not return. What then? Are we to submit our judgment to their passion—our interests to their caprice—our conduct to their direction—our honor to their keeping? I think not. I think the duty devolves upon us to take care of our own rights, our own interests and our own honor. It seems to be thought here . . . that our interests are all with the Cotton States—that our interests, commercial, manufacturing, industrial—of all sorts carry us South. Sir, I do not know what are the interests of the manufacturing portion of the community; . . . but I do know something about the pursuits of my constituents, who are an agricultural people. . . . What do my constituents, and in fact a large majority of the people of Virginia, raise for sale? . . . Why, sir, breadstuffs, cattle, horses, mules, and all sorts of live stock are the products of my people and of a large majority of the people represented on this floor. Now, the Cotton States do not raise any of the products. They want to buy them all.

The gentleman from Richmond city [Mr. GEORGE WYTHE RANDOLPH] . . . [argued] . . . that it is our interest to go with the Cotton States, because we want to sell to them and they want to buy from us. That is not a legitimate argument. They want to buy these products for they are necessaries of life to them, so much so, as to have led them in laying down their tariff, to admit them all duty free; and they are bound to do so always. . . . By going with the Southern Confederacy, we interpose a tariff between us and our Northern customers. By staying as we are, we maintain free trade with our customers North and South. . . .

But it is said that when we go into this new Confederacy, . . . Virginia will . . . become the Yankees of the South. Sir, . . . I have no sympathy for the indiscriminate denunciation that is heaped upon our Yankee brethren: none, whatever. I look upon them as a noble race of men, with all their faults and foibles. . . . I don't want to get rid of them; but I don't want to introduce the Yankee system of industry into Virginia. . . . I prefer our agricultural pursuits. . . . I don't want our people to be a manufacturing people. I don't want to be overrun here with these immense corporations. . . .

I would rejoice to see our country, in all respects, socially, industrially, politically united. Can this ever be accomplished? They say it cannot. I must confess that when I look along the path which my sense of duty calls me to walk in, and see the number of steps that are required for the accomplishment of the great object of my hopes, my spirit oftentimes quails within me and I tremble with apprehension, lest I may fall short of the great result. [Yet] I can only . . . march in that path of duty. I intend to look neither . . . for smiles of approbation or words of encouragement. I intend not to be driven back by frowns of opposition or threats of intimidation; but sustained by my own sense of right and my own conviction of patriotic duty, I shall march forward and leave the result to God. [Applause.]

9

Hugh Nelson's Unionist Speech, March 26

If no one needed more editorial help than John Baldwin, no one needed less such aid than Hugh Mortimer Nelson. This forty-nine-year-old attorney represented the Shenandoah Valley's Clarke County (47.2 percent enslaved). Nelson, who never held office before the convention, died in 1862 from war wounds incurred in Stonewall Jackson's Valley campaign. No other speaker in Part I of this book suffered death on the battlefields. Appropriately, no other speaker delivered such a crisp, spare warning about secessionists' mortal gamble.[1]

... Sir, I have the honor to represent ... the largest slaveholding county in proportion to her white population, west of the Blue Ridge. I have the honor to represent ... a people, sir, who, whilst they are loyal to the State of Virginia and to this Union, "know their rights, and knowing, dare maintain them." Sir, there are swords there "ready to leap from their scabbards"—there are still unerring rifles there ready to be directed with deadly aim, against any and all enemies; but, sir, we remember the order of the old hero, and we mean "to wait till we see the whites of the enemy's eyes." ...

I do not belong to that school of modern political philosophers who believe "that the Constitution is effete and gone to seed." I do not believe that any ten men in any parlor, or in all the parlors of Virginia and the United States together can make a better. I do not hesitate to say that I ... still cherish a fond attachment to this Union and ... still believe that the Constitution of the United States, if administered according to the spirit and intention of its framers, is the best government, for our people, that the world has ever seen. ...

Nor, sir, have I heard any complain against the administration of the government. . . . The Executive Department is charged with no usurpation. The Legislative Department—the Congress—has passed no unconstitutional laws interfering with any man's rights or liberties, nor has the Judiciary Department of the Government, by any decision, interfered

From Reese, *Proceedings* 2:344–55.

1. Gaines, *Biographical Register,* 61.

with our rights in the territory or elsewhere; on the contrary they have decided that . . . the slaveholder is entitled to protection in every part of the common territory during its territorial condition.[2]

What then are the true causes of the present crisis in our affairs, and for which we are asked to break up this Government purchased at the price of so much treasure and blood? . . .

1st. The passage of certain laws by some of the non-slaveholding States, called the Personal Liberty Bills.

2nd. The alleged intention of the majority in power, to exclude our peculiar institution from the common territory; and

3d. The fanatical spirit which prevails in the non-slaveholding States, which threatens ultimately to destroy that institution where it now exists—and this spirit as exhibited, in the election of a President, on a sectional platform, with the avowed purpose of its ultimate extinction.

Is there no remedy, Mr. Chairman, for these evils? . . .

The only remedy proposed by what we call the ultra party is immediate secession. Sir, what will be the effect of secession on the first of these evils, the escape of our slaves? Sir, we who live on the border of the slaveholding States are accustomed to take a practical view of this question, and are much less excited on this subject than those who live at a distance from the border, and who reason abstractly upon it. We know that, notwithstanding the Personal Liberty Bills, we lose comparatively few of our slaves since the passage of the fugitive slave law. Before the law was passed, they were leaving my county by tens and twenties at a time. Since 1850, notwithstanding the Personal Liberty Bills, we lose, as I stated, comparatively few. Sir, when I consider that secession will not move Virginia one foot further from Pennsylvania and Ohio, but will, in effect, *repeal* the fugitive slave law and place a foreign country close upon us, I cannot but conclude that secession, so far from remedying this evil, will increase it. . . .

Will secession secure us our rights in the territories? According to the theory of secession as I understand it, so far from securing our rights there, we abandon, for a time at least, the very territory we are contending for, and leave it all in the possession of those States which remain in the Union. I do not contend, sir, that we would abandon our equitable

2. Hugh Nelson, like Waitman Willey earlier, mischaracterized the *Dred Scott* decision. The Supreme Court only barred Congress from abolishing slavery in the U.S. territories. The question of what government, if any, was constitutionally bound to protect slavery in the territories remained open, and an open sore in national politics.

claim, yet the only remedy left to us would be to obtain it, either by war or by treaty, and I, for one, am free to confess that I think we can treat better *in* than *out* of the Union. For the present at least.

Now, sir, as to the third cause of complaint. Whilst I do not consider that the election of any man to the Presidency of the United States, according to the forms of the Constitution, is a sufficient cause, of itself, for breaking up this Union, yet if Mr. Lincoln unyieldingly persists in carrying out that spirit of fanaticism and that policy which will not only deny us our rights in the common territory, but must result in the ultimate extinction of slavery in all the States, much as I love this Union, I, for one, am prepared to say "away with it." I, sir, am prepared, at any cost, to sever every bond which binds us together. And in view of this, I say, sir, that the time has now come for us to settle definitely and forever this vital question.

Yet, sir, when I remember the large number of our fellow-citizens of the non-slaveholding States who have nobly stood up for us and gallantly fought on our side; when I remember that of the 3,400,000 votes, nearly 1,600,000 were cast against the Republican candidate, and even of the 1,800,000 who voted for Mr. Lincoln, many voted on other issues than those of Black Republicanism, I am not disposed to embrace them all, both friends and foes, in one common anathema. I will *not* call those *enemies* whom I know to be our warm friends; I will even dare in this presence to call them friends. Nay, sir, I cannot but hope that we shall not appeal in vain to the great conservative element of the North, to award us our just rights without an appeal to the *ultima ratio regum*.[3] I would have this Convention to present to the non-slaveholding States clearly and distinctly our ultimatum of adherence to the Union. I have already indicated those conditions in the resolutions which I offered to this body on the 20th of February.[4] ...

The ultimatum I would present in the calm and dignified language of settled purpose. If it be heeded, ... this great republic, returning to its ancient usages, acting within the scope of its constitutional limitations, will go on to illustrate the grand theory of popular sovereignty, and to perpe-

---

3. The last resort of kings, that is, war.

4. Nelson's most important February 20 resolution urged drawing the 36°30′ line to the eastern border of California but said nothing about territories "hereafter acquired." That omission, if Congress had approved Nelson's resolutions, would have opened pacifying possibilities that secessionists shuddered to contemplate. Nelson's resolutions can be found in Reese, *Proceedings* 1:106–7.

trate the great blessings of liberty, prosperity and happiness to us and to our posterity. If, unfortunately, it should be unheeded, then, conscious of having done all that forbearance can do, wisdom suggest, or patriotism demand, to save from destruction this glorious Union, we will—nay, of necessity we then must—withdraw from a Confederacy no longer compatible with our interest or our honor.

But, Mr. President, the question is asked on the other side, in case the Gulf States will not come back into this Confederacy will you go with the South or with the North? Do gentlemen forget or mean to ignore the border Slave States? Sir, I will not ignore them. They are a mighty empire, embracing within themselves all the elements of greatness and power—they contain at this time a population double that of the Gulf States, and I, for one, Mr. Chairman, am prepared to say that if I can get such constitutional guarantees as will be satisfactory to Virginia and the border Slave States, and which ought to be satisfactory to the Gulf States, much as I will deplore a separation from them, though they will have my strongest sympathies and my best wishes for their prosperity, I will not consent, as far as my humble influence can effect it, to take Virginia out of this Union. . . .

Sir, would you break up this Union because there are acknowledged evils in our system of government? Is there an human institution which is unattended with evils? Is it, sir, an easy matter to make everything in the actual world conform to the ideal pattern which we have conceived in our minds, of absolute right? Sir, I would ask the gentleman if he is really of the opinion that this government has been a source of evil, and only of evil, to Virginia? . . .

Mr. Chairman, I hope we have not yet passed our golden age; but, judging by the warlike sentiments I have heard on this floor, I think we certainly have arrived at the heroic period of our history. . . . Sir, gentlemen on this floor have intimated that even the ladies of Virginia are far ahead of the Union party of this body in their zeal for war; and I have heard it stated, that in one county the ladies had held a meeting and resolved, that they would come here and teach "our hands to war and our fingers to fight." . . .

Mothers, wives, sisters of Virginia! I doubt not that when your sons, your husbands, and your brothers are called to the battle, like the Spartan mother you will tell them "to return *with* their shields or to return *on* them." But when they are brought back to you in the cold embrace of death, will it assuage your grief to reflect that you have urged them on to an unnecessary contest in a deadly civil war? Will you call me coward when I tell you, that like Lucius, "my thoughts are turned on peace"— because, when the war does come, those who are dearer to me than my own life, my wife and children, will be much nearer to the seat of war, much more exposed to its dangers than you will be.

I come from the banks of the sparkling Shenandoah, "Daughter of the stars," as its name imports. . . . That valley, now beautiful and peaceful, . . . those green fields, where now "lowing herds wind slowly o'er the lea," may become fields of blood. Can you blame me, then, if I wish to try all peaceful means, consistent with Virginia honor, of obtaining our rights, before I try the last resort? I promise you, when the contest does come, if come it must, the people whom I have the honor to represent on this floor, will meet it like men. . . . When Virginia spreads her broad banner to the breeze and gives me my orders, no Mahomedan ever followed the sacred Banner of the Prophet with greater zeal than I will follow her standard. I hope, if need be, "I'll follow it to the death."

Mr. Chairman, I have said, that my sympathies are with the South— and I, for one, will never consent for the Government of the United States to attempt to coerce them, either directly or indirectly. Sir, if we can get such Constitutional guarantees as will be satisfactory to Virginia, and ought to be so to them—as I think we can—I would entreat them to return to this Union. Sir, I hope, nay, I have an abiding faith, that they will return. I pray to God that the time may not be far distant when all our difficulties will be adjusted, and we shall again be a united, prosperous and happy people. I think, Mr. Chairman, that Virginia, by the noble sacrifices and successful efforts she has from time to time made, for the formation and preservation of this Union, has well earned for herself, the proud position of a great pacificator. I trust her voice will again be potent to still the troubled waves, and that the North and the South will listen to that voice. . . .

Sir, I wish to stand under my country's flag with all its stars and all its stripes. I want the Pole star there—I want the Southern Cross to shine out brightly there. But should the Pole star retreat far into Northern regions, and veil its face in icy clouds—should the Southern Cross shoot madly from its sphere—I want Virginia to be that great central point in our political system, by her unfettered influences, to draw them all back, to revolve once more in harmony in their accustomed orbits. . . .

10

Thomas Flournoy's Unionist Speech, March 30

Thomas Stanhope Flournoy, representing the Piedmont's Halifax County (56.2 percent enslaved), had better fortune before and during the war than Hugh Nelson. Flournoy, forty-nine years old in 1860, would survive his own hard times in Stonewall Jackson's Valley army. Before the war he had been a U.S. congressman, 1847–49, and the Know-Nothings' candidate for governor in 1855. Flournoy received more votes than any previous candidate for the state's highest office. But his opponent, Henry Wise, received more ballots still, prefiguring Wise and the secessionists' victory over Flournoy and the Unionists six years later.[1]

... Mr. Chairman, ... I am no disunionist. From my earliest manhood I was taught to cherish a cordial, habitual and an immovable attachment to the Union. . . . I look upon the distraction and the division, and the feeling of distrust, jealousy and hate . . . in our land, . . . [augering] the permanent dismemberment of this great Government, . . . with feelings of the deepest sorrow. . . . The preservation of our Government, the restoration of . . . a proper, fair, just recognition of the rights of all, . . . would be consummation, in my humble judgment, devoutly to be wished. . . . Sir, in regard to the very institution, the interference with which has . . . our country now in the throes and agonies of dissolution—that institution itself, upon such a restoration of our government, would be stronger . . . and more enduring than . . . ever. . . .

A portion of the Northern people . . . began the agitation of this question . . . [by preaching] a crusade against the Southern Christians who owned slaves. . . . This war . . . turned the Christian mind of the South to the investigation of that subject. They examined it carefully, they examined it prayerfully, they examined it earnestly. . . . And where, now, Mr. Chairman, will you find, throughout all the Southern land, a man who

From Reese, *Proceedings* 2:590–602.

1. Gaines, *Biographical Register,* 34–35.

will tell you that slavery is an evil morally, socially, politically? You will find him nowhere. . . . Look to the advance made since 1832, when many now in this Convention advocated the passage . . . of gradual emancipation.[2]

The same change that has come over us is now beginning by small degrees . . . in the North. If the North could have foreseen, preceding the Presidential election, the division, the distraction, the discord, the ruin and bankruptcy that would have followed the elevation of a Black Republican to power, . . . is there a man in this assembly who believes that he would have been elected? None doubt . . . that the result would have been entirely different if the disastrous consequences . . . could have been foreseen. . . . We hear, day after day, time after time, that if Virginia will adopt . . . and send to the North her demand for adjustment, that the North are ready to accept it.

Let us, then, do it. If the North . . . shall accept . . . [our] amendments to the Constitution, . . . that vote . . . will . . . be the final and everlasting overthrow of this fanatical Black Republican party. . . . The very arguments we have been using in the South, . . . that slavery is right, morally, socially and politically, will have to be used by the men of the North, . . . [when] urging upon their people the . . . amendments . . . demanded by the people of Virginia. [Then] . . . the Northern people . . . will also . . . [conclude] that slavery is right. . . .

Is it now wiser to make an honest, earnest, decided effort to crush out and overthrow the party that is in power in Washington . . . to crush out our institutions? Or [is it wiser] for us to unite with the South, in producing the permanent separation of the States of this Union? Sir, I a thousand-fold prefer to make an attempt to crush out that fanatical abolition

---

2. Flournoy here referred to the 1832 Virginia legislature's traumatic two-week debate on abolishing slavery in the state, after the Nat Turner scare. This legislative confrontation, the longest but not the last Southern consideration of state abolition, ended when a largely eastern coalition narrowly defeated a largely western bid for a diluted abolition proposal. Flournoy was right that some 1861 convention delegates repudiated their 1832 emancipationist allies. Western Virginia's William Ballard Preston, for example, introduced the motion for the crucial antislavery amendment in 1832 and the crucial secession ordinance in 1861. Flournoy was also right that many Virginians, having espoused antislavery heresies in 1832, embraced proslavery orthodoxy in 1861 (as some prominent Unionists demonstrated in the convention debates). But some secessionists, including George Wythe Randolph, argued that such relatively new commitments to slavery remained shallow, especially compared to spottily enslaved areas' deep commitments to Union.

party in the North. Let my country rise above them, and set out afresh in its career of usefulness and glory. . . .

I regret that there is any son of Virginia so little capable of appreciating . . . her . . . proud position . . . as to look upon her as submitting to wrong, . . . and hazarding her honor and her interest, because, forsooth, instead of immediately seceding, she has endeavored . . . to adjust all our difficulties, and save our great country from permanent dismemberment, if not ruin. . . . Her sisters, the cotton States of the South, are under a debt of gratitude to her that they will never be able to discharge. She has thrown herself between the government at Washington and the seceded States. She has said to the powers at Washington, "Lay not your hand upon our sisters at the South." She has asked in all kindness to her sisters at the South to do no act that should bring about a collision between them and the General Government. She has said to that Government that if collision comes, if war ensues, if you endeavor to subjugate or coerce the South, Virginia is ready to make common cause with her Southern sisters, and, if need be, her sons will die in the last entrenchments of liberty, in their defence. . . .

The effect of this conduct upon the part of Virginia, which certain gentlemen . . . call submission, . . . has been that the Government at Washington has stayed its hands. . . . The Cabinet at Washington, with Mr. Lincoln at their head, have been consulting, day after day, hour after hour, and contriving and managing, not with manly, but weak and shifting policy, how to get their men away from the Southern posts, and away from the Southern States, because Virginia has thrown herself in the breach and warned them to commit no act of aggression upon the seceded States. . . .

While she has thus afforded protection to the Cotton States of the South, . . . her sister slaveholding States of the Border . . . are now looking anxiously to her—to us in this Convention—and asking us, by wise, prudent, moderate but firm action, to save and restore the Union if it can be honorably saved and restored. Sir, Virginia, while she protects the Cotton States of the South from war, listens to the counsel of her sister States in the border, and says, by the course of this Convention, that while we intend to preserve the honor and interests and rights of Virginia, . . . we will endeavor . . . to do it . . . with the whole South.

And not only they, but a large body of the people of the North, are looking to us with the most intense interest in our proceedings and deliberations, and asking us in God's name not to deliver them over into the hands of a reckless, ruthless, merciless fanaticism, but, by our firmness, by our prudence and moderation, to save them from the rule of such intolerable proscription.

That, sir, is the problem of Virginia. . . . She has a duty which she must perform. . . . That duty is, Mr. Chairman, to agree upon . . . proper amendments to the Constitution of the United States, and proper guaranties . . . for herself and for the South, and present them to the North as her final and last demand. . . . In making that demand, let her ask nothing that is wrong and fail to ask nothing that is right. Let us with due deliberation conclude . . . what our interests require—and let Virginia send it to the North as her conclusion, from which she will under no circumstances depart.

I know that . . . many of my friends . . . [favor] a conference of the border slave States, in order that they may all agree upon what . . . to present unitedly to the North as our ultimatum. Here I differ, and I am sorry to differ from those with whom it has been my pleasure to act upon every other question. Why, I ask, should we have further conference with the border slave States? . . . [Virginia] has had her consultation with them all—little Delaware included. After South Carolina, Georgia, Florida, Alabama, Mississippi, Louisiana and Texas, one by one had left the Union, . . . Virginia . . . called upon her sister border slave States, and not only upon them, but upon the Northern States, to meet her in council on the 4th of February, in the city of Washington, to consult upon such terms of guarantee and constitutional amendment as were necessary to protect her and her Southern sisters, to enable them all to come back into the Union. . . .

All the border slave States were in conference with Virginia in Washington city. . . . Then, sir, Virginia agreed in that conference with her sisters of the border slave States. She knew very well—they knew very well, that time had become an important element in the controversy, that it was time to settle it, and settle it as speedily as possible.

If time was an important element then, how much more important now. The material interests of our land are wasting. Our commerce is languishing. Our property is declining. Our people are restless. A spirit of revolution is getting abroad over the whole land, engendered . . . by the pecuniary distress which is bringing the laboring man, his wife and children daily and hourly to the risk of starvation. . . . Why, then, I ask, should we delay, and keep the country in still further suspense by referring the whole subject to a Convention of the border states, there to be discussed anew, in amendments, in alterations, in verbal criticisms, such as have occupied . . . this Convention for such a length of time, and which will, if the wishes of some men prevail, occupy us still longer, and even down, probably, to the first of May?

Why hang in suspense on the deliberation of the border Conference to settle and fix an *ultimatum* to be sent to the North which . . . will have to be adopted and submitted by us to a vote of the people of Virginia, and approved by them, before we send it to the North to be there acted upon—before the peace of the country is restored—a procrastination of settlement beyond endurance? . . . Let Virginia lay down her *ultimatum,* let her fix her final propositions, let her make them reasonable, right, just, covering the whole question, and forever expelling from the councils of the country the agitation of this important question. Let her present them to the North and fix some reasonable time in the future when the Northern people—not the Congress of the United States—shall vote on these propositions, and say whether they will preserve this Union by doing justice to the South, or whether they will refuse our just and fair demands and thereby incur the sin, the damning sin, of destroying the very best government that God, in his Providence, ever vouchsafed to man.

Sir, I would be delighted to see . . . the extreme Union men and the extreme secessionists come up to this proposition in the spirit of compromise and . . . with one voice. . . . The unanimous voice of Virginia . . . will be felt in the South, it will be felt in the border, it will be felt in the North. When you adopt your *ultimatum,* send it by Commissioners to your sister border slave States, and tell them why Virginia adopted it without further conference with them. Ask them in the spirit of fraternity and patriotism and justice to endorse this action of Virginia—to send it forth as their *ultimatum* too, and to let one voice reach the North, saying, in the name of the South, "here is our last proposition. . . . If you do not agree to it we will form our own government and take care of ourselves, as best we can, looking to the God of men and of nations to guide us, . . . [as] our fathers led us in defence of their liberties." . . . I think now I can hear echoed and reechoed from the seaboard to the mountains, and from the mountain tops to the beautiful Ohio, the language of the immortal [Patrick] Henry—"Give me liberty or give me death!"

I am not one of those who doubt or distrust the loyalty of any son of

Virginia. My own opinion is that no man can be a Virginian and be a submissionist. . . . No, sir, you may differ with me in the details, you may differ with me as to the course to be pursued to protect her honor, and to protect her rights, but I yet believe, sir, and shall continue to believe, that a Virginian heart rests in every Virginian bosom, and when the hour of trial shall come, and she is driven to stand on our defence, let her enemies come. If they refuse to give us our rights, and we cannot separate in peace, but must meet in hostile array, through all her border you will find—

Their swords are a thousand: their bosoms are one.

While I say to our Union friends that it is right and proper they should come up to the position, I also say to our friends who are for immediate secession: "Your remedy is unattainable." If it were a right remedy under present circumstances—which I do not believe—yet it is a remedy which cannot be carried out. Pass your ordinance of secession to-morrow, and submit the question to the people, and . . . the people . . . will see and know that your final proposition has not been presented to the North and rejected by the North. . . . [Then] they will vote it down by a larger majority than that by which they voted it should be referred back to them. . . .

But let Virginia present her *ultimatum*. Let her eschew immediate secession. Let her avoid the Border Conference, and explain her reasons why. Let her present her ultimatum to the North. Let it be endorsed by the border slave States. Let the North, with wild fanaticism, refuse to grant her fair, her just, her reasonable demands, and there will be but one voice all through the border, from Delaware to Missouri, that the time has come when we must take care of ourselves, when all the States of the South must join in one common Government, receiving as many of the far North-western States as will unite with us—all the States which lie in the draft of the Mississippi and its tributary waters; and we will form a Government of our own, which, in power and influence, may still take back, not the name of the Confederate States, but of "the United States." . . . [Then] the same flag, . . . with the fanatical New England stars stricken from its folds, will float over us, a free and happy people. We will thus perpetuate the blessings bestowed upon us by a more glorious ancestry than ever formed a Government. . . .

The proposition which I have presented to-day is a fair offer of compromise between the extremes of this body, and to which every man may come without the least sacrifice of principle. This Convention will then present a united, firm, unbroken front to the people of the States, and will bring with it the endorsement of the border slave States; and that voice will go to the North with a force which, if anything can, will awaken them, from the fanatical torpor which oppresses them. . . .

But, as I remarked, if it awakes them not and they refuse to listen to the voice of reason and the demands of justice, we . . . will then shake hands with and part from them, if possible, in peace. . . . Virginia would thus be placed in an impregnable position, where no finger of scorn, reproach or contempt could be pointed at her. . . . And when she shall go out, if go she must, having made this last noble struggle to save the country, the free States of the border will unite with the South. . . . The interest of all the American people will be concentrated in this great republic, while the fanatical States of New England will be left to themselves, to suffer the . . . dreadful recoil of fanaticism. . . .

11

James Barbour's Secessionist Speech, March 30–April 1

James Barbour represented Culpeper County in Virginia's western Piedmont (35 percent enslaved). A lawyer and minor slaveholder, he was a younger son of one of Virginia's most prominent families, a clan long closely allied with the nearby Jefferson and Madison families. Thirty-seven years old in 1861, James Barbour was the youngest speaker in this book and the only one who concurrently held a seat in Virginia's lower legislative house.

There, a year earlier, he had led the successful opposition to South Carolina's call for a southern convention, in the wake of John Brown's raid. Barbour's unsuccessful countervailing proposal: Virginia should decree economic nonintercourse with Northerners, in a bid to force them to renounce John Brown and all abolitionists.

Again a Unionist immediately after Lincoln's election, young Barbour was the first delegate to break with that coalition and therefore among the first to illuminate the majority bloc's fragility. Criticized for his "recreancy," Barbour fired back bitter assaults on his former comrades. His tone reflected not only a younger man's callowness and a new convert's stridency but also the contempt of supposedly realistic secessionists for supposedly naive Unionists. The irony: no one was more naive than Barbour about Yankee money-grubbers and their alleged commitment to peace and Union at any cost.[1]

. . . Few men as humble and as young as I am have ever . . . risked, on more than one occasion, all . . . political hope [and] all . . . political aspiration, . . . in giving an earnest, zealous, living testimony of attachment to the Union.

Sir, certain action of the Virginia Legislature last winter has been repeatedly criticised by gentlemen of this floor. . . . I believed then that . . . [South Carolina's] proposal for a Southern Conference was as idle

From Reese, *Proceedings* 2:602–11, 671–704.

    1. Gaines, *Biographical Register*, 15–16.

and as void of any *useful* purpose as the gentleman from Halifax [Mr. FLOURNOY], has just shown you a Middle State Conference to be. I believe it was intended to commit us to disunion! . . . Every leading gentleman of the party in the State, high in position, publicly and openly implored the Legislature to go . . . into that Conference. . . . But, sir, I did not shrink. . . .

[On] one more occasion, . . . I put my political all at stake upon the cause of the Union. When, after six months of confinement to my bed—when I had not even seen the people of my county for six months, and had no opportunity of consulting with them, I came down here to the Virginia Assembly, and there vigorously aided in the movement which inaugurated this Peace Conference. I stood, in the recorded language of the Virginia Assembly, determined to make one *final* effort to preserve this Union, and to wait until that final effort was made. My personal and political friends at home poured letters down upon me, assuring me I was not reflecting the will of my constituents. . . .

I went back home in my enfeebled condition and stood before them. I told them my purpose to stand by that one effort and to await its result. I . . . could not see them again until the election day [for this convention's delegates], while my opponent—one of the most worthy, able and eloquent men in Virginia—was traversing the county, speaking every day to the people. Yet I was sustained by nearly four-fifths of the voters. Now, sir, when I have thus, by positive act, testified, at the hazard of my own political existence on two occasions, my devotion to the Union, have I here to get up and sing psalms to the Union, to convince anybody that I have been its earnest devotee? I do not intend to condescend to that, sir.

Mr. Chairman, . . . the first object in every discussion is to find upon what points all parties in the discussion agree. . . . Is there a gentleman within the sound of my voice who is willing to let Virginia remain under the government and the Constitution as it is? I pause for a response. Then on all hands we are agreed that the property, the liberty and the rights of Virginia are unsafe under the government as it is; that you must have a new government, a new Constitution, a new Union for the protection of your people, and that it is your determined purpose to resume your sovereignty if you do not get it. . . .

Mr. Chairman, the majority of this Committee [on Federal Relations],[2]

2. The Committee on Federal Relations considered all secession issues privately during the convention's first month, while debate swirled publicly on the convention's floor. The

after having exhausted themselves in these investigations upon . . . the deplorable condition of the country, do what next? These wise patriots actually propose to adjourn over for six months! . . . The picked men of Virginia, . . . after they have spent six weeks in investigating this subject, now gravely come to the conclusion . . . that Virginia is living under a Government utterly unsafe. After this they come to the farther conclusion, that the best thing for us to do is to live on under it for six months more, and see if somebody will not come to our help in the meantime. . . . Merciful Father—what a melancholy contrast will the record of history present between the Virginia of this day and the Virginia of 1776, if this Convention act as your Committee counsel you to act. Well may her sons bow their heads in deep humiliation at such a spectacle. . . .

Suppose you send forth your *ultimatum* to the North, tell me, as a sensible man, whilst you are waiting for the response, where is it best to be? Where are you most likely to get a satisfactory response? . . . Under a government bitterly hostile to you; a government . . . broken down in all its departments; broken down in every respect? . . . Do you want to . . . remain under this Washington government, when you see an efficient and friendly government imploring you to join them; a government that is infinitely stronger even at this time? . . . And it grows stronger every day. . . .

If you will find men staking money upon the credit of a Government, you have the strongest evidence of the belief of the men in the stability and the strength of that Government. Now, let us, by this test, try the two Governments between which we are now situated. Abe Lincoln's Government is borrowing money and its stocks go off at ninety cents to the dollar. . . . What is the condition of the other [Confederate] Government—this thing that you say is . . . so low down that if you poke a paper resolution at it, you crumble it into ruins. . . . The Secretary of the Treasury of that Government . . . states that upon that loan of theirs of fifteen

committee's majority report, issued on March 9, bent ambiguously in the Unionists' direction. While it threatened secession if the Lincoln administration "coerced" seceding states, it urged negotiation toward a peaceful settlement unless "coercion" transpired. Although the majority report proposed an ultimatum to the North, it left the terms of the demands and the time limits for a Northern answer undefined. It also endorsed a border state conference without defining the conference's power. These ambiguities distressed the committee's outnumbered secessionist members, who issued an unambiguously disunionist minority report. The convention was still warring over these critical details when Lincoln's April 15 proclamation and Wise's extralegal strike changed the basis of discussion.

millions, . . . they have already a large proportion of offers, at and above par, and in his judgment the whole of it would go off at or above par. Was ever such strength exhibited by a new Government in the first few weeks of its existence?

Mr. Chairman, which Government would be the safest under which to live? The people who command the most money are able to equip the largest army. . . . The Government at Washington owes a hundred millions of dollars; its stocks have no par sales. When Virginia goes, certain as fate not only the other Border Slave States, but a large portion of the Border non-slaveholding States will go with her or go after her. And [given] . . . the credit of the Federal Government, . . . under existing circumstances, the secession of Virginia would crumble that credit into atoms. . . .

Their own official declaration shows that they are utterly bankrupt. Here is one of the circulars that they are sending around now to the men who have performed service for them. . . .

CENSUS OFFICE,
DEPARTMENT OF THE INTERIOR
WASHINGTON, MARCH 22nd, 1861

Sir: You are informed that the suspension of the United States Treasury has for some time prevented the payment of Marshals and assistants engaged in taking the Census. The first . . . and final payments will be made at the earliest moment possible. That you will receive full compensation cannot be doubted, and you are advised not to dispose of your claim at a sacrifice.

Very respectfully,
Your obedient servant,
J. C. G. KENNEDY,
Superintendent.

. . . The brave and high-minded people of this Old Dominion have no reason to fear a government thus deficient in the sinews of war. [In contrast to] the Abolition Government at Washington, . . . [Vice President Alexander Stephens sums up] the condition of the Government of the Confederate States at Montgomery: . . .

We have all the essential elements of a high national career. The idea has been given out at the North, and even in the Border States, that we are too small and too weak to maintain a separate nationality. This is a great mistake. In extent of territory we embrace 564,000 square miles and upwards. This is upwards of 200,000 square miles more than was included within the limits of the original thirteen States. It is an area of country more than double the territory of France or the Austrian Empire. France in round numbers has but 212,000 square miles. Austria in round numbers has 248,000 square miles. Ours is greater than both combined. It is greater than all France, Spain, Portugal and Great Britain, including England, Ireland and Scotland together. In population we have upwards of five millions, according to the census of 1860; this includes white and black. The entire population, including white and black, of the original thirteen States, was less than 4,000,000 in 1790, and still less in '76, when the independence of our fathers was achieved. If they, with a less population, dared to maintain their independence against the greatest power on earth, shall we have any apprehension of maintaining ours now?

In point of material wealth and resources, we are greatly in advance of them. The taxable property of the Confederate States cannot be less than $2,200,000,000, . . . five times more than the Colonies possessed at the time they achieved their independence. . . . The debts of the seven Confederate States sum up in the aggregate less than $18,000,000; while the existing debts of the other of the late United States sum up, in the aggregate, the enormous amount of $74,000,000. This is without taking into the account the heavy city debts, corporation debts and railroad debts, which press, and will continue to press, a heavy incubus upon the resources of those States. These debts, added to others, make a sum total not much under $500,000,000. With such an area of territory—with such an amount of population—with a climate and soil unsurpassed by any on the face of the earth—with such resources already at our command—with productions which control the commerce of the world—who can entertain any apprehensions as to our success, whether others join us or not?

Mr. Chairman, is a Virginia Assembly, after what we see and hear, going to sit with folded arms and decline to recognize a fact which is about to be acknowledged by all the powers of the earth? Look to the recent European news. Will not the powers of Europe do that which a Virginia Convention hesitates and pauses to do—recognize the fact that there is a national existence at Montgomery? Nations act on their interest, not on sentiments. England and France, because they do not like slavery, are not going to refuse to deal with and make money out of the most lucrative customer on the face of the globe. . . .

All the powers of the earth, unless the Convention shall make the State of Virginia an exception, must recognize the Government at Montgomery as a *de facto* Government. . . . Will you decline to deal with the Great Fact of this age, . . . in consequence of your great, affectionate attachment to the Government at Washington? Dare you close your eyes to the abolition influences that control the Government at Washington? . . . In the midst of a great Revolution you sit here picking straws and whittling sticks. . . . Will not your countrymen . . . exclaim, "How are the mighty *fallen, fallen* from their high estate!" . . .

That man who stands here to-day, and says that the action of Virginia now should be what he would say it ought to have been on the first of January last . . . closes his eyes to the great duties rising up before him. . . . I was willing, on the 15th of January, as one of the representatives of the people of Virginia, to place upon record . . . that a prompt tender of the Crittenden propositions would . . . be accepted by the people. . . . At that time this Government of the Southern Confederacy down yonder, was in its chrysalis state, and we then heard the declarations of all their representatives that, rather than to tempt the trial of a new experiment in . . . a new Government, those people would accept those Crittenden propositions. . . .

Those Crittenden propositions would, at this moment, be utterly impotent to dissolve that Government at Montgomery, and bring those seceded States back; and I tell you I have no idea of remaining in this Government unless it will bring them back. Nor have my constituents if I know their purposes. . . .

Do you think that . . . these little paper amendments . . . [will] become so seductive to them that they are going to throw off the habiliments of an independent Empire and come back to the oppression from which they successfully, manfully walked away? . . . With all those elements of power stated by Vice President Stephens, . . . how can you expect that Southern Republic to dissolve itself—strip itself of all the attributes of a separate existence, bow its head, come back here and subject itself to that oppression which it has just left? . . .

If there is to be a new alliance between those States of the South and those of the North, it is to be done by TREATY. . . . You propose that a peaceful negotiation shall be inaugurated. . . . The subject of the controversy is your property, and your rights. . . . And when that negotiation commences, Virginia is to be on the Northern side. . . .

This great controversy has reached its crisis. . . . The collision between the sections has become so violent—the struggle has become so vital—that, by general acknowledgement here, we have now to come to new terms of association, or separate forever. Then let the parties to the new compact stand honestly and fairly asunder. Let each stand for its own interest and give to its own side its full power and influence. . . . Let us take our natural, our honest side in the negotiation. . . . [Let us not] sit here holding tremblingly on, . . . sobbing, weeping like old women over this condition of things for six months, to see if, in the meantime, it will not get better.

Sir, is there any danger in joining that Government down at Montgomery? I think there is danger in remaining in the other one up here at Washington. Let me ask you this one question. And here excuse [me] for saying I only address those of you who are living men of this day. . . . The men who belong wholly to the past are unfit for the duties before us. It is a public misfortune that this element too strongly predominates in this assembly and paralyzes it.

But to my question. . . . Which Government will be the most likely to relieve you from direct taxation by ample revenues, derived from duties on imports? . . . The cotton crop exported from the United States, according to the latest treasury return, . . . is $161,000,000. The cotton crop used in the Northern States, according to the statistics of the Massachusetts Board of Trade, cannot be less than $40,000,000. . . . There is [thus] not less than $200,000,000 worth of cotton exported from the Southern Confederacy. . . .

Goods exported from the border States, including cotton, tobacco, and other cereal products, . . . amount . . . [to] $100,000,000, making the entire exports from the slaveholding States not less than $300,000,000, a year. These are facts. Three hundred millions of exports return at least as much imports. An impost tax[3] of ten per cent, would produce a revenue of $30,000,000, a year, would it not? Sir, living under such a confederated government you would be the lightest taxed people upon the face of the earth.

That is your condition down there, sir; and that is the place to which

---

3. A tariff on imported goods.

you are afraid to go. How is it up North? They are not able to pay the men that took the census last year! . . . They have no means of meeting their current expenses, and they have a debt of $100,000,000 besides. Do you suppose that Government will, or can, get on with an impost tax? No, sir, it cannot. It will have to resort to direct taxation to meet its own expenses. And you propose for this old Commonwealth of Virginia, now taxed 40 cts. upon every $100 [of property] and advised by the Auditor to increase that tax to sixty cents—I say you propose, in addition to this, to submit to a direct tax[4] for the support of the Northern Confederacy. . . . Poor as we are, we must support our Yankee kin. . . .

In this connection, let me ask you was ever a people yet made the object of war by the commercial powers of the earth, while that people controlled $300,000,000 of exports? Why, sir, that very circumstance will keep the peace, not only with the Northern Government, but with all the commercial powers of the earth. . . . When a Commercial nation makes war upon such a Republic, it makes war upon its own interests. . . . Sir, I have not much faith in the sentiments of Yankees. . . . But I have a vast confidence in their appreciation of their own interests; and if their own interests do not make them the most peaceful, the most subservient and obedient friendly power upon the face of the earth, to this Southern Republic, I am vastly mistaken. . . . We can hold them in more abject submission than you hold your own slaves at home. . . . I venture to say, sir, that the whole industrial system of New England would be prostrated by closing the Southern markets to their manufactures.

By opening these markets to the manufactures of the North, we have built up the power which now assails us. The Southern consumer has multiplied the population of New England, enhanced its wealth, invigorated its material strength, and increased its political power. If you writhe from the sting of this serpent, you must reflect that you nursed it into life and strength. . . .

One eighth of the whole population of Massachusetts is supported upon the boot and shoe trade. Its chief seats are at Natick and Lynn. Perhaps there are no such hot-beds of abolitionism in the whole North as Natick and Lynn. . . . Shortly after the foray of John Brown, the operatives in the boot and shoe factories of Natick unanimously resolved that it is the right and duty of the Southern slaves to rebel, and it is the right and

4. In this context, a property tax.

duty of the Northern people to encourage and support them in doing so.
. . . Many of those who are now listening to me have . . . on their feet, at
this moment, boots or shoes made by these bloody propagandists of the
Natick shoe factories. . . . No Virginia encouragement . . . [should] be
extended to that nest of pestiferous vipers. . . .

Let the present condition of things continue, and they will have two-
fold advantages; or, to use another expression, they strike two blows at
your industrial interests. As their manufactures increase ours will dimin-
ish, because of the impossibility of our competing with them. They have
already driven your mechanics from your midst. Let them go on, year
after year, and soon we shall be left without a tradesman of any kind,
and reduced to a condition of entire dependence on the North. They are
going on, driving your white labor out, while applying themselves vigorously to the task of driving your black labor from your midst; so that,
with powerful force, they are striking double blows at you. . . .

You annually expend beyond the limits of this Commonwealth not less
than thirty millions of dollars in merchandize consumed in this Commonwealth. . . . [Our money] ought to remain here at home. Where does
it go now? It goes to support the manufacturing and commercial interests
of the Northern States. . . .

What then would be the effect on our internal interests to retain for
home expenditure thirty millions annually? You would create employment for your white labor, which would restrain it from emigration. You
would give your own mechanics a monopoly of your own market. . . .
What if it does raise the price of some . . . [articles] generally consumed?
The property holder can afford to pay the little increase of price . . . [to
encourage] white labor, when the white laborer is needed to aid in the
protection of property.

This State . . . needs population as an element of power in the federal
government [and] as a means of defence under the State government.
We must at any sacrifice, therefore, retain our people at home. . . . Protect your own mechanics, . . . artisans, and . . . merchants from Northern competition, and you enhance your own strength and power, just
as fast as you reduce that of your adversary. Let us gather our imperial
resources. . . . While resolutely protecting slave labor, let us also give the
fullest encouragement to the labor of the mechanic and the merchant and
the artisan in our midst. . . .

The whole industrial system of Massachusetts and all New England depends upon the support of the South. I was in favor, last winter, inside the Union, of making them feel their commercial dependence upon us;[5] but that is gone, and you can now only make them feel it by a Union of the whole South outside this Northern Confederacy. . . .

That . . . Southern Republic [now stands outside], and what will be the position of Virginia in it? . . . Virginia would control almost one fourth of the entire vote in their lower House of Congress. . . . She will have about 11 in the Congress of a Northern Confederacy with 150 members. . . . And the entire border States, to which so much importance is here attached, stand in the next Congress with about 54 out of 150 representatives. . . . All the border States put together will not hold the same relative power in the Northern Confederacy that the State of Virginia alone would hold in the Southern. . . . Where will you, under this state of facts, place your constituents? In a hostile confederacy in which your power will be but 11 out of 150, or in a friendly confederacy where it will be 21 out of 89? . . .

Wise, astute, experienced statesmen, *you* discover that we are living under a system which it is utterly unsafe to trust; but at the same time you discover that you are utterly unfit to make a better one. . . . And, therefore, it is proposed to get up a Border Conference. . . . We must send out to Missouri, and to Delaware, and to Maryland, and to Kentucky, and to North Carolina, and find material outside the limits of the old Commonwealth, to see what will promote the interest of the Commonwealth of Virginia. . . .

The question is what we shall do to protect our slave interest in Virginia, and you ask Delaware to send somebody to advise with you as to what you shall do with your 500,000 slaves. . . . Delaware has 1,798 slaves, and her idea about taking care of the institution of slavery is to let Black Republican politicians attend to it. She has elected a Black Republican member of the next Congress, and her policy is a gradual extermination of slavery within her limits. . . .

Well, what next? Maryland has 599,000 white people, and 87,000 slaves; that is, there are seven white men in Maryland to one slave. . . . Arkansas . . . has 300,000 white people, and 111,324 slaves. The whites there

5. The previous winter, after South Carolina commissioner Christopher Memminger urged a Southern convention, Barbour, a state legislator, countered by proposing a Virginia embargo on buying Northern goods, to last until the Yankees repressed abolitionist agitation. The Virginia legislature rejected both Memminger's and Barbour's proposals.

are three to one. Missouri, with a million of whites, has 114,000 slaves—the whites being nine to one. . . .

Mr. President, will this Convention close its eyes to the astounding fact that when we get into that border States Conference, Virginia and North Carolina will own one half of all the slaves in the States represented there? And yet they will hold but two out of the eight votes in that Conference. Virginia will have one third of all the slaves represented in that border Conference, while she will have only one of the eight votes. . . . Virginia with her five hundred thousand slaves would stand there with only as much power as little Delaware would have with her 1798 slaves. Is that the way in this great crisis that the wise men of Virginia propose to take care of the slave interests of the State? . . .

What is to come of that border State Conference? If the greatest Abolitionist in America would apply himself to the task of devising a plan to injure the institution of slavery, he could have hit upon no better plan than that of entering a wedge between the border States and the seceded States. . . . Divide and conquer—that is the great maxim of an enemy. The North can do nothing with these fifteen slave States united. Drive the wedge between them, separate them, organize them into separate Governments, and make them colliding and warring organizations, if you can; and then, I ask, what becomes of the slavery interests? . . .

You go into this Conference. In case you shall not get what you want, you will erect a new Government. Then you will invite the North and the South together to come and join you in it! Here in the South is a Government in full working order, strong, powerful, and efficient, which at this instant may be said to be one of the most successful governmental institutions in the world; and you tell me you cannot find safety there. Oh, no, you want to organize another Government. These people of the Old Union are so tractable, so amendable to the will of Virginia, that when you establish your Government, all will come into it, the North and South alike. . . .

How long is it going to take you to go through all this formula you propose? Who is going to appoint these conferees? . . . The sovereign assembly of Virginia assembled here to take care of the slave institution of the State appoint your men; and the Black Republican Governor of Maryland—Governor Hicks—makes appointments in behalf of that State. . . . Virginia in the Conference counts one; . . . the Black Republican

Governor of Maryland counts one. . . . That is your mode of rescuing your institution of slavery. . . .

Your Legislature declared that this Peace Conference should be your final effort. That Peace Conference has adjourned and gone. Nothing has come out of it. . . . Now you propose to discredit the declaration of the representatives of the people of Virginia? . . . That Legislature, chosen by the people of Virginia, declared . . . "Virginia's last final effort to restore this Union." Now comes this bran-new set of Virginia representatives, and the first thing you do is to . . . declare that this [Border South conference] is to be our very last [Union-saving attempt].

It is very much like the play-bills, when some favorite performer is engaged. They announce for one night his last appearance, the next night "positively his last appearance," and the third night comes the benefit. I suppose as old Virginia has performed her last appearance you want now a better set of men to make her appear on positively her last appearance, and after both of these are over, I suppose we will have a benefit night. [Laughter.]

Who is going to believe a Virginia declaration about your determined purpose, when you discredit what two months ago Virginia proclaimed— that the Peace Conference was her final effort for the Union. You come forward now and declare that all you have got to do is to play a little longer. Every time the play bill comes out, you are going to play thunder the next time. Rolling up your sleeves and spitting on your hands, you are going to knock somebody down, bye and bye, and when the time comes you will postpone a little longer, and then, in place of a fight, wind up with a foot-race. For one, my judgment is, that the effect, whatever the design, . . . is to bring discredit on this Commonwealth. . . .

12

Robert Montague's Secessionist Speech, April 1–2

Lieutenant Governor Robert La-tané Montague, forty-one years old in 1861, represented the Tidewater's Mathews and Middlesex counties (together 48.4 percent enslaved). This descendant of one of Virginia's first families was one of the convention's few large planters and its highest-ranking current officeholder (Governor Henry Wise and U.S. President John Tyler being former holders of their higher positions). In 1859 Montague had defeated Waitman Willey for his state post. He would serve later in the Confederate House of Representatives and as a postwar Virginia state legislator and judge.[1]

. . . When this confederation was formed, . . . two great prominent ideas lay at the foundation of the whole system. . . . First, . . . to combine the common forces of the country for the purpose of repelling foreign invasion. . . . Second, . . . [to establish] commercial, social, and political equality between the States . . . and prevent any invasion . . . of one State upon the rights of another. . . .

How stands Virginia to-day, when you apply that [second] principle to her condition? She has been invaded by citizens of her sister States. That invasion cost your State between $300,000 and $400,000. . . . Your Legislature, last winter, appropriated $500,000 for the construction of an armory to manufacture arms and munitions of war. Your Legislature, at the present session, has appropriated $1,000,000 for arming your State. Here, then, is a tax of $2,000,000[2] imposed upon a people already ground down by a debt of $40,000,000. And for what, I ask? For what? Why, sir, to put your State in a position to defend herself against the members of her own family; to defend her equality; to protect herself against her sister States; or against the Federal Government, which is the common agent of all the States. Can this state of things last?

From Reese, *Proceedings* 2:729–36, 3:10–39.

1. Gaines, *Biographical Register,* 59.

2. Montague's faulty addition of his numbers ill served the wider accuracy of his general point.

Sir, your Government rests in the affections of the people. Its abiding place must be in the honest hearts of the great masses of the people. And when those hearts become perverted, and when hate and malignity take the place of affection and regard, your whole system is a failure, and it becomes the part of wisdom and prudence to organize another that will cure these defects. . . .

My able and distinguished friend from Augusta [Mr. BALDWIN] . . . made . . . the most remarkable [point] that I ever heard fall from the lips of a Virginia statesman. He declared that . . . to settle this question, and to give peace, and quiet, and tranquility to the country for ever, he would not sanction, by way of amendments to the Constitution, what was called guarantees of power, because that would admit the right of the minority, and not of the majority, to control the government, and that this was a government of majorities.

Mr. BALDWIN: My statement on that subject, was, that our government has its foundation in the virtue and intelligence of the people; that the administrative force of the government must be lodged necessarily in the hands of the majority; . . . and that any attempt to build the administration of the Government on any narrower foundation than the virtue, and intelligence, and power of a majority of the people would lead to its overthrow.

Mr. MONTAGUE: Exactly. I did not misunderstand my friend. . . . But, sir, I utterly deny that proposition. It is entirely at war with the theory and practice of the government. . . . The very aim, and end, and object of a government, is to protect the minority against the majority. A majority can always protect itself. If you give to the minority no guarantee of power to protect itself, against the aggressions of the majority, then your government is but a despotism of numbers, the worst of all despotisms— a government of strength and not a government of right. If my friend will turn to the Constitution, he will find that a minority of the people can break up the government whenever they please. . . . They have the power; and . . . the power shows that our government is not one of majorities. . . .

Only one gentleman, so far as I remember, had attempted during the progress of our deliberations to make an argument against this right [of secession]. . . . Other gentlemen have sneered at it . . . as ridiculous and absurd, . . . [or] denounced in open and bold terms all of us who . . . act upon it as traitors, and inquired if there was not such a thing as hemp for us. . . . While we have been denounced as traitors, while our doctrine has been denounced as ridiculous, while the doctrine of the fathers of the Republic is held up to the scorn of the world, I trust I shall be excused if I attempt to put this great doctrine on a foundation from which I think it cannot be overthrown.

Virginia was the first State on this Continent that ever exercised the great doctrine of secession. When did Virginia do that? On the 15th of May, 1776—prior to your Declaration of Independence. She did not go about to consult border States, to see what they would do. In the plenitude of her sovereignty, and in the depth of her patriotism, she severed her connection with the British Government. . . .

Old Virginia, who adopted the first act of secession on this continent, was the first to . . . bring about another great measure of secession. In January 1786, Virginia, by her Legislature proposed a Convention of Delegates from the States. . . . That Convention recommended that all the States should appoint commissioners to meet at Philadelphia, on the second Monday of May, 1787. . . . That Convention met and formed our Constitution. . . .

Now, what sort of government is this? . . . Just take up the celebrated report of Mr. Madison, which has been the political law of Virginia for sixty years, and . . . you will see that it is declared to be a compact between sovereign States. . . . Being a compact between sovereign States, the States who are parties to it can alone judge of its infraction, and of the mode and manner of redress. . . . "On what principle," [Mr. Madison asked in the *Federalist* #43,]

[can] a compact among the States . . . be superseded without the unanimous consent of the parties to it? This question is answered at once by recurring to the absolute necessity of the case; to the great principle of self-preservation; to the transcendent law of nature and of nature's God, which declares that the safety and happiness of society are the objects at which all political institutions aim, and to which all such institutions must be sacrificed. . . .

A compact between independent sovereigns . . . can pretend to no higher validity than a league or treaty between the parties. . . . A breach of any one article is a breach of the whole treaty. . . . A breach committed by either of the parties, absolves the others, and authorizes them, if they please, to pronounce the compact *violated and void*. . . .

The old articles of Confederation declared that the Union which they formed should be *perpetual,* and that it could not be altered or abolished without the consent of *all the States.* Yet the fact is, that nine States, upon the principles laid down by Mr. Madison above, did secede from that Union and form another—Virginia advised and started it, and this is her second act of secession. . . .

The right to secede is . . . Virginia's own doctrine. . . . I hope all true sons of Virginia will stand . . . [behind] one of the blessed doctrines of our glorious old mother, . . . [originating] in that high spirit of liberty which developed itself in Williamsburg in 1776. . . . If I am to be hung, if I am to be denounced as a traitor, . . . let it be for standing up and maintaining, in all their vigor and purity, the doctrines of the fathers of Virginia's immortal principles of civil liberty. [Applause.] . . .

Nobody will pretend that any force was resorted to by any power, of carrying the States into the Union. Now, sir, I ask, as it is admitted they went into the Union voluntarily, if there is anything in the Constitution which gives Congress or any department of the Federal Government the power to use force to keep them in? If there is, point it out. If any gentleman here shows me one word in the Constitution which gives Congress, or any department of the Federal Government, the power to keep a State in the Federal Union by force, I will yield the point. No, sir, it is not in the Constitution. You cannot find it there—*it is not there.* . . .

You gentlemen who belong to the Adams' school of politicians, hear what that great man, Mr. [John Quincy] Adams, said upon this question, and then, if you think proper, denounce the doctrine as "absurd and ridiculous." Will my friend read the extract for me? It is from an address delivered before the New York Historical Society in 1839, at the jubilee of the Constitution.

Mr. HOLCOMBE, of Albemarle, read the extract as follows:

> Nations acknowledge no judge between them upon earth. And their Governments, from necessity, must, in their intercourse with each other, decide when the failure of one party to a contract to perform its obligations absolves the other from the reciprocal fulfillment of his own. . . . We may admit the same right as vested in the people of every State in the Union, with reference to the General Government, which was exercised by the people of the United Colonies with reference to the supreme head of the British Empire, of which they formed a part. . . .

Thus stands the *right*. But the indissoluble link of union between the people of the several States of this confederated nation is, after all, not in the *right,* but in the *heart*. If the day should ever come (may Heaven avert it!) when the affections of the people of these States shall be alienated from each other; when the fraternal spirit shall give way to cold indifference, or collisions of interest shall fester into hatred, the bands of political association will not long hold together parties no longer attracted by the magnetism of conciliated interests and kindly sympathies; and far better will it be for the people of the disunited States to part in friendship from each other, than to be held together by constraint. Then will be the time for reverting to the precedent, which occurred at the formation and adoption of the Constitution, to form again a more perfect Union, by dissolving that which could no longer bind, and to leave the separated parts to be re-united by the law of political gravitation, to the centre. . . .

Mr. Adams . . . says we have had two precedents—one when we seceded from England, and the other when we seceded from the articles of Confederation; and when the day comes that the hearts of these people are divided, when the Government no longer rests upon kindly sympathies and affections, then it is time for them, as Abraham and Lot did, to separate in peace. Adams men present, listen to the voice of your father. Come up now; you cannot shut your eyes to the fact that the period has arrived when kindly sympathies no longer exist, and instead of keeping Virginia in a free-soil Confederacy, and keeping her down as a mere political dependency upon that central empire at Washington, use your efforts to bring about a peaceable separation of people that can no longer live together in peace and harmony. . . .

The gentleman from Monongalia [Mr. WILLEY] brought forward here one argument against the exercise of this right which I was extremely surprised to hear. . . . The gentleman says that Florida cost millions of dollars, that Texas cost millions of dollars, that Louisiana cost millions of dollars, and asks whether we shall now permit them to secede after having paid this large amount of money for them. . . .

I scout this argument. With perfect respect, I say to the gentleman that it is unworthy the consideration of any Virginian, to measure sovereignty, to measure the great question of self-government, and the great eternal principles of civil liberty, by dollars and cents. I repeat, sir, . . . such an argument . . . should not be used upon this floor. . . .

I will now . . . give one or two reasons why, in my judgment, Virginia ought at this time, ought to-day, to resort to the exercise of this right. I dissent from the gentleman from Augusta [Mr. BALDWIN] . . . that slavery is stronger to-day than it had ever been. It is stronger with its friends—it is stronger in the States where it exists; but everywhere else it has infinitely more enemies to-day than it ever had. The whole world is against you; the whole civilized world, including three-fourths of your own country—including every power in Europe, except Spain, and every power upon this continent, except Brazil—is against you. And with these facts staring the gentleman in the face, he gets up and proclaims that slavery is stronger to-day than ever.

If that were so, how can he reconcile it with the history of our own government? That government is seventy-five years old. In its beginning, slavery existed in nearly every State; and if slavery is stronger to-day than ever before, how happens it that your government is for the first time in the hands of the enemies of slavery? How did it get there? . . .

In 1790 petitions were sent from Philadelphia and New York to Congress asking them to abolish slavery. . . . In 1792 petitions came again. In 1797 they came. In 1805 they came. In 1817 they came. In 1819 . . . we had the war upon the Missouri question. In 1827 petitions came again. In 1831 they came again. In 1835 the war regularly begun upon the right of petition, and it was waged there until it was shifted . . . to a war upon the territories. . . .

In 1840 for the first time this anti-slavery element entered into the Presidential election. Twenty years ago [James] Birney, as their candidate, received 7,000 votes. In 1844 he again received, as the candidate of the anti-slavery party, 62,140 votes. In 1848 [Martin] Van Buren and Gerrit Smith received 296,233 votes. In 1852 [John P.] Hale received 157,296 votes. In 1856 . . . John C. Fremont received 1,324,812 votes, showing an increase in sixteen years of over 1,300,000 votes. In 1860 Abraham Lincoln got votes enough to elect him President. . . .

These facts show that there has been a persistent war from the very first session of the First Congress down to the present moment, made upon you and upon your interests. . . . [Can] any sensible man . . . arrive at the conclusion that these people, who have been contending now for nearly seventy-five years for the accomplishment of one object, will relinquish it, give it up, just when successful, and go back to where they started?

Answer that point, gentlemen. Can it be answered upon any principle of human reason, upon any principle that governs human nature? If it cannot, these facts show you that your existence as a free people, that your existence as a slaveholding people depends upon your separation from this Government, where, if you remain, you will be crushed out; you will become degraded outcasts among the nations of the earth. . . .

The generation that now governs the North have grown up in the last 30 years, and [almost] every man . . . believes in their hearts, honestly before God, that slavery is a sin. Judge Story, Chancellor Kent, and Daniel Webster, in his great argument before the Supreme Court of the United States have taught them the fallacious doctrine that this is a Government of one people and . . . that one section must be in part responsible for the sins of the other section. . . . Judge Story's book is a text-book in all their Colleges. Dr. Wayland, a great theologian, . . . has written a book upon Moral Philosophy; . . . his book is a text-book in all their Colleges; and . . . a whole chapter [is] put forth to show that slavery is a sin. Then, sir, there is Peter Parley, useful and instructive as his books are—yet . . . you will find pervading the whole works an anti-slavery feeling. . . .

Here, then, you have the masses indoctrinated with Parley's doctrine, and the educated young man indoctrinated with Webster, Kent, Story and Wayland's doctrine. Then you have—and I defy any gentleman here to deny it—a union of the masses, . . . to strike down an institution which they believe is sinful, . . . with the educated men and political leaders; and I again defy any gentleman here to point me to an instance in the history of the world, when the masses have united with the leaders for a given purpose, that they ever ceased from their efforts until that purpose had been accomplished, or they themselves have been destroyed in their efforts to accomplish it. . . .

Look again at the way in which these Northern people have been educated. They have had anti-slavery catechisms, anti-slavery priests, anti-slavery lectures; they have anti-slavery everything. Their whole system is pervaded with anti-slavery feeling and anti-slavery sentiment. And yet Virginia statesmen get up here and talk about the overwhelming tide that is to destroy the anti-slavery feeling of the North, by paper guarantees attached to the Constitution. You may just as well attempt to dam up the tumbling waters of the Niagara, with your little finger, as to attempt any such thing. . . . I must state to you, Mr. Chairman, that I was startled, astounded to hear gentlemen . . . crying, "wait, wait," "delay, delay," when every day, every hour, brings the event these Northern people desire to accomplish nearer to your door.

Can we live with people like these? . . . Is there so corrupt a Government upon God's earth as your present Government at Washington? . . . It has lived seventy-five years, and now you have to wipe it out and begin afresh or it will end in despotism; and those men who will not vilely and slavishly submit to that despotism will be slaughtered upon some battle field fighting in defence of the rights and principles that have been handed down to us from our ancestors. . . . I believe in God, I believe in His Providence, I believe in His direction, and I believe, as a moral, Christian man, it is my duty to do what I can to separate my State from these people at the North, who are striving day and night to destroy one of God's institutions. . . .

We are told that about 1620 there was a storm at sea, and that . . . God, in His providence and mercy, to save a ship from being engulfed in the ocean, led her into a safe haven at Hampton Roads. . . . She put out twenty odd savage Africans. Our people assembled. They were amazed. They saw there a simple-hearted, docile people that might be elevated to a high standard of Christian civilization. . . . Virginia responded, . . . and in consequence of her response these twenty odd savage Africans have grown to be four millions of civilized men now upon your continent.

As Virginia was thus the great pioneer of the institution and its great author, would it not be the rankest cowardice, the most disgraceful scene ever acted on the theatre of the world, for her, in this hour of distress and extremity of that institution which she has imposed on the land, to turn her back upon it and to permit Northern fanatics to exterminate it from the face of the earth? I do not believe that God will permit that to be done. You may talk about National Conventions, and Border Conferences, and you may send your committees to Washington every other day to confer with Mr. Lincoln, and to know when he is going to hit us: you may read letters from Secretary [of War Simon] Cameron, and Colonel Somebody, and Major Somebody else, each contradicting the other, to show that they are not going to remove guns from this city, but all will have no effect. God means, through the instrumentality of African slavery, to accomplish His great purpose of Christianizing and civilizing that race. You may throw impediments in the way, and thereby bring down punishment on your own hands, but you cannot stop it. . . . Every consideration of duty, of interest, of high Christian moral obligation, conspires to make us cause Virginia to secede at once, settle our difficulties peaceably afterwards, if we can—and if we cannot, forcibly.

If I find that you will not go with me, if you are determined to wait, wait, wait, . . . I will . . . go with you for the next plan which I think will best promote the great object I have in view. . . . I mean to stand by my principles and doctrines to the bitter end. If that day shall come—which God in his mercy avert—when you and I will have to be exiled or yield to this horde of Northern Vandals, . . . I will not be exiled. . . . I will stand on the shores of my own native Rappahannock, and there I will fall. . . . I will die in Virginia, and trust to God and to posterity to vindicate what is just and what is right. [Applause on the floor and gallery.]

13

George Richardson's Secessionist Speech, April 3–4

George William Richardson's brilliance as delegate from the western Tidewater's Hanover County (55.1 percent enslaved) demonstrated again that oratorical skill, rather than fame or wealth, yielded notoriety in this debate. This middle-class lawyer and petty slaveholder, forty years old in 1860, had never before and would never again hold office. He was as much a lifelong outsider as Robert Montague was a perpetual insider. Yet in this conclave, democratic for middle-aged and propertied white men, these two late-speaking secessionists waxed equally powerful oratorically. As an explanation of disunionist motivation, Richardson's fury about wounded honor also rivaled George Wythe Randolph's logic about economic exploitation and Jeremiah Morton's and James Holcombe's apprehensions about politically vulnerable slaveholders.[1]

Mr. Chairman: I . . . propose first to . . . glance at the origin of . . . the North and the South—to show [that] while the former section and a foreign power are, for the most part, responsible for slavery here, they have sought, with unhallowed hands, to destroy both the institution and those on whom they forced it. . . .

To the progress of a [southern] portion of this beautiful country there was an obstacle which at first seemed insurmountable. . . . Caucasians . . . found themselves lords of a country whose resources were to be developed in a climate, and under a sun beneath which their energies, mental and physical, drooped and withered. But the power which had guided them over the trackless ocean did not desert them here. Far away, . . . beneath the burning sun of Africa, there dwelt, in . . . barbarism, heathenism, and cannibalism, a race on whom, for the crime of their progenitor, had come down . . . the curse of . . . God. . . . To lift that curse, [so] that the degraded African might . . . share in . . . atonement, . . . the Redeemer . . .

From Reese, *Proceedings* 3:79–111.
1. Gaines, *Biographical Register,* 66–67.

[brought] him in contact with civilization here. . . . But, [so] that . . . [the South] might have no stain on her escutcheon, . . . [he made] others than her sons the responsible agents of the evil, from which was to flow in full and gushing streams blessings and benefits. . . .

To Great Britain, the country which now so bitterly denounces us for our domestic institutions, must be charged the existence of slavery amongst us. She established it here by positive enactment of law, spreading on her statute book that it was not only profitable, but right. . . . The North, lynx-eyed as to everything which advances her interest, took up and carried on the trade with an avidity which showed her constitutional thirst for and keenness in the pursuit of gain. Immaculate Massachusetts, as early as 1641, declared the lawfulness of African slavery and of the slave trade. In the other Northern States, slavery was established, but . . . these enterprising people took their part in the trade more in selling slaves to the South than in introducing them into their own country. . . .

To the influx of Africans, . . . the Southern Colonies presented an unbroken series of earnest protests. Noble, glorious old Virginia . . . passed no less than twenty-three acts to suppress it;[2] the other Southern States also endeavored to put an end to it, but veto after veto of royal Governors trampled upon the ardent wishes of the people. Not until the revolution had given freedom to these States were they enabled to end the traffic. . . .

I have glanced at these historical facts to show the injustice, the iniquity, the cruelty of the attacks on the South and her institutions, and I ask if the world can furnish a parallel to an outrage so atrocious. Not only are we assailed by that country which forced the institution upon us . . . but the honest, benevolent and immaculate saints of the perjured North, who sold us slaves for gold, proclaim that a sin in which they were *particeps criminis*[3] . . . and seek to destroy our institutions and cut our throats. . . .

Mr. Chairman, a fearful crisis is upon us—our agricultural, mercantile and commercial interests are prostrate—our finances are deranged—our once glorious Union is disrupted—seven stars have left our federative constellation, and others threaten to shoot from their spheres. . . . Amid these raging elements, what should be the course of the border States and of Virginia? In my humble judgment they should at once resume the

2. Richardson referred here to colonial Virginia's unsuccessful efforts, before the American Revolution, to end the colony's participation in the international slave trade.

3. Participants in the crime.

powers formerly delegated by them to the General Government, and in solid phalanx assert their independence. . . . If, when the South was a unit, we were unable to stem the tide of injustice and oppression, how hopeless will our condition be now, with this resistless majority of Northern and North-western States against us, and when seven of our sovereign allies have left the Confederacy? With these great political facts staring me in the face, I am forced to say that guarantees, which, for the sake of the peace, I would, at one time, have accepted, I would now consider myself unjust to my constituents to touch. . . .

To the Southern Confederacy alone can we look for a community of interest for strength, and for real sympathy in the maintenance of that most sensitive and vital of all our domestic institutions, slavery. We cannot be sure of the effective co-operation of the border States. Delaware, Maryland, Kentucky, Tennessee and North Carolina, notwithstanding the nation is in the throes of revolution, have refused to call conventions. . . . I fear there is too much reason to deplore the free soil proclivities of Delaware and Maryland; and Missouri on the 20th of last month, by a vote of 69 to 23, actually refused to declare her willingness to unite with the South. . . . Then we should not await the action of the border States. Delay and uncertainty are ruinous to our interests. . . .

At the very moment this Convention was discussing the modes of restoring union and fraternity, a Black Republican Congress passed, and a Black Republican President signed the odious Morrill Tariff, more unequal and oppressive to the South than that bill of abominations of 1832, which came near disrupting the government and destroying the confederacy.[4] Go with the Southern Confederacy, sir, and no such oppression awaits us. We will then rest under the wise and statesman-like Constitution of the Confederate States, formed by Southern slaveholders for the benefit of Southern slaveholders. . . . The Constitution of the Confederate States will be administered by a Southern Congress, a Southern President, with a Southern Cabinet, and construed by Southern Judges, all looking to the interest of Southern slaveholders; and not by a Northern

---

4. The more industrialized North favored protective tariffs on manufactured goods more than did the more agrarian South. Southerners had blocked protective tariffs ever since the 1832–33 Nullification Controversy. But the secession of the Lower South depleted Southern power in Congress, and the Northern Republicans quickly used their first-ever congressional majority to pass the highly protective Morrill Tariff.

free soil executive and abolition Congress, and a Supreme Court to be abolitionized as rapidly as death shall remove the remainder of the venerable States rights Judges who now grace its bench. . . .

I do not see that the withdrawal of Virginia from the Confederacy, without aggression upon the Federal Government, will produce war any more than the mere withdrawal of the Confederate States has produced war. I apprehend that if war springs up between the rival Confederacies, it will not be in consequence of the isolated act of secession, but in consequence of some controversy with regard to the forts, and the collection of the revenue. And if it be said that the Government has up to this time stayed its hostile hand to keep Virginia with the Northern Confederacy I answer that if she secedes, the same policy will probably be pursued to keep in that Confederacy the remaining border slave States. . . .

If there is any hope of reconstruction, it must be from the prompt secession of Virginia, and her union with the Southern Confederacy. . . . The Gulf States will never return without constitutional amendments, securing them thorough and absolute equality with the North. . . . But, if miraculously almost, the free soil party, from a returning sense of justice, should be willing to accord us this equality, nothing but a union of Virginia with the States of the Southern Confederacy will bring them back. . . .

Much as I have loved the old Union and would love it now, freed from oppression and wrong, I think we have no safety in it unless these seceded States return. Having ranged ourselves with them we would go back when they return; and if that is never to be, then we should remain under the wise Constitution of the Confederate States, with powerful allies, and not be reduced to the weakness, the impotence of being alone. If all the slave States will not join the Southern Confederacy, I would, at least, make it as strong as we can by the addition of Virginia. The Northern States will then see . . . that the subjugation of the South is hopeless; and (harshly as it may grate on their haughty and guilty pride) that unless the war on our institutions is ended and our equality admitted every where, the Union is gone forever. . . .

Great complaints have been made of the so-called rashness of these Cotton States, and of their failure to act in concert with the other slave States. Mr. Chairman, statesmen have to deal with questions practically. There is no propriety in standing upon stilts. . . . The question is not whether the Southern States have acted with perfect prudence and courtesy, but whether, under the facts as they exist, the interest of the State is with the Northern or with the Southern Confederacy.

And, it seems to me, that the imputation of rashness or want of courtesy at all, to the Southern Confederacy, is rather illiberal, in view of their invitation to us, both before and since their secession, to co-operate with them. Equally illiberal seems to me to be the complaint, that they have endeavored to coerce and drag us out of the Union. We must admit their sovereignty, or abandon our own, and sovereignty carries with it the right to secede. Now, does a State, when she thinks her safety and honor require her to withdraw from the Confederacy, coerce States that do not withdraw? She uses no force upon them. She merely exercises her own Constitutional rights—her own attribute of sovereignty. . . .

But it has been repeatedly argued here, that . . . the Federal Government . . . has made no aggression on the South; has taken no part in the passage of personal liberty bills, and has reclaimed some fugitive slaves. . . . [But] thousands of fugitive slaves have never been reclaimed. . . . Sir, if this is protection, God save us from injustice and wrong! . . .

The eloquent gentleman from Kanawha [Mr. SUMMERS], asked us if we were willing to make the Western section of the State the outside row of the Southern Confederacy—if we were willing to bring the Canada line down to the Border? Well, sir, I think the Canada line has been brought down practically to the border years ago. . . . Make them the "outside row"? Why, sir, I ask if they are not already the "outside row." . . . The border counties, with the number of slaves in each one, are as follows:

Monongalia 101
Wetzel 10
Marshall 29
Ohio 100
Brooke 18
Hancock 2
Tyler 18
Pleasants 15
Wood 176
Jackson 55
Mason 386
Cabell 305
Wayne 143

Perhaps those gentlemen can inform me what has become of their slaves. I ask whether the abolitionists have not carried them away? Pressing thus upon the border and driving slavery from those counties, what, I ask, is to prevent them from pressing on still further and pushing it from the counties which come next in order, and so rolling on the wave of sectionalism till they sweep slavery away through Virginia, through the Confederate States, and into the far South?

Now, sir, I want to stop this fearful wave—to roll it back from our Western brethren, their homes and families. To effect this, let the Southern States in solid column leave the Northern Confederacy, and establish on our free State frontier a line of military posts which will prevent further encroachments by the abolitionists. . . .

Sir, this idea that the maintenance of an army of 15,000 or 20,000 men is going to ruin our hoped for Southern Confederacy, is a most preposterous one. . . . Ruin such a country, sir, by the appropriation of a few millions of dollars for its defence? Why, do not some of the most prosperous and flourishing countries in the world maintain immense standing armies of hundreds of thousands of men; and could not our giant Southern country maintain twenty or thirty thousand? . . . When . . . the great Southern Confederacy is in successful operation; when the commercial navies of the world ride in her harbors; when, relieved from Northern taxation, she has grown to be independent and prosperous—she will no more feel the burthen of maintaining an army of fifteen or twenty, or thirty thousand men, than would a giant feel the stroke of a pigmy's arm. . . .

Sir, neither individuals or nations can submit, habitually, to insult and indignity, without degradation so fearful, that they become ultimately as base as the denunciations of the oppressors proclaim them. The spiritual dilapidation goes on; it may be slowly, but surely, and soon or late moral ruin is the result. . . .

I for one, will never consent to live or hold intercourse with men who claim that I am socially their inferior. The insolent pretension of those who—whether nations or individuals—have invariably the least right to make it; the bloated arrogance and impudence which prefers such a claim, will be met by true men with the scorn and defiance of border chivalry. . . .

The fanatical, meddlesome, overbearing disposition of the Puritans— their arrogant, conceited and wicked determination to . . . regulate and control the social rights and customs of other people, has deluged more than one country in blood. . . . In England, . . . so arrogant—so conceited, . . . so intolerant were they, that . . . a gallant people . . . drove them beyond the *ocean*. . . . On American soil, . . . they have chosen to make themselves the bitter enemies of peace, happiness and safety of the gentlemen of the South. . . .

This great country was formed by the compact of independent sovereignties, not the right, first, of libel, and then of destruction by one part of the institutions of the other, but with an endorsement of the institutions of the whole country. . . . These solemn covenants have been fraudulently and foully repudiated, . . . [leaving] every ism which degrades man to a level with brutes. Infidelity, Spiritualism, Mormonism, Free Soil, . . . Free Speech (which with them is the right of rank and reeking . . . and atrocious slander on the South); Free Love (which means to roll back the tide of refinement and virtue for . . . the hell of vileness and iniquity): [all this] has, in the blended spirit of avarice and fanaticism, not only assailed our fair fame abroad, but our very household gods at home. . . .

Great names adorn our Southern annals—Washington and Jefferson, Madison and Monroe, Carroll and Rutledge, and a host of others. Splendid mausoleums mark the resting places of these great men, and they have still nobler monuments in the hearts of their countrymen. But the sacrilegious effort is made to blacken their sacred fame because they were slaveholders. . . . Sir, facts, stored in the memory of every gentleman in this hall, give the lie to these atrocious slanders.

Who is there, reared in Virginia, . . . [without] a thousand pleasant memories of the patriarchal institution of the State—of the good will between the servants and the families of their masters—of the many errands of kindness on which he has been sent to old or sick domestics of the household, and of the scenes in which these domestics would bless with their latest breath the benevolence of their owners? Raise the curtain of the past, and . . . in memory rises the aged and honored head and patriarch of the house, whose feeble steps, whose personal goodness, whose position of common ancestor, commanded for him the pious love and care of his descendants. He recalls . . . that mother's love still encircles him like the atmosphere of a holier and better clime. Her tears fall upon his head like the dews of Heaven. . . . The memory of that mother's counsel and that mother's love will better defend him from dishonor than a thousand bristling bayonets.

Time rolls on, and these sacred forms depart. . . . Green grows the long grass and sweetly bloom the flowers planted on their graves by the hand of affection. . . . With throbbing brow the descendant of that house says these were mine, and though dead their pure virtuous memories live. But Abolitionism, that fiendish libeller, says *cursed be they for they were slave-holders.*

Sir, let us say to these oppressors of the South, . . . "Thus far shalt thou go and no farther." We demand stern, full and exact justice. Cease your assaults on our institutions; . . . bow to the decision of the Supreme Court; sweep from the statues of your States every enactment warring on our property; cease your attacks on the laws which have established slavery in places under the jurisdiction of the Federal Government; confess that we came into the Union on terms of perfect equality with you and that wherever in the common territories our flag floats, our property has the same right to protection that yours has; regard us and let your legislation regard us as equals, not tributaries. . . . [Then] the seceded South may return. The Union may again stretch its grand proportions from Maine to California, from the Atlantic to the Pacific. Deny us these, our rights, and our separation from you is eternal.

14

Chapman Stuart's Unionist Speech, April 5

As the preceding three secessionist speeches indicate, disunionist orators dominated the convention's proceedings during the final days before the war. But during this increasingly tense period, Unionists still possessed the numerical advantage. Chapman Johnson Stuart's brief outburst summed up a crucial reason for the secessionists' continued shortfall.

Chapman Stuart, not to be confused with Alexander H. H. Stuart from the Valley's Augusta County, represented the Trans-Allegheny's Tyler and Doddridge counties (together containing only fifty-two slaves). Although one of the few convention speakers who owned no slaves, the forty-year-old Stuart professed utter loyalty to slavery—and prescient conviction that secession would devastate the east's peculiar institution.[1]

. . . I said yesterday that my constituents were ready and willing to stand up in defence of the rights and institutions of the people of the Eastern portion of the State. In saying so, I did not wish to be understood as meaning that the people of the West were willing to take the course pressed by those whom we call the ultra men of the Eastern portion of the State, but that the people of the West are sound on the question of slavery, and are willing, at all hazards, to demand and have secured to you your rights; but I do not wish to be understood as being in favor of secession, or the constitutional right of secession.

We believe in the right of revolution. We believe that when the Constitution has been perverted to our injury and oppression, we have the right to throw off the shackles and appeal to our natural rights. But revolution presupposes, in my opinion, a remedy, and if the fact of dissevering

From Reese, *Proceedings* 3:168–70. In this case Reese reversed his usual procedure, placing the revised version of a speech in the main body of the *Proceedings* and the original version in the endnotes. We find his logic compelling (ibid., 775–76) and have followed his lead.

1. Gaines, *Biographical Register,* 72–73.

our connection from the Federal Government would be a remedy for the evils of which we complain, then we would be in favor of it.

But I cannot see for my life how, under present circumstances, secession or revolution would be a remedy for the evils of which you complain. Will it relieve us from any of them? If we had to complain of the perversion of the Constitution by the Federal Government, to our injury and oppression, then revolution, if successful, would be a complete remedy. But if the complaint is in regard to the action of separate States, then secession from the General Government would be no remedy. If it were even successful, we would still find ourselves in identically the same position in which we now are. The institutions and laws of those States derogatory of the rights of the South, would still remain on their statute books.

The people of my district . . . all stand up as one solid mass . . . to contend and fight for our rights in the Union. We believe that secession, instead of being a remedy for the evils complained of, would be an aggravation of those evils. The great question that has given rise to complaint is the slavery question. And I have told you that although we have no direct interest in that question, we were loyal and true to the interests of the people of the eastern portion of the State.

We take the position that slavery is right, legally, morally, and in every sense of the word. But the Convention will recollect that the sentiment of the whole civilized world, at this day, is arrayed against the institution of slavery, and it is nothing but the prestige and power of the General Government now that guarantees to the slaveholder his right. We find a large portion of the people of the Northern States standing up also to vindicate and support our rights. I believe that at this day there is a majority of the people of the free States in favor of the right of the Southern portion of the Confederacy to the institution of slavery.

They appeal to us to come to the rescue and help them to save the Union. They have fought for our rights in days gone by, and now they appeal to us as friends, for whose rights they have ever stood firm and true, to come to their aid and help them to save the Union. If we pursue the course indicated here by the secession party, we will cut ourselves loose from our friends in the free States, and array them against us and our institutions. If we say to those in the North, who have heretofore stood up for our rights, "We will have nothing more to do with you," can you expect or hope to retain the good will and kind feeling of that people?

No, sir. By pursuing this course, you will, in my humble opinion, drive from us our heretofore best and truest friends, and unite them in one solid mass against our institutions. Then we will have the whole world arrayed in sentiment against our institutions, with a power right on our borders three times our strength, made our enemies by our own acts. Can we expect our friends in the North to stand by us after we destroyed our common Government and brought ruin upon them? It is hopeless to expect so. Then I hold that secession or revolution is no remedy for the evils complained of, but will tend as an aggravation of them, and will, if persisted in, lead to the extermination of slavery. . . .

PART II

TAXATION DEBATED

On April 5 Chapman Stuart entwined his assault against secessionists' counterproductive revolution with an attack against slaveholders' counterproductive tax breaks. Unless you remove the state's constitutional ban on full taxation of your slaves, Stuart warned eastern slaveholders, "you might as well undertake to remove the Alleghany Mountains from their base, as to induce the people of the Northwest, for present causes, to secede from the Union."[1]

According to Virginia's constitution of 1851, slaves twelve years of age and over could not be valued at more than $300 for purposes of tax assessments. Property in slaves under twelve could not be taxed at all. All other property (including all nonslaveholders' property) could be assessed at its full value (known as ad valorem taxation).

At the convention western delegates meant to secure equal taxation of slaveholders' property. Westerners conceived that more than cash was at stake. Unequal taxation, they protested, consigned whites without slaves to degrading inequality, akin to slaves' shame.

Eastern slaveholders also saw more than money at stake. Equal taxation, they feared, could help drain the state of slaves. Many bondsmen had long been exiled from the less tropical northern South (including Virginia) to the more fertile Lower South's cotton and sugar kingdoms. Thomas R. Dew, one of Virginia's first proslavery apostles, had warned long ago that Virginia sooner or later would be "too far north" for slavery.

Equal taxation of slaves could turn later into sooner. The 57.3 percent of Virginia whites who lived west of the Blue Ridge owned only 12.8 percent of Virginia slaves. Give that white majority the ad valorem principle, and then slaves could be valued at the Lower South auction level, $1,500

From Reese, *Proceedings* 1:443–44.
1. Reese, *Proceedings* 3:116.

per slave. The fivefold increase in Virginia's existing $300 value placed on slaves over twelve, plus full taxation of previously untaxed slaves under twelve, could force many more slaveholders to sell many more slaves downriver.

Nonslaveholders generally had scant sympathy for abolitionists and less for blacks. But the intensified drain of blacks southward from Virginia might be an unintended consequence of nonslaveholders' push for equal treatment. On taxation, slaveholders preferred to treat nonslaveholders like unequals, or as the yeomen saw it, like slaves.

Still, upper-class squires, coveting western support for disunion, dared not altogether alienate their antagonists. As the following debate reveals, some easterners even offered to grant ad valorem taxes if westerners granted secession. The offer only intensified western anger. Ad valorem taxation, if right, must be guaranteed even if yeomen called secession wrong. In fact, many westerners, outraged by eastern stonewalling on equal taxation, considered seceding from Virginia if Virginia seceded from the Union.

15

William G. Brown Initiates the Taxation Debate, March 7

Although westerners had introduced taxation resolutions in the convention earlier, the issue only reached center stage on the convention's nineteenth day. Then William G. Brown, representing northwestern Virginia's Preston County (0.5 percent enslaved), moved to establish a "Committee of Finance" to consider "State . . . taxation." Brown followed up with the convention's first (albeit brief) inflammatory speech on ad valorem taxation.

. . . My noble friend from Northampton [Mr. MIERS FISHER] the other day . . . offered a resolution looking to the appropriation of millions for the defence of the State. I know, sir, that he will come to the rescue and will aid me in . . . [raising] the funds. . . . I want . . . all species of property subjected to the *ad valorem* system.

While I am opposed to all steps that will involve us in war, yet I declare to you, sir, in the event that war must come, every dollar's worth I have shall be subject to taxation, . . . to arm and clothe the true and brave men that we may send to the field. I . . . want to send them, sir, in a condition . . . [to] do honor to the old Commonwealth. . . .

I am satisfied, sir, that Eastern citizens are prepared now, in that generous spirit which I hope animates them, to subject their property to equal taxation. I want those true and brave men of the East, who have delivered such patriotic speeches here, to come forward and help us now to raise the sinews of war. Sir, I do not want our army to be fed with patriotic speeches and resolutions. I want them to have good coffee for breakfast; I want them to have good blankets to keep them warm; I want them by all means to be well armed. . . . I hope the Eastern Secessionists . . . will join me. . . . I know they are really sincere in their secession sentiments, and . . . we all know that a war cannot be carried on without the necessary means to prosecute it. . . . It is therefore the duty of those who favor secession to . . . provide these means.

16

Waitman Willey Introduces His Motion, March 16

Immediately after William G. Brown's speech, the convention tabled his motion, 69–41. Nine days later, however, Waitman Willey made a similar motion for a special committee to consider ad valorem taxes. Willey delivered as provocative a speech as Brown's, and this time the debate exploded.

I hold in my hand some resolutions which I propose to offer for the consideration of the Convention. . . .

We have now been earnestly engaged for more than a month in the great work of inaugurating a national conciliation. . . . But, sir, while we are thus engaged in settling our national difficulties, . . . would it not be wise . . . to remedy the causes of difficulty and strife at home? Whilst we are engaged in an effort to roll off the burthens of oppression from outside of Virginia, would it not be well to remedy the odious distinction or unequal burthens which are resting upon our own citizens; and whilst we are endeavoring to throw oil upon the troubled national waters, would it not be well . . . to make the necessary efforts to compose domestic strife, to produce conciliation and harmony throughout the length and breadth of our own State.

One of these odious and unequal burthens, Mr. President, is that anomaly in our organic law, whereby a large portion of the property of this Commonwealth is wholly exempt from taxation. . . . Allow me to remark, in this connection, that I am a slaveholder myself; and I ask upon what principle of public policy—upon what principle of public justice—upon what principle of right and propriety, is it that this large amount of the most valuable personal property in the Commonwealth of Virginia is wholly exempt from taxation? I . . . feel a sense of mortification when I remember that the property of my non-slaveholding neighbor is subject, every cent of it, to rigid tribute, whilst my property, equally valuable, is

From Reese, *Proceedings* 1:765–66.

exempt from taxation. Why is it that because I am a slaveholder I shall be exempt from the burdens of the Commonwealth, and my neighbor, equally worthy with me, though not a slaveholder, is to bear the burdens which I ought to bear, and which by virtue of my possession of my property I am able to bear?

17

The Confrontation That Willey's Motion Provoked, March 18–19

Two days later, proponents and opponents of ad valorem taxation clashed over Willey's proposed committee. Even an easterner's proposed compromise, offering to trade eastern support for tax reform for western support for secession, only propelled charges that each side meant to blackmail the other.

William G. Brown *again*

. . . It has been charged, sir, upon the North-western portion of the people, that I in part have the honor to represent, that they are Abolitionists. . . . Sir, if that were true I should not have a seat upon this floor. I am not only interested directly in the institution of slavery, but have vindicated it as one highly conservative; one that is ordained of God himself for the purpose of redeeming the African race from barbarism. I have said before my people again and again, that but for the opinions of the Christian world, . . . I would be willing to see the last African picked up and brought under the influence of Christianity and civilization; and yet, sir, no opinions of this character that I have expressed before my people have militated against me . . . whenever I sought their suffrages. It is unkind, therefore, to charge upon that people hostility to slavery. Let me tell you, sir, that your . . . particular property and . . . every kind of property . . . is much safer in the care and keeping of that people that have been denounced as Abolitionists here, than in the care and keeping of that mixed crowd that you see on your streets here shouting in a disorderly manner and at unusual hours. If that institution is never injured until the people of North-western Virginia disturbs it, it will never be injured or disturbed.

It is true, sir, that they believe, honestly believe, . . . that property that seeks the security of the laws of the land, should bear its equal proportion of the burdens of Government. . . . They are unwilling to see partial

From Reese, *Proceedings* 2:6–8, 8–11, 14–16, 16–17, 19–22, 23–24, 47–55.

legislation in reference to this institution, especially at a time when our interests have been so much disturbed in consequence of the rights of that peculiar property being disturbed or assailed. Let me say, sir, that we will stand by you to the last; we will stand by the principle of justice to the last; we will defend you against aggression from your enemies; but let me beg of you to remember that we have rights, that we are peculiarly sensitive upon this subject of equality. We may not have as much property as you, we may not have as much of that peculiar kind of property as you have, but we are unwilling to see one man pay $500 taxes and his neighbor pay $5 upon property of probably equal value. . . .

Miers Fisher *representing the Tidewater's Northampton County (49.4 percent enslaved)*

. . . Will my friend from Preston, while insisting that the North-West will not consent to occupy a position unequal to other portions of the State, maintain with equal firmness, that they will submit to no inequality in representation or taxation in the General Government? From what has taken place here, we are to infer that at least some of the gentlemen from the North-West are willing to submit to inequality in the Federal Union.

Now, sir, I am indisposed to submit to inequality either in the State or Federal Union. If my friend will . . . give us an ordinance of secession, and go before his people pledging himself in good faith to make the effort to induce them to confirm that ordinance, I will go into a consideration of this question of taxation and representation. I will say for myself, sir, whether my constituents will endorse it or not, that if these gentlemen give me an ordinance of secession that shall be adopted by their people and the Commonwealth, they shall have taxation upon slaves under twelve years of age, and all slaves over that age shall be taxed according to their value.

Shall we continue to allow the stamp of inferiority for ever to be put upon us? . . . Shall we . . . relieve . . . [our] degraded and degrading position . . . in this Federal Union? . . . [Every] gentleman in this Convention . . . [must] recognize the fact that our rights have been invaded, our interests paralyzed, our honor infringed, by the Northern States of this confederacy. Let them come up and relieve us from this degraded condition. . . . Then we will enter into a consideration of the State question which seems to occasion peculiar trouble to the gentleman from the North-West. . . .

Benjamin Wilson *representing the Trans-Allegheny's Harrison County* (*4.2 percent enslaved*)

Mr. President, I regret very much to have heard from gentlemen on this floor so much distrust manifested of the disloyalty of the people of that portion of the State which I have the honor to represent. . . . It is true there are some Abolitionists in North-western Virginia, but I venture to assert that you have more Abolitionists in the city of Richmond than there are in the whole of my Congressional District. . . .

An extensive and valuable property in Eastern Virginia . . . is now exempt from taxation. . . . If something is not done to make taxation more equal we will soon have a conflict, a dire and awful conflict in Virginia. Not a conflict between the people of the sea-coast and of the mountains, but an irrepressible conflict, I fear, between the laboring man and the slave owner.

Look at our tax laws. A man who toils day by day for his daily bread, and if his wages amount in the year to five hundred dollars (I believe) he is heavily taxed; while opulent slaveholders, resting upon pampered wealth and fortune own a valuable property in young negroes that is not taxed. Is that just and equitable? . . .

More true and more loyal friends of the negro interest are no where to be found than in the Western part of the State. But if we are to fight the battles of that interest, we contend that they should be subjected to the same rule of taxation as other property. We have no bargain to make, no measure to propose, but such as we believe will best promote the interest of Virginia. . . .

Thomas Branch *of the Tidewater's Petersburg City (31.1 percent enslaved)*

. . . The question of secession now agitating the people of the State of Virginia and the whole country is sufficient to occupy the whole of our time and attention at this moment. . . . I regard the maxim as true, that every man should pay taxes according to his ability to pay them. If that rule is carried out, the principle involves every species of property. . . .

The property in slaves should be valued according to their worth to the planter in working them in Virginia, and not according to their worth in Texas or Mississippi. If you value a negro in Virginia to be worked on a plantation here, according to the value of a negro in Mississippi, . . . you lose all the negroes. They will be taken into those States where they can be worked more profitably. . . .

We cannot afford to lose our slave labor by over taxation. The time has not yet arrived to agitate this question, but when the Convention shall have determined that the State shall leave the Union, then there should be a re-organization of the organic law upon the basis above stated. . . .

Allen Taylor Caperton *representing southwestern Virginia's Monroe County (10.4 percent enslaved)*

. . . We are here endeavoring to obtain from the Northern people such concessions and such guarantees as will enable us to continue in the Union. . . . Those people will grant those guarantees very much in pro-portion to their apprehensions . . . that if the demands are not accorded, we will separate from them. . . . [But they will dismiss] the earnestness of this declaration . . . if we exhibit . . . a domestic trouble in reference to [slavery] . . . which in all probability might so divide the State as to prevent any unity of action in regard to . . . separation. . . . [Thus] I am in favor of saying to the Northern people that we are for the time deter-mined to sink all questions of domestic strife, and to dispose of the great national questions, . . . before we act upon anything touching merely our State interests.

But, Mr. President, the question is not now whether the principle of taxation embodied in our State Constitution is right or not. Upon that proposition, I find myself with the mover of the resolutions. . . . But I am opposed to action now, because it is not the proper time for such action, on account of the peculiar circumstances under which we assembled. . . .

The people in [the eastern] . . . portion of the State are more alive, more apprehensive, more filled with dread consequences of the great trouble now upon us than the people inhabiting the Western portion of the State. . . . The people of Eastern Virginia are . . . worked up to such a pitch that they are willing to do now what they would not do under other circumstances, in order to have united action in resisting . . . the North. . . . It would [not] be right and proper . . . to avail ourselves of this occa-sion. Would we value concessions obtained under duress? . . .

Now, sir, when the proper time comes, we will unite with these gentle-men, . . . to obtain . . . reform . . . of taxation. This I do not regard as the proper time. I regard the effort now as having an injurious effect upon . . .

our national difficulties . . . [and] as not fair towards our neighbors of the East. . . .

Marmaduke Johnson *representing Richmond City (30.9 percent enslaved)*

. . . My friend from the county of Harrison [Mr. WILSON] . . . [said] that there are now more abolitionists in the city of Richmond than there are in North-Western Virginia. May I ask my friend by what authority he makes this assertion?

Mr. WILSON: . . . Your public prints have informed me of the fact, and from what I had seen and heard, I stated it as my belief that there were as many abolitionists in the city of Richmond as in my Congressional District; but I desire my friend to know that we have very few out there.

Mr. JOHNSON: I trust that there are none there, as I am confident that we have none here. . . . My friend . . . should seek authenticity for his information, beyond the calumnies which are daily circulating in the newspapers of . . . Richmond. . . . I am not prepared to say that there are any in the District from which the gentleman comes. One thing is certain, that there were votes recorded in his District for Abraham Lincoln, and that the poll book will show none in . . . Richmond.

I trust that I may not be understood as . . . [assaulting] any section of the State. . . . I think we are dwindling . . . very much . . . when we . . . criminate and recriminate one another upon local prejudices. We have a higher duty to perform here—we have a holier and more sacred function to discharge. Our country is in danger. The cause of republican liberty is at stake. The most magnificent temple of republican freedom that ever glittered in the sun, and that was ever vouchsafed by God or ordained by Him, is now tottering; and, for one, I protest against complicating the consideration of that great, comprehensive question with the question of taxation, or with any other local questions calculated to excite local prejudices. What good can be produced? What harm will not be produced? . . .

We have now from the lips of the gentleman from Northampton [Mr. FISHER] a proposition made upon this floor, to the West, that, if they will . . . disrupt the ties which bind us to our Union and the Constitution, then they can have their own terms upon the subject of taxation. . . . And he had the temerity, at the same time, to say that he did it without consultation with his own constituents. I trust in God that he will not be sustained by his constituents upon that reckless proposition, but that he will stand solitary and alone. . . . Gentlemen from the East and from the West, whatever may be their local interest or their opinions upon the question of taxation, should lay aside all petty considerations, for I regard the subject of taxation in the present crisis as no more than the smallest particle of attenuated matter. . . .

Samuel Woods *representing the Trans-Allegheny's Barbour County (1.2 percent enslaved), in a speech finished on March 19*

The gentleman from Northampton [Mr. FISHER] . . . [invites] Western gentlemen to . . . give him an ordinance of secession by way of offset for . . . equalizing taxation. . . . [But] I came here not to bargain, or beseech for my rights, but to ask, demand them, and insist upon them, because I hold in regard to the rights of citizens of Virginia in Virginia, that a right that is not worth asking for ought to be abandoned. I am not willing to consent to occupy an inferior position in the Confederacy of the United States, if I can help it, nor to consent that my people shall occupy an inferior position in the councils of their native State. . . .

Mr. President, the gentleman from Monroe [Mr. CAPERTON] . . . said to us upon this floor yesterday, that we ought not to extort from Eastern Virginia, in this hour of her peril and her calamity, those rights of ours which he, almost in the same breath, . . . asserted to be eminently just and proper. . . . It never occurred to my mind before that our friends . . . in any portion of the State, while admitting the existence of a right, and at the same time admitting that they withheld it from those entitled to it, could be induced to relinquish it, unless extorted by fear. I think it is unjust to our friends in Eastern Virginia, and I expect them to come up manfully to this subject, and indicate, by a liberal and generous support of this proposition, the just appreciation that they have of the affection of Western Virginia. . . .

I have never been able to appreciate the justice of that system of taxation . . . [which] enables me to relieve myself of all taxation by merely changing the character of my property. The common masses of the people throughout the country are at a loss to understand . . . [why] property, when consisting of lands, shall be taxed to its full value, but when that land is exchanged for negroes under twelve years of age, that property is exempt from taxation. And I have no idea that they will ever be able to understand such a proposition. . . .

I ask again, is it not sound policy for Virginia to adopt a system of equal taxation in view of the condition of things that is upon us? . . . The people of the West will have justice done them. . . . We make no threats; we appeal to your native magnanimity; we appeal to your sense of justice and right, and we still believe that that appeal will be met with . . . fraternal spirit. . . . We deem it of the utmost importance to Virginia, at this crisis in her history, that there shall be no division of sentiment among her people, no cause of division, whether ostensible or real, but that she shall be united as one people, from the Ohio to the Chesapeake. . . . I cannot look to the possibility of a rupture of the good old Commonwealth of Virginia without feeling that her glory will have departed forever. Everything which makes a Virginian raise his head with pride . . . will have passed away, and he must hang his head with shame . . . [as] a citizen of a State which, by wrong and injustice, accomplished her own destruction. . . .

18

Willey's Climactic Taxation Speech, March 28 and April 2

After the initial burst of hostility, the debate on ad valorem taxation dragged on as inconclusively as the confrontation over secession. The convention's rules, limiting debate on taxation to a couple of morning hours, helped delay a decision. But as with disunion, dread of a settlement, one way or the other, led many to procrastinate. As March turned into April, Willey's final appeal for a committee on taxation underlined the stakes in the convention's imminent (he thought) decision.

Before the vote is taken on . . . [my] resolutions, . . . I should explain . . . the reasons which induced me to offer them. . . . Our organic law either wants amendment or it does not. . . . If the principle of taxation, as now provided for in the organic law, . . . be wrong, why should we continue to live under the wrong? If it be oppressive, . . . why should the people of this Commonwealth be required to live longer under that oppression? . . .

It is objected against the consideration of this proposition now, that this is an inopportune occasion, that it brings into the deliberations of this body matters calculated to increase dissensions. . . . I had no such object in introducing this measure. . . . I offered it as a peace measure. I believe . . . it will have a tranquilizing influence. . . . It will show to the people of the Commonwealth . . . a disposition to extend full justice to them. It will remove from the public mind a question . . . which has been sowing the seeds of irritation deep in the public mind ever since Virginia had an organization as a Commonwealth. . . .

Further, . . . it is not a sectional question. . . . It is a question between the non-slaveholding and the slaveholding portions of the people of Virginia. In the streets of Richmond I see a white man with his horse and dray. . . . I find by the statutes of Virginia that his dray and horse, his household furniture, and the head on his shoulders, are all taxed. I go into the county and see the white man laboring on his farm, with his

From Reese, *Proceedings* 2:506–8, 3:3–7.

stalwart boys earning an honest livelihood. His little stock, his plough and horses, and mules, and furniture, the head on his shoulders, and the heads on the shoulders of his sons, are all taxed. I look again in our cities and see the sturdy arm of the white laborer pushing the plane. His very tools, and all that he has, are taxed—taxed to their full value. . . . Why is it that the property, the entire property, of this class of our population should be taxed, while the man most able to pay taxes, whose property consists in slaves, should have a very considerable portion of his property wholly exempt from taxation? . . .

The whole number of taxpayers in the Commonwealth of Virginia at this time, was, in round numbers, 207,000, . . . [including] 153,000 non-slaveholding tax-payers and 54,000 slaveholding tax payers. . . . The number of tax-payers . . . living East of the Blue Ridge was in round numbers 90,000, . . . [including] 47,000 owners of slaves and . . . 43,000 . . . non-slave-owning tax-payers. . . . You have in Eastern Virginia within four thousand of as many non-slaveholding tax-payers as there are slave holders.

And yet, Mr. President, it is said that this is a sectional question; it is said that this is a question brought here by Western men for the purpose of sowing dissensions and strife in the deliberations of this body. I demand to know whether the 43,000 non-slaveholding tax-payers in Eastern Virginia have not a right to be heard upon this floor as much as the non-slaveholding tax-payers West of the Blue Ridge? Sir, it is not a sectional question. Gentlemen cannot make it a sectional question. . . .

There is from $150,000,000 to $200,000,000 of the most valuable property in Virginia wholly exempt from taxation, . . . while we have resting upon us the crushing burden of $40,000,000 of public debt. Let it be remembered, sir, that this debt is annually increasing. Let it be remembered that our . . . last Legislature have appropriated . . . $500,000 and the present Legislature $1,000,000 for the purpose of putting this State in a condition of defence and to redress grievances upon this very property, so exempt from taxation—in short, to defend the institution of slavery. . . . We of the West willingly pay our quota of the taxes; but . . . I wish to know whether Eastern gentlemen require us to submit all of our property to taxation, and fight the battles of the country too, while your property, which we are defending, is to be exempt from taxation? . . .

We are not only grinding the people down with the burdens of heavy taxation. . . . We are [also] allowing [state] . . . improvements to be stopped short of completion, in consequence of the want of the means to complete them.[1] The ever-increasing tide of Western wealth and travel and traffic is coming down against our Western mountains like the waves of the sea against the shore, seeking the shortest way to the ocean and to Europe. . . . [Yet] this tide of traffic and wealth, from . . . the want of the means of direct outlet to its natural places of deposit at Richmond, Alexandria, Norfolk, and on the banks of the Chesapeake, is diverted from its natural channel and is turned away through the Northern ice and snows to New York, or down through the swamps and miasma of the South; thus securing Black Republican power by the diversion of capital from our State, concentrating it in the North, increasing Northern population and power, and increasing the ratio of representation against us, decade after decade, while we stand here with this immense amount of property untaxed, which if taxed, would be sufficient to obviate all these evils. The roar of this great tide of Western wealth, rolling down against our Western mountains, is falling upon our ears daily and yearly, demanding a passage to our Eastern shore cities and seaports, while we stand here folding our arms and saying, "let no profane commissioner of the revenue lay his impious hands upon our slaves. They shall not be taxed." I submit, therefore, Mr. President, whether under these circumstances, it is not the true policy of our Eastern friends to come at once to the rescue of their own interest. . . .

I wish, in conclusion, simply to add, why delay this measure of redress? Why delay the removal of this obnoxious oppression? Upon what principle of political expediency, or personal right, or public law, or public justice, can this discrimination be made in favor of the large slaveholders against the many non-slaveholders in the Commonwealth? I hope the question will be taken, and I give way for the purpose of allowing it to be done.

1. Western Virginians had long complained that the eastern majority blocked state funding for internal improvements (including roads, canals, and railroads) that would traverse the mountains to further westerners' trade with eastern Virginia. Meanwhile, the sectionally skewed legislative majority financed state internal improvements within eastern Virginia.

19

The Final Presecession Confrontation on Taxation, April 10–11

On April 10, more than a week after Willey (mistakenly) thought that the convention's vote on his proposed committee was imminent, Henry Alexander Wise initiated the final confrontation on Willey's motion.[1] Wise had lately been the state's especially flamboyant governor. He had long been one of Virginia's most remarkable leaders. For decades, he had been especially loved (or hated) for his demagogic speeches.

This famous orator, however, had been curiously unimportant in the convention's previous forensic duels. Perhaps Wise was too ill to make an extended oratorical effort. Or perhaps the secessionist thought that action must now replace speeches. At any rate, his belated short blast at the westerners provoked the final verbal fireworks on taxation, just as his belated short blast at the Unionists would imminently usher in the convention's final secession confrontation.

On taxation, Cyrus Hall answered Wise for the westerners. Then Williams C. Wickham answered Hall for the easterners. Wickham's emphasis on preserving slaveholders from westerners' economic threat flowed out of his position, like Jeremiah Morton's, as one of the convention's few large planters.

Henry Wise *representing the eastern Tidewater's Princess Anne County (41.3 percent enslaved)*

. . . As to this principle of equal, uniform, ad valorem taxation, . . . I . . . favor . . . that principle, without exception or qualification. But . . . it is unjust to the people of Virginia, either East or West, to seize upon a moment like this, . . . to divide us upon our own internal questions. Sir, . . . we should be ready to waive any minor point of difference and to unite upon the great questions now before us. . . .

From Reese, *Proceedings* 3:514–15, 526–28, 594–99.

1. Craig M. Simpson, *A Good Southerner: The Life of Henry A. Wise of Virginia* (Chapel Hill, NC, 1985).

There is another reason why I will not act upon it. I say to Western gentlemen that I want to see whether they will act in defence of my rights as a slaveholder, before I ever come to any more compromises upon this negro question. I want to know whether they are going to stand by me upon the main question, before I answer how I stand with them upon any incidental question. . . . I must say, that there are some men here from the East and from the West both, that I cannot rely upon any more to defend my rights upon the negro question; and I especially intend, before giving to these gentlemen additional power to tax slave property, to be well satisfied that they are willing to unite with me to defend the rights of slave property.

Cyrus Hall *representing the Trans-Allegheny's Pleasants and Ritchie counties (0.5 percent enslaved)*

. . . The gentleman from Princess Anne [Mr. WISE] . . . said that he had not come here to discuss the question of amending the State Constitution, but he had come here to save the life of Virginia. I must say to that gentleman that if he wants to save the life of Virginia, give to the West her just demands; don't tax everything in the shape of property, belonging to the poor man of the West, and at the same time exempt from taxation . . . property belonging to the wealthy men of the East. This system of unjust and unequal taxation in the Commonwealth is at this very hour doing more to crush out the very vitals of Virginia than anything else. If this cause of complaint was removed there would be harmony in this Convention instead of strife and division. . . .

Our people are becoming exceedingly restless and impatient. . . . If you refuse much longer to grant them their just demands, . . . they may come to the conclusion that this slave interest in Virginia, instead of being a blessing to them, is turned into an engine of oppression. Sir, instead of keeping our people sound upon the slave interest of Virginia, you gentlemen of the East, will give the right of way for the extension of the underground railroad over Virginia soil. . . . Sir, instead of keeping the terminus of this Abolition improvement on the Western bank of the Ohio River, in a short time you will find its terminus in the valley of Virginia, just ready to commence to tunnel the Blue Ridge. And when the work has progressed thus far, it will, . . . unlike other internal improvement companies, [not] find its capital exhausted—its capital will increase during its construction. I beg of you, for your own sake and for the sake of Virginia, don't by your own acts destroy your own cherished institutions.

Sir, some of my friends from North-western Virginia are charged with being Abolitionists; but what grounds have you for making this charge? . . . I suppose it is from the fact we have so little interest in the institution of slavery. Sir, we want an interest in the slave property of Eastern Virginia, and the only way you can make me and my people interested in the slave property of the East, is by taxing it according to its true value like other property. I am interested in dollars and cents, and when I get this moneyed interest in your slave property, you will not doubt my soundness, nor the soundness of my people on the slave question. . . .

This question was thoroughly discussed in the canvass in my section of the State, and it was understood by my people that this would be the most favorable time . . . to demand their rights at the hands of their Eastern brothers. You are calling upon us to sever our connection with the Federal Government. For what cause? For the purpose of protecting this slave property of the East, which you refuse to let contribute like other property to the support of the Government. . . .

Every gentleman from the Northwest that has addressed this Convention upon this subject, has, in most unmistakable terms, told you that if you fail to equalize the taxes in Virginia, you would do more to divide the people of Virginia by that act, than any other course you could pursue. If you want harmony in Virginia in this crisis, you must acknowledge the people of the West [as] your equals in every respect. . . . If . . . we are going to have a fight with the North about this slave property of yours, . . . I want that property . . . to support us while we fight. . . .

Williams C. Wickham *representing the western Tidewater's Henrico County (35.2 percent enslaved)*

. . . The delegate from the counties of Pleasants and Ritchie [Mr. HALL] . . . [declares] that unless Eastern men will grant the power to tax negroes of all ages ad valorem, his constituents will not give assistance for the protection of slave property in Virginia, but that on the contrary the underground railroad will be run through his country down into the Valley of Virginia. That to induce them to aid in the protection of slave property you must give them an interest in that property—and that interest must not be in the form of protection, which would enable them to hold slaves, but in the form of a cession to his people of the power to impose ruinous

taxation upon the slaves held chiefly by us of the East. Sir, no such proposals for the barter of Virginia's rights have been heard on our side of
the house. . . .

I differ entirely from the delegates in this Convention from the West,
on the question of taxation upon negroes. . . . In the whole State the tax on
slaves in 1859 was $326,487.60, and if the proposed increase were made,
estimating the average value of slaves at $500 apiece, . . . that tax would
amount to $1,000,000. In other words, the slaveholding interest of the
State would have to pay an increased tax of $673,512.40 per annum. . . .

This Convention has been called mainly for the purpose of securing
protection to slave property, and I say to gentlemen that the imposition of
this tax on young negroes would be a more dangerous blow to the institution of slavery in the State of Virginia than any single act that could be
done by the government. The imposition of $672,000 a year as additional
taxation on slave property would be a far greater injury than the loss of
$100,000 a year by fugitive slaves—which is, I believe, the estimated loss
in the whole of the slaveholding States. It seems to me that it would be
most unwise, now that we are attempting to secure slave property, to inflict a blow upon it which will inevitably drive it, to a certain extent, from
the Commonwealth of Virginia. . . .

20

Willey's Motion Adopted, April 11

After Williams C. Wickham spoke, the convention at last voted on Waitman Willey's motion to set up a committee to consider ad valorem taxation. It was now thirty-five days since William G. Brown's initial speech on the subject and twenty-six days since Willey had introduced his motion, a measurement of delegates' wariness. It was also only hours before the commencement of the Civil War at Fort Sumter, a measurement of delay's futility. At this juncture enough eastern delegates decided that slaveholders had more to lose from alienating western nonslaveholders (and over a mere committee) than from risking a committee proposal for ad valorem taxes. The convention approved Willey's committee, 63–26.

This action caused further delay. A committee had been established to consider the subject: a possible entering wedge. But the committee could reject ad valorem taxation, just as the convention could reject a committee's ad valorem proposal. The final vote, determining whether Willey's wedge would enter and revolutionize the tax code, would have to wait until the convention (at last) ended its stalling on disunion.

PART III

DECISIONS

In early April, while the taxation issue widened the division between eastern and western Virginians, events beyond the state threatened to drive most delegates together on secession, and thus to increase the western dissenters' rage at their unequal power.

The more extreme western Virginians aside, most delegates agreed that secession was legitimate, even when they disagreed on the tactic's expediency. If circumstances changed, the agreement could trump all disagreements. Because the people of a state supposedly had a right to withdraw their consent to be governed, Abraham Lincoln must never lash withdrawing citizens like unconsenting slaves. If the supposed tyrant coerced seceding brothers beyond Virginia, and if the Virginia convention then followed legitimate procedures in withdrawing the state's citizens' consent to be governed, a skittish Unionist could turn into a ferocious Confederate, regardless of whether the convert owned slaves.

The turning point could come whenever Lincoln's army or navy fired guns at Lower South rebels. Combat most likely would commence at Fort Sumter, inside Charleston harbor, or at Fort Pickens, near Pensacola, Florida, the only important Lower South federal posts that the Confederacy had not seized before Lincoln assumed the presidency.

Six weeks before the new president's March 4, 1861, inauguration, South Carolina authorities had barred food from being sent to Major Robert Anderson and his fifty-nine federal troops at Fort Sumter. For six weeks after March 4, President Lincoln stalled on whether to attempt to augment Anderson's dwindling food supplies. Meanwhile, the new president's secret orders to reinforce Fort Pickens fell victim to his military aides' blunders.

During this interim period of illusory peace, the Virginia convention continued to discuss how the Old Dominion could perpetuate a peaceable Union. On April 4 the state's convention voted 88–45 against immediate secession (and thus to continue the meandering debate on

Union-saving measures). But the two-to-one margin for the Union could easily be reversed. A controlling block of conditional Unionists would switch sides unless the crisis generated their desired conditions. The conditions ranged from a successful border conference to adequate Northern concessions on slavery to, above all else, no federal coercion of the Confederacy.

On April 4, the very day when the convention massed against immediate disunion, the Unionists' rising star was absent from the victory. John Baldwin was at the White House, learning how fragile his coalition's triumph might be. President Lincoln and Secretary of State William H. Seward had invited the nationally prominent Unionist delegate George Summers to Washington to discuss the desperate national situation. When Summers refused, citing his convention duties, Unionists instead sent the nationally obscure Baldwin.

Although the disappointed president and secretary did not know it, the substitution signaled a changing of the guard within Virginia's Unionist circles. The renowned Summers's rather mediocre oration during the convention's February–March period of expansive speeches had contrasted with the unheralded Baldwin's oratorical triumph. The rise and fall of the two careers would imminently become more apparent, with George Summers fading from view at the peak moment of secession and John Baldwin sharing the climactic spotlight with the disunionists.

At his April 4 secret meeting with Lincoln at the White House, Baldwin discovered the likelihood of federal war against the Confederacy. When the president "said something about feeding the troops at Sumter," Baldwin later recalled, "I told him that a relief expedition would cause guns to be fired." Whoever fired first, continued the Unionist, Virginia, "strong as the Union majority in the Convention is now, will be out in forty-eight hours." That cannot be true, answered the president.[1]

1. John B. Baldwin, *Interview between President Lincoln and Colonel John B. Baldwin, April 4th, 1861* (Staunton, VA, 1866), 11–13.

21

The Quest for Lincoln's Intentions, April 6

On Friday, April 5, John Baldwin was back in the convention. There he told fellow moderates about his discouraging White House interview. The next day, conditional Unionists commenced their official quest for Lincoln's intentions.

William Ballard Preston's Initiative   *The moderates' leader at this stage of the convention was the renowned William Ballard Preston. Preston, at age fifty-five, was one of the convention's oldest leaders. He had served in both houses of the Virginia legislature, in Congress, and in Zachary Taylor's cabinet as secretary of the navy. On Saturday, April 6, this representative from the southern Trans-Allegheny's Montgomery Country (20.9 percent enslaved) moved that the convention appoint three commissioners to visit President Lincoln and ascertain his intentions.*

Mr. President, . . . there is no power on the part of the Federal Government to coerce one of these seceding States, [and] the people of Virginia will never consent that the Federal power, which is in part our power, shall be exerted for the purpose of subjugating the people of seceded States to the Federal authority. . . . [My] resolution proposes that this Convention shall elect a committee to proceed to Washington, for the purpose of presenting these principles, avowed by this Convention, to the President of the United States, and to respectfully ask from him an answer thereto, with the hope of breaking a silence that has been so long protracted, so profound, and so mysterious as to create the greatest solicitude and alarm throughout the country. . . .

I am not alarmed, Mr. President, by the newspaper accounts or by the telegraphic dispatches. I have not regulated my conduct by such sources of information. We have, [however], waited here for more than a month,

From Reese, *Proceedings* 3:272–75, 283–91.

with an anxious desire, on the part of us all, to preserve the peace, and on the part of many, a very ardent wish that there should come from the President of the United States such a clear and distinct enunciation of the manner in which he intended to exercise his power and to discharge the trust that has been reposed in him by others, that the country at large might understand and know it, clearly and distinctly. This long silence is operating most injuriously upon every interest in the land. . . .

Is it an intrusion to ask him what his policy is to be? Has it come to this, that the Government of the United States will feel its dignity wounded, or its rights infringed upon, because a sovereign State in Convention asks him to speak the word which they desire—the word of peace, of forbearance? Suppose he does not answer. Silence at such a time as this would be regarded as very significant, and it is in consequence of that silence that I desire the appointment of a Committee to go to Washington. . . .

Virginia's Division Foreshadowed   *Preston's conditional Unionist motion alarmed western Virginia's unconditional Unionists. John Jay Jackson, representing the northern Trans-Alleghenys Wood County (11.6 percent enslaved), prophesied that Lincoln's answer would disappoint Virginia's commissioners. Then secessionist demagogues would use the disappointment to secure disunion. Jackson warned that western Virginians would defy such eastern irresponsibility.*

Jackson's defiance enraged the east's Robert Montague, whose retort infuriated the west's Waitman Willey. As the spectre of a shattered state loomed, the Valley's John Baldwin and James Baldwin Dorman (representing Rockbridge County, 23.1 percent enslaved) managed to secure an adjournment until Monday, April 8, in hopes that Sabbath reflection would cool hot tempers.

Mr. JACKSON: . . . I utterly dissent from this resolution. . . . Sir, if you . . . send these Commissioners to Washington, will they be received with more consideration than was . . . [JOHN] TYLER—who was sent by Joint Resolution of the General Assembly of Virginia, to Mr. Buchanan? Mr. Buchanan received him very politely, treated him very much like a gentleman, but told him substantially, that it was none of his business. Certainly he reported that the interview was wholly unsatisfactory. And now, sir, I put it to you, when you send this committee to the city of Washington, what answer can you reasonably expect? . . .

Does any gentleman here believe that the President of the United States is a Nero—that he is fiddling while Rome is burning? Does any gentleman believe that if the President of the United States could relieve this great country from the throes and convulsions that now agitate it, he would hesitate a moment to do it? . . . I have no doubt he is pursuing that policy which, in his judgment and in the judgment of his Cabinet, is calculated to promote the public good. Your resolution . . . [insultingly announces] that he is dark, that he is mysterious and that he ought to be more communicative to us and to the country. Sir, why should he withhold information unless the public good requires that it should be withheld? What other answer could he give to your committee . . . without rendering himself infamous in the public mind?

But, sir, that is not my chief objection to the resolution. I ask gentlemen to bear in mind—I ask Western gentlemen to bear it in mind, that when your committee come back, as I think they will do, . . . with an answer that is wholly unsatisfactory, and then comes up this Ordinance of Secession, we shall be expected to rush off like a flock of sheep, right into the embrace of the Southern Confederacy, where sir, so help me God, I do not mean to go. . . . I declare that you cannot under any circumstances make us go to South Carolina.

A MEMBER: Suppose Virginia goes, what then?

Mr. JACKSON: If Virginia desires to form this middle confederacy, . . . we will stand with her; but when you ask us to break up our markets, impoverish our people, destroy our domestic interest, to drench our homes in blood, to exile from our altars and stultify ourselves in the sight of the whole world by admitting that which we know is not true, that there is any sufficient cause to break up this Union, I tell you we will not do it. . . . We will stand by you as long as you will permit us to do so, but when we can no longer do so, then we will take care of ourselves. . . .

Mr. MONTAGUE: The gentleman speaks for himself and his constituents. . . . The plain English of it is that while these gentlemen stand here and vote with us, their votes counting equally with our votes—while they declare that justice and equity require that our slave property shall be taxed *ad valorem* with all other property, yet in the same breath they tell you that if a majority of the people of Virginia decide to carry Virginia into the Southern Confederacy, they are determined to divide the State, and join the free soil Confederacy. . . .

Mr. JACKSON: The gentleman misapprehended me. I said nothing of the kind.

Mr. MONTAGUE: What did you say?

Mr. JACKSON: I said this—that we would stand by you in securing you the Constitutional guarantees necessary for the protection of your rights; that if you were content with that we would stand by you, but that if you intended to hitch us on to South Carolina we would not go with you.

Mr. MONTAGUE: Yes; and you, and not we, are to be the judges of the efficiency of those guarantees.

Mr. JACKSON: This Convention was to be the judge of that.

Mr. MONTAGUE: You would stand by us and give us such guarantees as you might judge proper, if we would stay with you in a middle Confederacy or remain in the Northern free-soil Confederacy; but if we would not do either, then you would divide the State. That is the plain English of the matter. Now as you have appealed to the West, I appeal to the East, to note carefully and mark well what has occurred here this evening. . . .

Mr. WILLEY: Mr. President, we are not to be controlled in our action here by threats or promises thrown out to the West, on this or any other question. We . . . do not wish to be precipitated into a measure . . . fraught with the deepest and highest importance. I am very much mistaken about this measure if it will not precipitate us into revolution before fifteen days. . . .

As to the insinuation of the gentleman from Middlesex [Mr. MONTAGUE], in regard to the want of fidelity in the Western character, I hurl it back, as I have hurled back such insinuations from the beginning. I say here, that if the worst comes to the worst, it will be again as it has been heretofore: Western men will have to fight your battles. It is on our own mountain men that you must rely at last for the vindication of Virginia's rights, Virginia's honor, and Virginia's integrity. . . . I ask whether it may not be worth the consideration of Eastern gentlemen to pause and reflect before, by any action of theirs, they alienate their best friends—the friends of whom they may soon stand in the greatest need? . . .

Mr. BALDWIN: . . . I regretted exceedingly to hear the sort of discussion indulged in in regard to the sections of the State. . . . We have had, from the members of the West—of the extreme West—a firm declaration of a purpose to resist the will of Virginia; aye, sir, and we have had from members of the extreme East, a declaration of a purpose to resist the declared will of Virginia. Coming from the great central heart of the State, I represent a people who have no sympathies with any of these extreme views on either side. . . .

Mr. DORMAN: . . . I beg leave to say, without referring to one side or the other, that it is the most unfortunate debate that has occurred within this Hall since the Convention met, and I want to see it stopped as soon as possible. I . . . make a motion to adjourn. I hope the Convention will take until Monday morning to consider this question, and avoid now a discussion which, if persisted in, will do us a great deal of harm. . . .

22

The Beginning of the End, April 13

The convention delegates reconvened on Monday, April 8, having moved, at this pregnant moment, back to the Hall of the House of Delegates for the duration of the convention. Inside that customary home of the Virginia lower house, delegates passed William Ballard Preston's commissioner motion. Then they elected him, along with the Valley's Alexander H. H. Stuart and the secessionists' George Wythe Randolph, as their commissioners to visit President Lincoln immediately.

The weather canceled the immediacy. A prolonged rainstorm postponed the commissioners' arrival in Washington for four days. The president could not see them for the better part of another day.

Back in Richmond, the five-day delay furthered an exasperated sense of irrelevance among the convention delegates. They had long assumed that all American eyes were on Virginia and that the Old Mother would rescue the nation. Instead, all Virginia eyes were now on the nation's capital, and the state's rescuers were out there somewhere in the fog. Richmond folk could only read wild rumors on the telegraph wire, inspiring ever angrier debate in the convention.

The fog of misinformation no less than the weather began to lift on Saturday, April 13, when Virginia's three commissioners at last gained their audience with Lincoln. The president declared that "if, as now appears to be true, . . . an unprovoked assault has been made upon Fort Sumter, I shall hold myself at liberty to repossess, if I can," any and all federal forts that the Confederacy seized, before or after his Inaugural.[1]

Lincoln did not tell the commissioners that a week earlier he had ordered relief ships to fortify Pensacola's Fort Pickens, with no advance warning to Confederate authorities, and to reinforce Charleston's Fort Sumter, with the advance warning to South Carolina's governor that more than food would be landed if the Confederacy resisted the relief of starv-

---

From Reese, *Proceedings* 3:722–23, 723–29.
1. Reese, *Proceedings* 3:735.

160

ing men. After Lincoln's ultimatum had arrived in the governor's office, and after the Confederacy's president, Jefferson Davis, had been consulted, Confederates blasted Fort Sumter. The rebel assault commenced on Friday, April 12. The Union garrison surrendered Fort Sumter the next day, just as Lincoln was meeting with Virginia's commissioners.

That fateful day, the Richmond telegraph office received the tidings from Charleston. In the convention former governor Henry Wise, ecstatic that combat had begun, insisted that the delegates must now act rather than talk. "I hope, sir," exclaimed Wise, that because a "raging . . . war is now" applying "fire . . . to the terrapin, he will crawl, at last, and that you will heat the poker till you fry the very fat off his vitals."[2]

But on Saturday, April 13, most Unionists answered that the telegraph might again have delivered wild rumors, or that South Carolina fanatics, not Lincoln, might have started the Fort Sumter combat, or that the regrettable episode in far-off Charleston might not recur, or that Virginia's compromise proposals might silence any lingering gunfire. To Wise's astonishment, delegates spent the Civil War's initial day debating peaceful maneuvers as if nothing had changed.

Jubal Early's Ironic Appeal   *To posterity's astonishment, an imminent Confederate warrior epitomized how far the Virginia convention stood from joining the Confederacy on that day of Fort Sumter's surrender. In the summer three years thence, General Jubal Anderson Early would be marching a rebel army through Virginia toward vulnerable Washington, in one of the Confederacy's last forays north. But on April 13, 1861, citizen Early remained a Unionist. The representative from Franklin County (in Virginia's western Piedmont, 31.6 percent enslaved) expressed sympathy for his friend Major Robert Anderson, Fort Sumter's federal commander. Early also proclaimed that Virginia would never allow Confederates to march through the Union-loving state on the rebels' way to assaulting the Union capital.*

. . . I must confess that upon this day my heart is bowed down with sorrow, not so much that the flag of my country has been compelled to give way to another; not so much that a gallant friend and comrade of

2. Ibid., 678–79.

mine in former times has been compelled to yield to the force of over-ruling numbers, as that I find Virginians ready to rejoice in this event. . . . When a man in whose veins every drop of blood that flows is that of a Virginian; when the son of an officer of the Revolution, who fought for our liberties—yes, sir, fought for South Carolina—when, I say, the son of that man, with a handful of starving men, has been fired into, and has been compelled, at the cannon's mouth, to lower the flag of his country, I confess that my heart is bowed down with sorrow to find Virginians ready to rejoice. . . .

Mr. Chairman, this act has done nothing to advance the cause of the Confederate States. In . . . Virginia, the mass of the people will never be found sanctioning their cause. . . . If there be any Virginians who advise or encourage the idea of marching an army from the Confederated States through our borders to Washington, they mistake the tone and temper of our people. I trust that the issue may never be forced upon us; but when it does come, mark it, that the invasion of our soil will be promptly resisted. The spirit of manhood has not deserted the sons of Virginia. . . .

The Early-Goode Near Duel *The secessionists' Thomas F. Goode (representing the southwestern Piedmont's Mecklenburg County, 61.8 percent enslaved) answered that if the convention's majority would not allow the state out of the Union, eastern armies would shove the Unionists out of power. From there, the Early-Goode duel with words grew uglier, almost culminating in a duel with pistols.*

Mr. GOODE: The gentleman from Franklin [Mr. EARLY] . . . very much misconceives the sentiment of the people of Virginia, if he supposes that the act of the Confederate States of this day, at Fort Sumter, has placed an impassable gulf between them and us. What it may place between the majority of this Convention and the Confederate States, I will not undertake to say, but I fear that there was already between them a gulf, wide, deep, and impassable. But be this as it may, I tell the gentleman from Franklin that the great popular heart of Virginia is now throbbing in sympathy and unison with those gallant men who, upon Carolina's soil, are battling unto death for the common rights of the South. Sir, I tell gentlemen here that . . . [whatever] the action of this Convention, . . . when the dread struggle comes, the freemen of Virginia, from the Ohio to the Chesapeake, will gather around the flag of the Confederate States, as the Scottish Highlanders around the cross of fire—that side by side and shoulder to shoulder, they will go forth beneath its folds to victory or death.

Sir, the gentleman from Franklin intimates that the Confederate States would not be allowed to march an army over the soil of Virginia. I tell the gentleman that they will, if need be, march an army over Virginia's soil, I tell him that the battles of the Republican Administration at Washington, are not to be fought alone on Southern soil—our Southern brethren will not wait until fire and sword is carried into the heart of the Southern country. They will not wait to be cut down around their own altars and firesides, and amid their wives and children. The tramp of Southern soldiers will soon be heard on the Northward march. And I tell gentlemen, that with thousands of Virginia freemen at their side, they will carve their way, if need be, through Virginia soil, against all comers. . . . We of the East do not mean to be held in this Union by any power, within or without the State—out of it we intend to go.

Mr. EARLY: Mr. Chairman, I thought we had on this floor gentlemen who called themselves State Rights men. When I hear a gentleman belonging to that party get up on this floor and invite an army . . . to march through Virginia, . . . I ask what becomes of the doctrines of State Rights? . . .

Sir, I imagine that gentlemen don't know how large the State of Virginia is. There was an old man, a citizen of my county, who has been reared in the hollows of the mountains, where the peaks run up very high, and you see only a little of the sky above. He had never been further than ten miles away from home. He . . . took it into his head to become a candidate for the Legislature. Well, he started, and when he got a little below our Court-house, the country began to open up before him, and he was led to exclaim, "Great God, if I had known the world had been half so large, I never would have started out from home." [Laughter.] If these gentlemen who talk about revolution were to go up into our mountain peaks, and look out upon the broad expanse that would be spread before them, they would be astonished and amazed to see how large the State of Virginia is, . . . how many people we have, . . . [and] the fallacy of this idea of a change in popular sentiment.

Sir, the gentleman who claims to be of the States Rights school has threatened, whatever may be the voice of this Convention (do I understand him to say of the people?) that he still will join the banner of this Southern army. . . . Will the gentleman who claims to be the especial champion of Virginia's rights, place his voice, his wishes, in opposition to the wishes of the people of Virginia?

Mr. GOODE: Does the gentleman desire an answer?

Mr. EARLY indicated his assent.

Mr. GOODE: I said to the gentleman then, that be the action of the Convention what it may, we of the East will neither be held in this government under a Republican administration by the powers at Washington, nor by the powers that, perchance, may lie West of the Alleghany mountains.

Mr. EARLY: Then, sir, the gentleman is not only going to secede from the Union, but to secede from the State of Virginia; and I say, what becomes of his claim of devotion to Virginia, her altars, her honor and her interest? . . . The gentleman, under this new doctrine of State Rights, sets up his opinion and the opinion of his constituents, against the will of the majority. Great God, sir, if the honor of Virginia is to be confided to such hands, I want to know what will become of it. . . .

Mr. GOODE: I beg to ask the gentleman . . . whether in his closing remarks, it was his intention to cast any imputation or reflection upon me? . . . I understood him to say substantially . . . "God help the people, if their interests and honor were to be confined to the keeping of gentlemen such as I." I shall press the question . . . whether he designed to cast any imputation or reflection upon me?

Mr. EARLY: . . . The gentleman has no right to ask me such a question. . . . I think the gentleman is carrying this thing rather too far. . . . The idea I intended to convey was, that if the position taken by the gentleman from Mecklenburg was an evidence of States rights, God defend us from any such States rights as that. . . . I hope every gentleman will understand that what I said was intended to reach a political aspect of the case, and not to apply to the gentleman personally.

23

Decision Barely Averted, April 15

On April 13 Thomas Goode accepted Early's claim that no insult had been intended. The resumption of pleasantries after near gunfire epitomized the convention majority's determination on April 13, after hearing telegraph rumors about Fort Sumter's fall: to continue with business as usual, despite rising anxiety. Shortly after Goode and Early declared a truce, the convention adjourned for the second straight tense Sunday.

As the convention reassembled on Monday, April 15, telegraph wires hummed with far more disruptive news than perhaps temporary bloodshed at a distant fort. President Lincoln's proclamation of that day called up 75,000 troops (including, Secretary of War Simon Cameron simultaneously wrote, 3,500 Virginians) to smother the Confederacy. Virginians had been summoned to kill fellow Southerners. Secessionists urged the convention to answer with a secret session that would adopt disunion and plan military action.

Robert Scott's New Unionist Strategy *The Unionists' Robert Eden Scott (representing Fauquier County in the northern Piedmont, 48.2 percent enslaved) concurred that if Lincoln had turned coercive, Virginia must fight a tyrannical president. But Scott reminded the convention that the people must ratify a convention's secession ordinance. He thus opposed a secret session, closed to the people. Scott also hinted at the Unionists' fallback position if the news of Lincoln's proclamation was verified. Previously, Scott had urged the convention to summon a border conference, without mentioning secession. Now, he would call on the people (instead of the convention) to decide between secession and a border conference.*

From Reese, *Proceedings* 3:736–44, 758–59, 761–63.

. . . I am ready to pursue no course, to advocate no policy, which I am not ready to explain to the public. I see no reason why we should change, at this time, . . . [our] course of [open] public deliberation. . . .

So long as hostilities should be confined between the Administration at Washington and the Confederate States . . . [to] forts in Southern harbors, I could see no imminent danger of a general war; but now it seems that the President of the United States has issued his proclamation making a requisition for 75,000 soldiers, . . . designed for no other purpose than active general war. . . . We have already declared—deliberately declared—that under no circumstances, in our opinion, ought the people of this State to consent to be made parties to an unnatural war against our Southern brethren. . . . I know nothing, Mr. President, as to the authenticity of the proclamation which the papers of this morning give to us, but . . . if . . . the administration is about to inaugurate a general war, . . . we must disconnect ourselves from this Federal Government. . . .

[But] . . . in what manner, and at what time it shall be done, are questions of grave import. . . . Mr. President, by the law which convened this Convention, we are required to submit to the . . . people at the polls any measure . . . to change the relations of this State with the Federal Union. . . . I take it that whatever diversity of opinion prevails amongst us in respect to other matters, there can be none in respect to this. . . . [Because] secession, at last, will have to be determined by a vote of the people at the polls, I cannot see for what reason in the discussion of this question, we should resolve ourselves into secret session. . . .

The opinion is now entertained, and up to this time has been entertained by a decided majority, that we ought to adopt no final and decisive measure without a previous consultation with the remaining border slave States. On the part of other gentlemen, the opinion has been entertained that our true policy requires . . . separate State action. . . . [Because we must] submit our final action to the ratification of a popular vote, . . . we might now submit . . . the alternative propositions . . . to our constituents and put it in their power to determine whether they prefer . . . separate State action, or . . . the co-operation of the border States.

I conclude that . . . I know of no good to be attained by secret session, as I see that to whatever conclusion this body may arrive, the verdict of the people is to be taken upon it. [We] cannot act in secret [because] by the very law which summoned us, . . . the people at large have taken the determination of this question into their own hands; and if we submit fairly to them the [alternative] . . . of separate State action, or action through the co-operation of the border States, I cannot see how the policy of either party here is to suffer injury. . . .

Henry Wise's *Pro Salute Populi* *Against Robert Scott's plea for continued open session, Henry Wise urged a secret session, because the welfare of the people must be the supreme law (pro salute populi). Even in a democracy, Wise implied, even when the people have required a popular referendum on a convention's decision, convention delegates must protect the people's military welfare in an emergency involving war and peace. Wise here hinted at the convention's climactic question: whether democracy's requirements must be suspended when a republic's survival seems to be at stake. The Spontaneous People's Convention, that collection of primarily young hotheads assembled at a rival Richmond hall, urged Wise on. The sports threatened to kidnap the governor and seize federal installations if the convention preferred democratic niceties to revolution's necessities.*

Gentlemen do not seem to apprehend the correct idea of secret session. . . . Men . . . go into secret session because . . . there is a secret in the subject itself. I ask the gentlemen if any subjects are fuller of secrets—of mysteries upon mysteries—than the subject of peace and war? Have you not incidental [military] questions upon which the people are not to vote at all—[military questions] incidental . . . to the main question [of secession]? . . . Have you not to consider steps and preparations *pro salute populi*? Are you, the guardians of the people, called to look over their safety, seeing them about to be destroyed, to wait to ask the people whether the preparation shall be made to save them? Are you going to tell the enemy that has proclaimed war . . . [how] you are going to defend the people, and the preparations you are going to make? The circumstances have not been considered by those who . . . [oppose] secrecy in those matters.

Oh! the sweet mysteries of peace—Oh! the dreadful mysteries of war! Sir, for God's sake quit talking. . . . The time for action has now come. Action, sir, with lips not only unopened but compressed to immovable firmness. . . . What Virginia will do? Sir, with a view to answer that question quietly, deliberately, we are asked to go into secret session.

John Baldwin's Desperation for Delay   *Alarmed at the*
movement toward a secret session, John Baldwin urged the convention
to adjourn for the day, to await confirmation of Lincoln's intentions. He
barely prevailed.

. . . I have not heard yet any sufficient reason assigned for so striking
a departure from what I regard as one of the fundamental principles of
free government—that the discussion of the representatives shall be held
in open session subject to observation—of the constituent body. . . . I take
it to be a sound principle that all . . . policy . . . adopted by this Convention . . . must go before the people for their ratification or rejection. . . .
[Upon] these questions, . . . they [should] . . . know at every step and every stage of our progress, the reasons which have been assigned by those
advocating certain lines of policy, and the reasons which have led us to
our conclusions. . . . Sir, I look upon it as a grave responsibility for any
representative body to take, to withhold from their constituency a full
observation of all that they do. . . .

I think we are not at this time in a position, in point of information,
to justify us in departing from the ordinary course of the proceedings of
this body. I do not recognize the propriety of turning to the right or to
the left upon unauthenticated telegraphic despatches. I think that all of
us have a right to ask of our associates in this body, that we shall not be
pressed into any extraordinary course of proceeding upon half gathered
information. . . . I am not willing to take for granted every dispatch and
every rumor.

I can have no hesitation, when it comes to war or subjugation against
the South, as to what position I shall occupy; but I claim that before I
take . . . any position that is to transfer the seat of this war from the South
to Virginia, I . . . [must] see before me as clear as the sunlight the events
and facts upon which I am called to act. It is a momentous responsibility
that we are called on to take; and I want to consider the question in open
session, and with the deliberation necessary to gather all the facts upon
which we have to act.

Eve of Decision, April 16

24

By the next day even John Baldwin conceded that yesterday's telegraph wires broadcast the awful truth. Thus the convention went immediately into secret session.

George Wythe Randolph's Militarism *In secret session George Wythe Randolph picked up Wise's logic, without Wise's Latin vocabulary. Military necessity, urged Randolph, required not only instant secession but also immediate seizure of federal military treasure, in the name of the people and before they ratified the convention's secession ordinance. Otherwise, the federals would sneak military matériel out of their Virginia installations—Harpers Ferry Arsenal and Norfolk's Gosport Navy Yard— thereby undermining Virginia citizens' subsequent vote for war.*

. . . We are in the beginning of the greatest war that has ever been waged upon this continent. That war will be conducted with the entire force of the Federal Government, and will, unquestionably, in the start, command the entire support of the Northern people.

The object of that war . . . is ostensibly defensive—merely to re-possess certain forts and arsenals which have been seized by the Confederate States, and to collect the revenue. But . . . you may as well attempt to circumscribe a fire in a prairie as to attempt to confine a war to the neighborhood of the forts intended to be re-possessed. We see by the President's proclamation that 75,000 men are to be called into action. . . . We have every reason to believe . . . [that] the administration [wishes] that at least one-third of that number should be concentrated upon the frontier of Virginia and at the City of Washington. . . . Unless this State views this just now as a military question, and unless she considers military preparations as of the first and primary importance, we will be a subjugated people.

As for a position of neutrality in this shock of arms, if any were base

From Reese, *Proceedings* 4:4–8, 12–21, 30–33, 38–50, 51–52, 58–60, 60–71.

enough to desire it, he could not attain it. Why, you are called upon already to furnish your quota of [3,500] men! You are now furnishing your contingent of money to pay that [Union] army. . . .

There is only one course which would ensure neutrality. If they would permit you to separate yourselves from the United States without connecting yourselves with other States, you might stand idle, and dishonorably witness this war upon your own frontiers. But as long as you are connected with one side or the other, you must be a party to the war. There is no alternative; you have got to fight—and the question is, which side will you fight with?

If, in place of girding your loins for battle, you go into council with irresolute, divided, unprepared States, you will . . . [render] your military preparations . . . wholly inefficient. . . . As a military question, waiving all political considerations, looking solely to . . . maintain our liberties, I believe that the very first step . . . must be to relieve ourselves from all further constitutional obligations to that government. . . .

Two things, Mr. President, . . . are to be done quickly, and to some extent secretly. . . . In the first place, here is a dock-yard which it would be important for us immediately to possess. I took occasion to walk through it on Thursday, while in Norfolk, and to converse with the officer in charge of it, and to find out what they were doing. I ascertained that there are stored there 30,000 barrels of gunpowder, besides several hundred guns of heavy calibre. If you seize all that immense dock-yard, with all its ship timber, its vessels in the streams, your armament is complete. You have got what you most need; an ample supply of powder, vessels in stocks and materials for a navy force. If you stand idly by—even now they are stripping it of everything and moving it off—all that material will be employed to subjugate instead of defend you. . . .

There [are also] . . . at Harpers Ferry 48,000 Minié muskets and a much larger number of smooth bore muskets. It would be an easy matter to prevent the removal of those by breaking up the railroad track of the Baltimore and Ohio Rail Road. . . . The question now is whether you will give up these arms to the enemy or keep them yourselves.

There is another great object to be looked to. . . . It is absolutely necessary, without delay, . . . to see that you do not bring into the field undisciplined, unorganized battalions against disciplined and organized battalions. . . . [That necessity requires] the agency and control of experienced and regular officers, and these you cannot get so long as you are connected with that government, and they are in its service. . . .

Let this war go on while you are in the Union, and you will lose . . . many brave and experienced officers; you will lose all opportunity of organizing and disciplining your own troops while organization and instruction is going on on the other side; so that those 75,000 militia men will be made efficient soldiers by the time you have done your counsels, and then you will have to commence your preparations when, perhaps, it may be too late.

Mr. President, I don't see how it is possible for us to maintain our independence in the face of that power, unless we at once and without a delay of twenty-four hours, commence immediate preparation. Shall we do this by going to Kentucky, which has not appropriated a dollar to raise an armed soldier? By going to Tennessee, which does not consider the cause of sufficient importance to assemble a convention? . . . By going to Missouri, which is almost on the side of the enemy? By going to Maryland, where a Henry Winter Davis is elected while the South is battling for equality?[1] Shall we best vindicate our liberty and independence by counselling with irresolute, divided and distracted States? Or by throwing ourselves at once into the arms of the only organized government which is ready to do battle with us and for us?

I don't object to conference with the border States. I think it respectful; I think it proper; but I do most earnestly protest . . . against delaying the action of Virginia. . . . These States can be brought to concur with us . . . sooner by going out [of the Union], and by sending commissioners . . . to explain to them that the emergency was so great that you could not wait . . . than . . . by assembling in Convention and discussing the question, whether you will fight on one side or the other, or fight at all? That question is settled. You have got to fight; and the further question is settled as to which side you have got to fight on; and the next question is, whether you will act promptly and efficiently? . . . We do not need advice now. We need . . . bayonets, not counsel, in the extremity in which we now find ourselves. . . .

1. Henry Winter Davis was a Maryland congressman whose ambiguous attitudes about slavery stopped short of abolitionism and whose ardent support of perpetual Union knew no bounds.

Sir, the destiny of Virginia is committed now to our hands. . . . Don't let us distract the people by submitting to them alternate propositions. We are sent here to tell them what we think they ought to do, not to throw upon them the decision of a military or other question which ought to be considered here with closed doors. Whether the State would be benefited by co-operation or separate action, we are the people to decide. We know the grounds upon which to decide. We have the information, and they look to us for advice; and, in my judgment, we should be wanting in our duty to them, if we failed to indicate to them the line of policy which, in our judgment, they ought to pursue. . . .

Alexander H. H. Stuart's Open-Ended Unionism   *For two months Alexander Hugh Holmes Stuart had been surprisingly less important in the convention than his fellow Staunton resident, law partner, cousin, and brother-in-law, the less wealthy John Baldwin. Although Baldwin had only previously served in the state legislature's lower house, Stuart had sat in the state senate, Congress, and Millard Fillmore's cabinet. But at the convention Baldwin became the family's star performer, and Stuart usually applauded from the shadows.[2]*

The shadows were no place for the Shenandoah Valley's most famous Unionist, not after he joined the convention's commission to Lincoln, listened to the president threaten to reinforce Fort Sumter, and then heard George Wythe Randolph and Henry Wise rattling the swords. Sandy Stuart, joining his brother-in-law in representing Augusta County (20.2 percent enslaved), answered Randolph and Wise by declaring that Virginia must not seize federal military installations before its citizens approved secession.

Stuart also alarmed secessionists by suggesting that a border conference might lead to an independent border state confederacy. More alarmingly still, he denied that the Virginia convention need adopt a contingency plan if a border conference failed. This was unionism opened to the skies, with no prospect of joining the Confederacy in sight.

---

2. Gaines, *Biographical Register,* 72; *ANB;* Alexander Farrish Robertson, *Alexander Hugh Holmes Stuart, 1807–1891: A Biography* (Richmond, 1925).

. . . I was so entirely taken by surprise by the appearance of the proclamation, that I did not for a moment believe that it was authentic. I believed that it was a sensation document, gotten up by some mischievous
persons; and such was my confidence of that fact, that as soon as I read
the document yesterday, I repaired to my room, prepared a despatch to
the Secretary of State, to ask him whether it was genuine or fabricated.
I received a response from him late last night that it was genuine. . . . I
therefore think . . . that there is no hope of an amicable arrangement with
the Administration. . . . My hopes in the perpetuation of the Union, as
it now stands, have [also] been greatly weakened, if they have not been
entirely destroyed.

In this emergency, . . . three lines of policy . . . lay before us: One is
to remain in the Union as we are, and to lend our forces and our arms
to the subjugation of our Southern sisters, . . . without . . . guarantees of
protection . . . consistent with the interest and the honor of the Commonwealth. Sir, if we remain as we are we abandon, in my judgment, all hope
of obtaining any such guarantees; we abandon all hope of security, and
we lend ourselves to the purposes of a dominant, sectional majority. I am
not, then, sir, for adopting that line of policy.

But there are two . . . [alternatives]. One is to secede immediately, and
the other is to ask the co-operation of our sister States which have not yet
seceded. . . .

Here is a war waging. Here is an immense preparation made on the
part of the United States Government for carrying on that war. The present seat of that war is at a remote part of the Union. It is now confined to
the region about the city of Charleston and the city of Pensacola. . . . What
would be the effect of the immediate secession of Virginia? It would be to
transfer the seat of war from the Gulf of Mexico, and from the extreme
Southern part of our Atlantic coast, to the bosom of Virginia. . . .

I could not conceive of any greater favor that you could confer upon
this Black Republican administration. . . . The miasma arising from the
swamps of Florida, and the swamps that surround Charleston, would
sweep out of existence more of the [federal] invaders than the [soldiers]
. . . of the . . . Confederate States. All the provisions for the support of
the Northern armies would have to be transported thousands of miles, at
great expense; and it is under great difficulties that they could be supplied
at all.

But, sir, by Virginia's seceding you transfer the seat of war to this fertile and salubrious country. You transfer it to a country that furnishes every supply that is necessary for the support of the troops; to a climate that is entirely salubrious to the Northern troops who would be engaged in prosecuting the war. Yes, sir, you bring it home to your own fair cities and families.

You go into this war without any aid from any quarter. We have no alliance with the Confederate States, nor [with] our sister border States not yet seceded, and Virginia would stand alone between the Federal Government and the Confederate States of the South. She would be the battle ground. Her fields would be laid waste, and her citizens would become the victims of the conflict.

And, sir, what is our state of preparation? Where is our ordnance? Where is our musketry? Where are our rifles? Where, in fact, are any of the munitions of war, which are indispensable for our security? . . . My friend over the way, from the city of Richmond [Mr. RANDOLPH] has suggested the idea of the capture of the Navy Yard at Gosport, and of the Armory at Harpers Ferry. Let me call his attention, and that of the Convention, to the relations which we now bear to the Federal Government.

An ordinance of secession does not terminate our relations with the Federal Government. An ordinance passed by this body . . . goes forth simply as a matter of advice to the people; and, without the ratification of the people, it is not worth the paper on which it is written. What, then, are we to do? Are we acting under the obligation of an oath to support the Constitution of the United States, as I venture to say almost every man in this body is? I ask gentlemen, under these circumstances, if they are prepared, in view of the obligation of that oath, to make, as it were, a flagrant and unprovoked war upon the Government of the United States by seizing upon these public arsenals? . . .

In my opinion, secession is not only war, but it is emancipation; it is bankruptcy; it is repudiation; it is wide-spread ruin to our people; nay, sir, it must be more. It may result . . . in another dissolution, . . . more painful, even, than the overthrow of the Union itself. It may result in a dissolution of the bonds which bind together the different great slopes of the State. . . .

Here we have our State divided into two great mountain shoots—one sloping to the Atlantic, and the other to the Ohio. We find the trade and the social relations of that [westward] mountain slope intertwined and associated with the great West. We find almost all their relations connected with the non-slaveholding States of the great West. These people, then, will be called upon to sever connections of the most intimate character—connections which affect vitally every interest which they have—connections which are indispensable to their enjoyment, their social happiness and prosperity. . . .

But, sir, there is another aspect of the case. We have already held out to our sister States that have not yet seceded, the idea that we intended to co-operate with them. . . . How would we be regarded, if . . . we should now precipitately rush ourselves out of the Union without consulting them? Did we not all complain of the action of South Carolina, in going out of the Union without consultation with any of her sister States? . . . Now, sir, I for one am not for following the example of South Carolina. . . .

Here is Virginia surrounded on three sides by States that have not seceded, and on the other side bounded by the Atlantic ocean. How would we stand if North Carolina, Maryland, Kentucky and Tennessee refused to secede? . . . If a nation is going to war, does it not always seek . . . alliances offensive and defensive? When we were struggling for our independence did we not seek an alliance with France to aid us in our struggle for liberty? . . . But if we have this conference, if these other States should come into line with us, if we show an unbroken front, then I cherish the hope that the North, according to the argument which has been urged by our friends, the secessionists, will see that it is a hopeless task to attempt to subjugate these eight States, in addition to the seven seceded States; and that, instead of the bloody war which we now expect, we might have a peaceable adjustment of our difficulties.

Sir, I am in favor of making this appeal. . . . I am in favor of addressing this invitation to our sister States to meet us in Conference at Frankfort on the 27th of next month. I want to have a full and fair interchange of opinion in secret session with them there. . . . I believe that the relations of business interests and those social ties which connect the Border States, on either side, will exercise the most potent influence on either side of the dividing line; and I would be willing to tender to Illinois, Indiana, Ohio, Pennsylvania, New York and New Jersey, such amendments to the Constitution, or such a new Constitution as we are willing to live under. I would invite their aid and concurrence. I would invite them to join us under a new Constitution, framed with such guarantees as would give to us effectual security for all our rights. I would invite them to disconnect themselves from the extreme North and North-west, and, unlike some of my friends, my information leads me to believe that such an appeal would be responded to by these States.

Sir, fanaticism is a great evil, and I would avoid contact with it as I would a plague; but business relations, private interests, social ties, the ties of brotherhood, the ties of intermarriage and of communication, in every form and shape in which they can take place, must, to a great extent, counterbalance this odious fanaticism; and in severing those political ties, I would seek to withdraw these States from their allegiance to the Federal government—I would seek to induce them to become part and parcel of our new government. I would seek to have a tier of friendly States between the slaveholding States and the States of the extreme North and North-west. By pursuing this policy we would, I believe, ultimately effect a reconstruction of the Union upon such terms as we would dictate. We could compel the young States to come . . . [in on] our terms or to remain outside of this great Central Confederacy. . . . Our Southern sisters would quickly unite with us; because . . . they would feel there would be security from every foe, external and internal. . . .

Sir, pass the Ordinance of Secession now, and you incur another hazard. You incur the hazard that the people themselves, not quite as sensitive to the highest notions of chivalry as the members of this Convention, but looking with a more unimpassioned view at the practical results, the interruptions to business, the burthensome taxation, the onerous military service, all the privations of every description which they are to suffer, might be induced to vote down the Ordinance of Secession. And where would you then stand? The gentleman before me [Mr. MORTON] says forcible revolution would follow. Revolution against whom? . . . The gentleman would not be willing to turn his sword against his brother, who, cherishing a feeling of attachment to his country, might entertain a different notion of what is best for its interest. . . .

Mr. MORTON: Will the gentleman permit me to ask him a question?

Mr. STUART: Certainly.

Mr. MORTON: The gentleman, I understood, in . . . [his] first proposition, . . . repudiated the idea of continuing in this Union.

Mr. STUART: Yes, sir.

Mr. MORTON: The gentleman has not told us what would be his course in the event of a rejection or the abortion of the Border Conference. Suppose the Conference should fail, what position would he then have Virginia occupy?

Mr. STUART: I might answer the gentleman in the language of the Scripture: "Sufficient unto the day is the evil thereof;" but I will say that his conclusions are so remote, so nearly relate to an impossibility, as scarcely to need any discussion. If we treat our sister States with ordinary respect, I can hardly look to such a contingency, or deem any measure necessary to provide for that contingency.

Even the Trans-Allegheny Divided: John Jackson Again Answers William Ballard Preston
Despite Alexander H. H. Stuart's oratory, his erstwhile Unionist colleague William Ballard Preston, of the southern Trans-Allegheny, introduced an "Ordinance of Secession," to "take effect . . . when ratified by a majority of the votes . . . cast at a poll . . . on" May 23.³ The northern Trans-Allegheny's John Jackson was again first to protest against a Preston initiative. Jackson's latest protest demonstrated anew that the Trans-Allegheny suffered from its own north-south split. Jackson stormed not only at his ex-Unionist colleague's secession ordinance, not only at the southern Trans-Allegheny's disregard for the northern Trans-Allegheny's plight, not only at the dangers of disunion, but also at the evident plot afoot to seize forts before the people had spoken on Preston's ordinance.

I have done . . . all that lies in my power in order to effect reconciliation and restore peace and unity. I have now been conducted by gentlemen upon this floor to the brink of a yawning gulf, and I feel to-day as if I was at . . . the funeral of my country; aye, sir, a funeral which must be but the forerunner of many a disaster, and much suffering.

I have no heart; no, no, sir—none whatever. I stand here an old man; I have loved my country; I have served my country; I have served this Commonwealth long, faithfully, earnestly— . . . with my whole heart. . . . I stand here to-day having taken the oath to support the Constitution of the United States twenty-seven times. . . . Was it of no consequence that I called the eternal God to witness that I would be true to the Constitution of Virginia as well as the Constitution of the United States? . . . In a few years more I expect to be confronted with Him. . . . Is it compatible with

3. Reese, *Proceedings* 4:24–25.

my obligations, not only to my country but . . . to God, that I shall obliterate this magnificent fabric of self-government?

The man who was cradled under the stars and stripes; who was nurtured and cherished under them; who grew to manhood under their benignity and protection, and who now stands in the enjoyment of every civil right which he needs—I say that a man so blessed should pause and reflect upon these benefits before taking this fatal step. It was a great work to create man, but it was . . . the work of a demon to drag him from his high eminence, and pervert him from his noble destiny. It was a great work to create this Government; but it is the work of a Lilliput[4] alone to destroy it. . . .

The gentleman from Richmond [Mr. RANDOLPH], astounded me beyond measure this morning, when he intimated that it is . . . in the power of this Convention to make an act of war which will change the relations of the people of this Commonwealth to the government of the United States. Have they not declared that you can do no act changing the relations of the people of Virginia to the General Government, without submitting it to them? If you seize upon ships—if you seize upon the Armory at Harpers Ferry—is not that an act of war, changing the relations of the people of Virginia to the General Government? . . . Why go through the sham of sending to the people an ordinance of secession, when you yourselves have struck the blow at once by seizing upon ships, arsenals, &c.? Why, sir, it is a solemn farce. . . . True, the ordinance will have to be submitted to the people; but a determination will already have been formed by this act of war, to go out. If the people vote down this ordinance, what then? Why, you are already at war with the General Government. . . . And in the teeth of this, with facts like these apparent to the world, you are going before the people with the sham ordinance, asking them whether they will secede or not! . . .

We are going to destroy this Government, under which we have prospered as no people ever prospered before, and which we are bound to hand down to posterity as it was given to us—and for what? Because South Carolina chooses to throw off her connection with the General Government. Virginia does not suffer more now than she did twenty years ago, and I can see no other reason for this effort on her part to

---

4. The tiny inhabitants of the imaginary island Lilliput are described in Jonathan Swift's *Gulliver's Travels*.

destroy this Government, than this action on the part of South Carolina. . . . According to the best lights of my understanding, . . . the Government of the United States is acting on the defensive; and, viewing the matter in this light, can you expect me, representing a people who have their family connections on the other side of the Ohio, in sight of them—who are allied with the people of that State by inter-marriages—do you expect me to abandon them all, and to throw them away by giving satisfaction to your proceeding? . . .

If you want your action to have the moral weight it ought to have, accept . . . the proposition of the gentleman from Fauquier [Mr. Scott]. Do it, and you can have Virginia a unit. You can command our hearts, and our hands, and our all. But, sir, if you are determined to precipitate this matter, you must not expect us to be led like beeves to the slaughter. I tell you that when "grim-visaged war" is staring us in the face, the old men of the country will wake up and . . . will hold to a just accountability those who shall bring upon us this terrible disaster. . . .

Robert Scott versus George Wythe Randolph   *Robert Scott furthered John Jackson's protest against William Ballard Preston's secession ordinance by introducing a substitute ordinance, giving the voters on May 23 a choice between Virginia's secession and its participation in a border conference. In the interim, declared Scott, the state could purchase arms, a legitimate alternative to illegitimate seizure of federal firepower.*

Scott emphasized, more strongly than he had the previous day, that he no longer hoped that a border conference would save the Union. Rather, he prayed that a conference of the eight slave states still in the Union would best secure unanimous southern secession. But as Alexander H. H. Stuart had demonstrated, many who massed behind Scott's alternative to Preston's ordinance still wished to save the Union with a border conference (and with no promises to leave the Union if the conference failed or to join the Confederacy if the Union failed).

George Wythe Randolph then ridiculed Robert Scott's new supposed form of secessionism. Randolph completed his retort with threats of Scott's greatest immediate fear: the convention would dispatch Virginia troops to capture federal military supplies before the Virginia people could authorize secession and war.

Mr. SCOTT: . . . From my earliest manhood I have cherished . . . our Federal Union. . . . But, Mr. President, these feelings have . . . fled. I no long believe that the Union . . . can be preserved. I . . . look upon a dissolution as inevitable; nay, more, . . . as a necessity, and as desirable. . . . When I see the President . . . declaring war upon seven States of the Confederacy; and when I see the people of the non-slaveholding States . . . making themselves parties to the war, . . . I am ready to . . . cut loose from them. . . .

[But] I do not regret that, under the commission by which we exercise the powers of this body, the decision is to rest ultimately with those who are most concerned. . . . Whatever conclusion we come to, must remain unexecuted until it receives the approbation of the people. Our power extends no farther than to recommend what in our judgment the people ought to do; we cannot command, we cannot bind them.

When . . . I took my seat in this body, no one was more intent than myself upon propositions of adjustment. But . . . no one can think that . . . in the present temper of the Northern mind, there is the remotest possibility that any favorable response will be made to any . . . constitutional amendments that might emanate from this body. . . .

Nevertheless diversities still exist among the members of this body, and to an equal extent among the people. The diversity . . . to a great extent is sectional. . . . It would be deplorable indeed if the sectional controversy which is sundering the bonds that have connected the South with the North, should infuse its venom into the domestic relations of our own State, and poison the peace of our own firesides.

The question arises whether, in the presence of these differences, it is prudent and wise to recommend [instant disunion]. . . . If Maryland, Kentucky, North Carolina and Tennessee would unite in a common action with us, every section of our State would agree in opinion and . . . sectional antagonism would disappear. . . . It is mainly owing to the apprehension that Virginia is to be torn from her natural connections with these States, or some of them, that, in some parts of the State, opposition to secession has taken such firm hold. . . .

When we return to our constituents and tell them that we have adopted an ordinance of secession, they will naturally [ask], . . . will it bring on war? . . . I appeal to my friend from Montgomery [Mr. PRESTON], [and] to my friend from Richmond city [Mr. RANDOLPH], to tell me what answers are to be given.

Mr. RANDOLPH: I would say to them, no; the war is already brought on, and it is necessary for you to defend yourselves against that war.

Mr. SCOTT: They would tell me that they saw no war and felt none, and they would still desire to know whether war will come of it. It will not do for the gentleman from Richmond city to tell me that war already exists. Whatever of war there is consists merely of hostility about some of the Southern ports, to which, under present circumstances, it must necessarily be confined. . . . Between the President and the Southern States, the border States will stand in the attitude of armed neutrals, forbidding assaults through their territories; and, with full representation in Congress, they will exert a strong influence in restraining intemperate action. . . . We shall have no war in the border States; standing together, they will cause their neutrality to be respected. We shall have no war upon the soil of Virginia.

If the President persists in hostility against the Southern States it will remove all diversities of opinions among the people of the border States. . . . Union sentiment is prevalent among the people of those States, but it is not strong enough to stand . . . [warfare] in opposition to their protests. The sympathies of all are with the Southern States, and in the end we must make common cause with them. It is but a question of time and manner. While we adhere to the Union our ports will be open; we can sell wherever we can find purchasers, and buy wherever commodities are to be found. We can purchase arms and munitions of war; all of the border States can put themselves in military array, and when fully armed, and acting together, their determination to unite their destinies with the Southern States will be respected by the Northern States and submitted to in peace.

Precipitation will defeat these ends, and separate action, without precipitation will . . . lead to war. . . . Are we prepared for it? We have not more than thirty thousand stand of efficient arms, with a very small quantity of powder and balls; we have but few percussion caps and scarcely any military organization. We have no military head. All of these . . . may be speedily obtained if we remain a member of the present Union.

But when we secede what will be our condition? The enemy will be in possession of Harpers Ferry, of Fortress Monroe, of Fort Calhoun and of the Gosport Navy Yard; and our harbors will be blockaded. In what manner will we obtain supplies? . . . Tennessee and North Carolina may join us, but they, too, are without arms. Maryland cannot join us; the government will occupy her territory and take military possession of her strongholds . . . or [must] abandon the city of Washington. Kentucky and Missouri may not choose to join us. . . .

With suitable preparation for the conflict, I cannot doubt that all the Border States will act together, and that much of that division which now distracts their people will disappear; but if the conflict be precipitated in advance of preparation, no one can foresee the disaster . . . which . . . may result. We want friends and we want allies. We want to make friends and allies of the people of these Border States. Let us, then, consult with them, and concert the plan of action. . . .

Those most opposed to . . . secession . . . are content to abide by the determination of all the border States in council. If these States together declare for secession, they and their constituents will acquiesce, and they will vote now for such consultation. Why may not all agree to convoke these States in council? The time required cannot be long, and it need not be lost. We can improve the time by purchasing . . . arms and munitions that we . . . need. In this way we may obtain union at home, we may satisfy those who otherwise would be dissatisfied, and move . . . more surely and safely . . . [toward] the most ardent secessionist. . . . I think it a straight road to secession, and I am frank to avow it. . . . I cannot believe that intelligent and patriotic representatives of the border slave States would . . . subordinate the great interests of their section to the overbearing dominant majority of the North. . . .

Between the two policies, the Convention is divided—some are for instant secession and the adoption of an ordinance, others are opposed to secession, but will acquiesce in the determination of a border State Conference. Now our action in the premises is not to be final. . . . [An] ordinance of secession . . . must be submitted to the ratification of the popular vote. . . .

It would be just as well, therefore, to submit . . . both policies to the people. . . . Those who prefer the policy of immediate secession can vote [that] . . . instruction to the Convention, while those who prefer the policy of consultation and concert of action with the other border States can vote [that] . . . instruction. . . . In no way can anything be lost . . . to the cause of secession. . . .

Mr. RANDOLPH: . . . The gentleman declares that he is in favor of secession; and how does he propose to get out? By seceding? No; but by getting the States, that everybody knows will not secede, to join with Virginia in a consultation which is destined to end in nothing but mischief, by delaying action and allowing the enemy an opportunity of fastening his fangs tighter upon us. The gentleman tells us to defer secession until Maryland, North Carolina, Tennessee and Kentucky tell us that they are ready to go out, and all this time we are getting weaker—in my judgment weaker, morally and physically, in the eyes of all honorable men—weaker in the eyes of our own citizens. Unless you go out forthwith, you will have to contribute your blood and treasure to subjugate the Confederate States. If we have to fight, let us fight in behalf of Southern rights, and not to sustain the enemies of our section.

In my humble judgment, the Ordinance of Secession, so far from being a war measure, is the most pacific course that could be adopted. The enemy is coming down upon us with his entire force, and, in my opinion, no man ever yet escaped danger by turning his back upon it. Face it like a man. Call your sons to the field, give them the best arms you have got, and put your trust in your cause and in the God of battles.

I do not pretend to say that secession will save your liberties and existence; but if you do fail, you leave a page in history that your descendants need not be ashamed of. My humble belief is, that a bold, manly, decided course will operate a moral influence upon the North that will bring them to a stand until mediation comes between. But if we give way, the storm will burst upon us and destroy us.

Sir, when General [Winfield] Scott arrives here to morrow to offer you his counsel and his sword, are you to tell him to go back and wait until we consult the border States?[5] . . . Are you going to tell him that his services are not needed; that you are not ready to fight; to go back and wait till you send for him? I, for one, never will vote for any such proposition. If I stand alone, I mean to record my vote, this night I hope, for immediate secession; and I mean to follow it up with a resolution, calling upon the Governor of this Commonwealth to organize the whole military force of the State, in order to repel invasion, defend our soil, and maintain our honor, until assistance can come from some other quarter.

5. In reality, fellow Virginians could never convince Winfield Scott, hero of the Mexican War and general in chief of the U.S. Army, to join Robert E. Lee in commanding Confederate rather than Union troops.

Waitman Willey's and Jubal Early's Alarm *Waitman Willey led western Virginians' movement behind Robert Scott's alternative to secession. Eloquence such as Willey's helped slow eastern Unionists' desertion from the cause, as Jubal Early demonstrated.*

Mr. WILLEY: . . . I had, sometimes, in the indulgence of a patriotic hope, wished that I could have lived a century hence, to see the advancement of our civilization. . . . Instead, . . . I live to see . . . the commencement of our disintegration and down fall. I have lived to see the hour when the proud flag, under which we have lived in safety and honor for nearly a century, and which waved victoriously over many a battle field, is to be trailed in the dust, and I have lived to see the hour when Virginia, who gave the first impulse to the . . . revolution, is about to put her foot on that flag, on the very soil that gave it glorious birth.

Sir, I . . . protest against this measure, in the name of my constituents; in the name of the people of Virginia; in the name of liberty, and in the name of God. . . . You . . . ordain this day that my constituents and the people of North-western Virginia should be delivered over to death and destruction. . . .

I have a wife and children; I represent a constituency that have wives and children; I represent an old, patriotic father, born amid the thunders of the Revolution, whom I went out of my way to see as I came down here, with the frosts of ninety-five winters gathered upon his revered head; and the last words he told me when he gave me his blessings were: "My son, save this Union, or never let my eyes rest upon you again."

You cannot . . . more effectually dissever the people of Virginia lying along our North western border from those on the other side of the line, than will this ordinance of secession. These 450 miles of border State line will interpose a barrier between fathers and sons, fathers-in-law and sons-in-law, that no effort of ours can overcome.

Mr. WISE: You will all associate as before; there will be nothing to prevent it.

Mr. WILLEY: No, sir. Secession is war, and the man on this side of the line that does not rally to the call of his State, is a traitor; and if I meet a man from the other side of the line with weapon in hand, and fail to shoot him, in disregard of the order of a superior officer, I will be hung as a traitor. . . .

Why can't we wait until we consult with our border sister States? We will not have to wait much longer than . . . for the ratification of your ordinance. . . . If this ordinance of secession goes out naked and alone, it will either be voted down by the people, or it will . . . divide this State; it will destroy the loyalty of the best friends that ever your slaveholders had; it will destroy the sons of sires who shed their blood in your defence. . . . I protest against this hasty measure. . . .

Mr. EARLY: . . . [All] day, . . . I have felt as if a great crime was about being perpetrated against the cause of liberty and civilization. During . . . this Convention, we have frequently referred to the example of our fathers in the Revolution. They took no precipitate course of action. They protested and remonstrated for years . . . before they decided upon the final act of separation from the British Government. The State of Virginia herself never adopted the Declaration of Independence until after our armies had been in the field for twelve months. . . .

Sir, I see no reason why we should act more precipitately than those men. . . . What must be the result, the inevitable result of this proceeding? War, sir—such a war as this country has never seen, or, until recently, has never dreamed of. I should like to know, if we are engaged in war, what are the means of transportation of arms from this portion of the State to North-western Virginia? How will men and arms come from North-Western Virginia to this portion of the Commonwealth? . . . A gentleman on this floor has told you that North-western Virginia is almost entirely destitute of arms. It may be necessary to send them; it may be necessary for us to call upon them for men to defend us in the West, and how can we do so with propriety without furnishing them the means of defence?

Am I going by my vote to place the country in such a position as this? I certainly am not. . . . I cannot forget that the whole State of Virginia is my country. . . . There is not a portion of the State, from the Eastern Shore to the Pan Handle, that is not dear to me. I cannot, by my vote, adopt . . . the evils which I believe secession and war in its footsteps will bring upon the Western and North-western parts of this State. I trust, therefore it may not be the decision of this Convention to hurry us into a vote upon this question this evening.

Samuel Staples versus John Baldwin   *Despite Early's and Willey's efforts to salvage the Unionists' lately dominant coalition, Lincoln's proclamation had shocked too many delegates away from moderation.*

Samuel G. Staples, representing Patrick County in the southwestern Piedmont (22.1 percent enslaved), explained the reason for the fateful shift of opinion.

With some three dozen formerly cautious antisecessionists repudiating caution, the convention had a new majority and a new pace. Where the old Unionist majority had savored delay, the new secessionist majority would not tolerate dawdling. Now, almost all secessionists shunned debate, they limited each debater to ten minutes, and they clamored to put the question. As secession seemed likely this very night, John Baldwin issued yet another anguished protest.

Mr. STAPLES: . . . The gentleman from Montgomery [Mr. PRESTON] has proposed that . . . secession be adopted by the Convention and submitted to the people for ratification or rejection. To this proposition the gentleman from Fauquier [Mr. SCOTT] offers an amendment, . . . to submit to the . . . people the [choice] . . . of secession or a conference of the border slave States. I shall vote against the proposition of the gentleman from Fauquier, because I can see no good result to be obtained by a border slave State conference. . . . Virginia . . . alone must be the arbiter of her own destiny. Besides, Mr. President, the rapidly shifting scenes of the day admonish us of the imperious necessity for instant action. . . .

Ten days ago, I was known as a Union man—attached to the Union . . . by . . . hallowed memories . . . and by . . . glorious hopes. . . . I was elected under a pledge to resort to all honorable, constitutional means to preserve it in its integrity and purity just as our fathers formed it. It was formed by them . . . in the defence of the great principle of self-government, . . . "that to secure these rights governments are instituted among men, deriving their just powers from the consent of the governed; that whenever any form of government becomes destructive of these ends, it is the right of the people to alter or abolish it and to institute new government, laying its foundations on such principles, and organizing its power in such form as to them shall seem most likely to effect their safety and happiness."

In support of these time-honored principles, in defence of which the revolutionary patriots poured out their blood like water, . . . I cordially endorsed the reasons that impelled the seceded States to dissolve their connection with the Federal Government; yet, I doubted the propriety of their course. . . . Sound policy dictated a united movement . . . of all the Southern States, in order to procure from the Northern people an acknowledgement of our absolute equality in this government and of all the rights guaranteed to us by the Constitution. At the same time I declared my unalterable opposition to any attempt . . . of the Federal Government to coerce any of the seceded States back into the Union as in direct violation of the fundamental principles of the government and as in conflict with the acknowledged right of every people to regulate their own institutions in their own way. . . . Actuated by these patriotic motives, the Union party voted for and adopted the following resolution:

> The people of Virginia will await any reasonable time to obtain answers from the other States to these propositions, aware of the embarrassments that may produce delay; but they will expect, as an indispensable condition, that a pacific policy should be adopted towards the seceded States, and that no attempt be made to subject them to the Federal authority, nor to reinforce the forts now in possession of the United States, nor recapture the arsenals or other property of the United States within their limits, nor to exact the payment of imports upon their commerce, nor any measure resorted to, justly calculated to provoke hostile collision.

All we asked of the Federal authorities at Washington was, a pacific, a conciliatory policy. . . . We could not consent that the Federal power, which was in part our power, should be exerted for the purpose of subjugating the people of any of the States to the Federal authority. . . . Virginia had a right to demand this, and nothing less. . . . Her people never did and never will consent to the . . . power of the General Government to coerce any seceded States back into the Union. . . . It is, Mr. President, this principle, held sacred in the bosom of all true Virginians, that has aroused the people of Virginia to arms, to resist the usurpation of Abraham Lincoln and the dangerous doctrines contained in his proclamation of war against the seceded States. . . .

The people of Virginia could never consent to take part in a contest against their Southern brethren, who had done nothing more than change their form of government to suit themselves. The question is now narrowed down to this: Shall Virginia unite her fortunes with the Northern . . . war of subjugation and conquest? . . . We are now called upon to make a choice of our destiny—to bow our proud necks to the yoke of the tyrant, or rise up as one man, and burst the manacles that bind us. . . . I shall cheerfully vote for and subscribe my name to this ordinance of secession, regarding it as the proudest act of my life; one . . . by which the liberties under which we were born will be . . . transmitted unimpaired to our posterity; and the heritage of our children will be one of honor, and not of shame—of freedom, and not of slavery.

Mr. BALDWIN: . . . I am surprised and disturbed to see the course pursued here upon this floor by men who, like myself, were elected as Union men, representing Union constituencies, and men who have, from the commencement of the session of this body, concurred with me in opinion and co-operated with me in action. . . . They have a perfect right to change their views; and I would be the last man to question the sincerity of the change, or the patriotism of the motives. . . .

But . . . I do complain . . . that these gentlemen . . . have . . . changed their views and policy without conference . . . with those who have concurred with them. . . . [They also] prevent me and all the rest of their [former] associates . . . from having any opportunity whatever to debate this now most important . . . business. . . . These gentlemen, . . . [having] thought with me all the time that the true plan was, that of a Border Conference and co-operation with the slave States yet remaining in the Union, . . . refuse even to . . . [submit] this policy for the approval of the people. . . . They should either allow us an opportunity of fair and open debate in regard to this matter, or allow us the opportunity of appealing to the people, who sent them here as Union men and co-operationists, to determine which is the true policy, the one that they have matured up to within a day or two past, or the one with which they have recently become enamored. . . .

[As] soon as gentlemen who have been cautious, deliberate, prudent in counsel and action consent to go for secession, they seem to . . . become the most rabid of all, sir. There seems to be something in the hour; there seems to be something in the fever with which our people have been seized; there seems to be something in the excitement which pervades the community, . . . hopeless . . . to . . . stop or check, . . . [promising] nothing but calamity. . . .

Sir, if I had the time, I think I could show that the scheme of co-operation . . . is the only . . . hope . . . of avoiding instant and overwhelming . . . civil war, the only hope . . . of escaping from utter and irretrievable destruction. . . . But, sir, it seems that we are to be pressed to a vote upon this proposition to-night. . . . In view of the responsibility that I owe to God and man, I cannot concur. . . .

25

The Convention's Secession
Ordinance Adopted,
April 17

Alpheus Haymond's Plea   *On the evening of April 16, John
Baldwin managed a last pause. His still-Unionist colleagues barely passed
an adjournment motion, 76-66.*

*The next day, secessionists ended delay. With westerners now the only
speakers, protests against eastern secessionists dominated the secret
session. Alpheus F. Haymond, representing Marion County (0.5 percent
enslaved), brought the west's futile oratory to a climax.*

. . . I have never been a disunionist. I have been in favor of perpetuat-
ing forever, if possible, the Constitution and our Union. . . . I had engaged
in this body, with my whole heart and my whole soul, . . . to bring about
a restoration of the country to a condition of peace, harmony and mutual
good will. . . . This hope, I regret to say, was not fulfilled, and the terrible
consequence, it appears, is now upon us. . . .

In the North-western portion of Virginia, from which I come, dissatisfaction will be produced by the passage of this ordinance, because of
their isolated and defenceless condition—the result of the policy pursued
towards that section by past legislation. While the bounty of the Commonwealth has been poured out upon every other section of the State,
that section has been neglected; and, sir, so much so that we have not
the means of communication with your city, or the commercial ports of
Virginia. We cannot get to this capitol without coming through the State
of Maryland, having no other means of travel to this point than the Baltimore and Ohio rail road. My people have no trade whatever with any
other point except the cities of Pittsburgh and of Baltimore, and in that

From Reese, *Proceedings* 4:77–80, 106–8, 116–18, 124–27.

state of things, I apprehend that, with the disruption of interests which will follow the act of secession, deep and bitter dissatisfaction will prevail among them upon the consummation of this act of dissolution.

Now, sir, I have been in favor of a Border State Conference. Why, sir? Because if Virginia moved and Maryland would not, the mountains and hills which, until within the last few years, have shut us out from the world, would again encircle us, and the only outlet which we have had would be effectually blocked up. We would be shut out from every market, and our condition would be no better than was that of the primitive settlers of that vast North-western region. . . . Universal bankruptcy will spread all over my country. . . . Not the least of the evils . . . will be, as I very much apprehend, the manumission of every slave in our midst by the enemy.

I am a Virginian in every aspiration, and feeling, and sentiment. I stood by you at all times in defending your rights. I would like to do so now. I would like to see a united Virginia, and to that end I should have been pleased to see you pay some attention to our interests; for it is only in that way that you can reconcile our people to the sufferings and disadvantages to be entailed by dissolution. Why not now adopt some measure upon which we can all unite? Will you save us by adopting the border State Conference proposition, or hand us over to a heartless enemy by passing the ordinance of secession? . . .

John Hughes's Conversion   *At this final presecession moment, only one Trans-Allegheny speaker sought disunion. John N. Hughes, representing Randolph and Tucker counties (together 3.2 percent enslaved), explained one last time why Lincoln's proclamation had shattered the Unionist coalition.*

. . . Heretofore, I have co-operated with the Union party on this floor. I have had an earnest, abiding faith that all our difficulties might be amicably settled, and that peace and quiet might once more reign throughout the borders of this noble old Commonwealth. I have clung to the last broken plank of our once noble ship of State, until it has sunk beneath me; and I have now but one remedy left. . . .

An emergency has arisen which compels . . . prompt, immediate, decisive action. . . . I am opposed to making any more propositions to a tyrannical and overbearing foe that desires to make slaves of me and you. . . . I can submit no longer. . . .

Look, if you please, at the action of the last Black Republican Congress, sixty-seven members of which signed a recommendation in favor of the notorious Helper book, which advised our slaves to rise up and cut our throats.[1] . . . [Look too] at a proposition introduced into the Congress of the United States that the Black Republican party must not interfere with slavery in the States; and what do you find in the teeth of this movement? I blush to state the fact—that almost 100 Black Republicans in that Congress voted against that proposition, . . . [in] effect . . . declaring war upon slavery in Virginia and the South. . . .

Notwithstanding all this, I was willing still to compromise, still to adjust our difficulties, still to meet them in a spirit of brotherly love. . . . [Yet] while we showed to Abraham Lincoln that there was a majority of this Convention who were determined to preserve this Union; while we were engaged in this good work of seeking to effect an adjustment, Lincoln . . . adds insult to injury; he makes a requisition upon Gov. Letcher for Virginia's quota of troops to make war upon the Southern States. When that is the case, after having done all that, as an honorable man, I think I can do . . . to adjust these difficulties—I feel compelled to give my vote in favor of action—decisive and immediate action. . . . [A] declaration of war upon our people . . . [compels a] vote in favor of the Ordinance of Secession.

Chapman Stuart's Warning   *As the convention's vote on secession approached, Chapman Stuart explained one last time why a secessionist military strike before the voters' verdict on the convention's decision might help provoke a western rebellion.*

. . . [Gentlemen ask], were we Western Virginians and not Virginians! Let me say to that gentleman that I am a Virginian. My great ancestor

1. Hughes here refers to the Republican congressmen who endorsed Hinton R. Helper's *The Impending Crisis in the South: How to Meet It* (New York, 1857). Helper, a North Carolina racist nonslaveholder, intended to arouse slaveless whites, not enslaved blacks, against the slaveholders. But whatever his intention, angry Southern politicians called his antislavery appeal an incendiary menace to racial peace. They would not allow an endorser of *The Impending Crisis* to become Speaker of the national House of Representatives. Their intransigence led to the two-month-long Speakership crisis in late 1859–early 1860. The same apprehension about Southern antislavery agitators, if supported by Northern Republicans, provoked the secessionists' concern, evident in some speeches above, that President Lincoln would use federal patronage to build a Helper-like Southern Republican Party.

sought refuge in Virginia from foreign bondage and oppression. My grand ancestor fought through the Revolutionary war as a Virginian. My father fought through the war of 1812, and I, Mr. President, stand here to day a Virginian—a direct lineal descendant from revolutionary stock—ready and willing to live or die for my country. . . . I am not willing to perjure myself and commit treason against my Government until that Government has been perverted to my oppression and injury. Not until I and my people are enabled to justify ourselves in the sight of God and man for such a fearful act, are we prepared to do this thing.

I am now called upon to pass upon a question of more vital importance to the people of Virginia than . . . ever . . . before . . . during her existence as a sovereign State; and that, too, with closed doors and with indecent haste. Why this unusual haste to press this question on the Convention? The ordinance of secession offered for adoption proposes to submit the action of this body to the people for ratification some forty days hence. An ordinance of secession cannot be effective until ratified by the people. Then, what possible harm could result to this Convention or the people, if one or two days should be consumed in discussing the two propositions now before this body? We have consumed months in debating abstractions which were of no earthly importance; and now . . . a question that . . . involves life and death and all the material interest of this Commonwealth . . . is to be pressed through under an unusual excitement. Little does it become the dignity of Virginia statesmen.

The people will demand, and have a right to know, the reasons that influenced the actions of their representatives. We hear some of our brother members say they desire to be heard before this House. Let me say to them, if their voice is to be silenced here, that this is not the only tribunal. There is another last and final appeal to be made before those of whom we are their servants. There, if not here, we will be heard.

I see one object the friends of the ordinance of secession have in view, in pressing it to so hasty an issue. . . . The property within the limits of Virginia, belonging to the Federal Government, is to be seized. Hostile collision is to be induced by that act between the people of Virginia and the General Government. War is to be inaugurated here, without consulting the people. . . .

Our mission here . . . was to deliberate and consult together . . . and to submit our action to the people for their adoption or rejection. What matters an Ordinance of Secession after we have brought upon our people open war with the General Government—the very thing we were sent here to prevent? Peace was our mission. The people reserved to themselves the right to say whether we should have war or peace. They reserved to themselves the right to pass upon every act of ours looking to a change of our federal relations. . . . [Does not their reserved right cover] the seizing and wresting from the possession of the federal government the property in our limits, changing our relations with that government; and that, too, in the face of the avowed declaration of the President that he would hold the public property, peaceably, if he could, forcibly, if he must? Will not the members of this Convention hesitate before they recommend such a course? If you will not, let me warn you, that your unwanted usurpation of power will arouse a spirit of resistance in Virginia, that you are not now prepared to realize. . . .

Henry Wise's Strike and John Baldwin's Outrage *Shortly after Chapman Stuart's warning, the convention cleared the way for William Ballard Preston's secession ordinance by rejecting Robert Scott's proposed substitute, 77-64. Less than two weeks earlier, the convention had rejected secession, 88-45. The Unionists' victorious April 4 coalition could have lost twenty-one supporters and still secured Scott's substitute on April 17. Instead, twenty-six delegates switched sides.*

Shortly after this rather close Unionist defeat, Henry Wise ascended to the podium. He placed his huge horse pistol before him. He waved his large pocket watch at the delayers. Then he announced that at this hour Virginia troops were marching toward the two key federal military installations in Virginia, Harpers Ferry Arsenal and Norfolk's Gosport Navy Yard.

No matter that the convention had not yet voted for a secession ordinance. No matter that the Virginia voters had not yet approved any convention ordinance. No matter that Wise's term as governor had recently ended. The private citizen with the horse pistol had organized the twin ambushes, would help dragoon the sitting governor into approving the fait accompli, and had ordered the troops forward, in the name of the people's supposed necessity to stop federal armaments from being removed.[2]

Meanwhile, the Spontaneous People's Convention's extralegal delegates

2. Harold R. Woodward Jr., *Defender of the Faith: Brigadier General John Daniel Imboden, CSA* (Berryville, VA, 1996), 23–24.

paraded in the streets. The demonstrators threatened to lynch softhearts who blocked Wise's extralegal path. Their prey, the legally elected convention delegates, had moved nine days earlier to the State Capitol, designed by Thomas Jefferson. Inside and outside that monument to republican balance, the unbalanced atmosphere highlighted the question that John Jackson hurled at William Ballard Preston. Would the destruction of Jefferson's Union proceed with a republican legitimacy that opponents must accept?

Inside Jefferson's architectural masterwork the convention reporter recorded only a bare outline of Wise's ragged tirade. Left out was the former governor's veiled confession that he led the plot. Still, enough was recorded to explain why John Baldwin, thinking he heard the true origin of an imminent preemptive military strike, immediately protested against the apparent suspension of the people's right to decide between Union and secession, and between war and peace, before state troops rendered popular decision superfluous.

Mr. Wise: I know the fact, as well as I can know it without being present at either the time or place. . . . There is a probability that blood will be flowing at Harpers Ferry before night. I know the fact that the harbor of Norfolk has been obstructed last night by the sinking of vessels. I know the fact that at this moment a force is on its way to Harpers Ferry to prevent the reinforcement of the Federal troops at that point. I am told it is already being reinforced by 1,000 men from the Black Republican ranks. I know the fact that your Governor has ordered reinforcements there to back our own citizens and to protect our lives and our arms. In the midst of a scene like this, when an attempt is made by our troops to capture the navy yard, and seize the armory at Harpers Ferry, we are here indulging in foolish debates, the only result of which must be delay, and, perhaps ruin. . . .

Mr. Baldwin: Sir, the gentleman from Princess Anne [Mr. Wise] says that we are already in the midst of war. The Governor of this State at his instance and the instance of others, has already directed assaults to be made upon Harpers Ferry and Gosport Navy Yard.

Mr. Wise: I did not say that.

Mr. Baldwin: I understood him to say that the Governor, at his instance, had directed steps to be taken with a view of taking Harpers Ferry and Gosport Navy Yard. If that is the case, I feel it to be my duty to tell my people not to march under an order that the Governor had no right to give.

Mr. WISE: I will state to the gentleman that . . . to protect his people from being cut to pieces by the Wide Awakes[3]—his people . . . have marched to Harpers Ferry, I hope in time to prevent the Wide-Awakes from getting the 20,000 arms at that place. . . . It is now too late to recall these people, if the gentleman could, and I hope he never would recall them, if he could. The Augusta [Baldwin's county] troop are acting nobly in this matter, and I only wish my people had the honor of taking that stronghold.

Mr. BALDWIN: I have no doubt that my people will be found ready, at all times and under all circumstances, to uphold the honor of their country. . . . But, sir, I am speaking here as the representative of the people in a constitutional government, in regard to an act which the people themselves, by a majority of 60,000, directed should not be consummated without their voice at the polls; and I say that to consummate this act in defiance of the solemn action of the sovereign people of Virginia, I care not how patriotic the impulse, . . . is in derogation of the sovereign rights of the people of Virginia, who have appointed to settle it at the polls. . . .

3. These especially antislavery Republicans, "wide awake" to slavery's moral blight, were apt to take their message to the streets in mass meetings and parades.

26

The Climactic Wise-Baldwin Debate, April 17

Within the hour the convention voted 88-55 for William Ballard Preston's secession ordinance, to take effect when the people endorsed it on May 23. Eleven more Unionists broke from that lately dominant coalition after Robert Scott lost the pivotal test vote.

The ensuing convention debate would have been anticlimactic except for its oratorical brilliance, its relevance to western Virginia's still unmade critical decision, and its illumination of a timeless democratic puzzle, never more pressing than in the early twenty-first century. The forensic masterpiece has escaped the attention of almost all previous writers[1] (including, alas, these editors). But when Henry Wise and John Baldwin explored the dilemma of military necessity versus constitutional necessities, their confrontation elevated the convention's verbal clashes to a historic importance.

Mr. BALDWIN: I do not wish . . . for one moment to obstruct . . . [this body's] business. . . . But I do desire . . . to draw the attention of this Convention to great and high considerations affecting the scope of our power. . . . I do . . . appeal to the House . . . to allow . . . fair debate . . . as to whether we are a body limited by the Constitution of the State and the act of Assembly under which we organized; or whether, . . . these being revolutionary times, we are invested with all manner of power. . . .

Mr. WISE: . . . This Convention is authorized to change the whole Constitution of the State. . . .

Mr. BALDWIN: Not without the sanction of the people. . . . The people themselves in calling the Convention together, stated . . . [our] limitations. . . .

Mr. WISE: . . . Suppose that they have required us to submit all questions back to them, is there any man here, when the car of war is rushing

From Reese, *Proceedings* 4:158–62, 171–78.

1. For the most discerning of the scarce exceptions, see Crofts, *Reluctant Confederates,* 321–22.

over the people themselves, crushing them like the car of Juggernaut under its wheels; when the whole frontier West, North and East; when the edge of every bay and estuary in the bay is endangered by invasion; whilst your steamers are seized in New York; whilst your people have risen up and sunk hulks in the channel at Norfolk—will you tell me, sir, whether the *salus populi*[2] does not require us to take the responsibility of doing *ad interim*[3] whatever we can do for their defence . . . between now and the election in May? . . . Sir, the safety of the people for every law, moral, divine, political or popular, justifies the overriding for a time at least of acts and statutes and even the Constitution itself.

Mr. BALDWIN: Not under our system.

Mr. WISE: Under our system . . . civil war attacks the safety of all; attacks the very vitals of the State, the happiness of the people, and destroys the very ends which the Constitution itself was established for. Now, to tell me that this Convention is bound, before it can do anything to . . . defend the people, . . . before it can prevent this navy yard from being taken with all its immense stores, shipping and ordnance; before it can take steps to capture the forts which are held by the Federal Government, and all the arms which are lying on our territory, among a people destitute of arms; to tell me that before all this is done we must await the sanction of the people . . . is to present to me an argument too conservative for any man to recognize in a crisis such as . . . is now upon us.

My friend from Augusta [Mr. BALDWIN] I have no doubt is conservative. As a general thing, in peaceful times, in ordinary exigencies—even extraordinary exigencies—his principle is undoubtedly a safe conservative principle. The question now is, when invasion is upon us, whether we dare stop to await the vote of the people upon an action which the *salus populi* imperatively demands at our hands with the least possible delay? Such a policy would be disastrous. . . .

Mr. BALDWIN: . . . The gentleman from Princess Anne [Mr. WISE] informs us that *salus populi* is a sort of higher law known in free government. I deny it. I deny that we have any higher law under our system of government than the Constitution. . . . I deny that there can be any *salus populi* in . . . violation of fundamental constitutional principles. The gentleman seems to think that we are in revolutionary times now, and that,

2. Welfare of the people.
3. In the meantime.

therefore, the great principles of free government are all to be forgotten. It seems to me if ever there was a time when it was necessary for us to appeal to the great cardinal principles of constitutional power, it is in a time like this. The fact that this is war time, is offered as an apology for a violation of the Constitution; but if we once adopt the principle of the *salus populi suprema lex,*[4] there is no knowing what we may practice in the name of this *salus populi.* In the various revolutions recorded in history, we know what was practiced under the euphonious name of liberty. It is the beauty of our government that all the functions of government are limited by constitutional restrictions. . . .

An intimation from this body, that it felt itself free from the . . . obligations . . . to refer back its action to the people, would raise a revolution among our own people. . . . They would instantly check so gross an assumption of unyielded power, and rise in their majesty and turn this body out of doors, if necessary, at the point of the bayonet. . . .

This Convention, like the people themselves, are under obligations to observe the Constitution of the State until it is lawfully changed. . . . It cannot be lawfully changed until it is submitted to the people and ratified by them. It is under these guarantees that the people consented to organize this Convention.

I imagine, if the people felt that they were calling a Convention to change the Constitution, without reference to their subsequent sanction and approval, they would never have constituted such a body under Heaven. They constituted this body, believing that it was . . . under the restraint of the Constitution of the State, . . . [and that] they had prohibited it from changing the fundamental law of the State, except by a vote of the people. . . .

Mr. WISE: . . . If the argument of the gentleman and his principle be correct, you can do nothing whatever, until after the election in May. . . . Are we to stand still—we, the conservators of the people—and do nothing between now and May? . . . If the invaders come down upon us, you are certain to have no election. If the invading army is to cross the line, West, North, and East, by sea and by land, where and how is the election to be held? Invasion can and will suspend the constitutional power, in the elective power of the State, from doing anything.

Take the other horn of the dilemma. Let the people say, we have se-

---

4. The welfare of the people is the supreme law.

ceded; our Convention has advised us to secede. In order to defend ourselves, in case we elect to secede, we will take the arms necessary to defend ourselves—we will take the forts that now threaten our lives and liberties; we will take the Navy-yard, that holds all the ship timber, the best in the United States. If we will take that Navy-yard now, we will have plenty of arms and ammunition. If we do not take it, when we vote to secede, we will have no ships, no muskets, no ordinance, no powder. Yes, sir, there lies 3,000 barrels of powder,[5] and the gentleman's argument is that you can do nothing in self-defence; but must permit the enemy to invade us without raising a hand in resistance. The enemy has told you that he intended to invade if you dare to secede; and has told you . . . that he intended to re-possess all the forts and arsenals, as if in utter contempt of the declared purpose of Virginia to resist any such attempt. The amount of the gentleman's argument is, that we are to do nothing; that we are to let the powder go, the navy-yard go, all the arms at Harpers Ferry go, the Thermopylæ[6] of the State go; and all this because of a mere stickling upon a point between tweedledum and tweedledee. . . .

I believe that you cannot have an election next month. My opinion is, that so many of the counties will be engaged in preparations for war, and so many absent in the camp, that . . . no election . . . will exhibit the true state of feelings. . . . I say, then, our policy is to seize at once upon the arms and ammunitions . . . within our reach. This doctrine of adherence to technical constitutional requirements, suited to ordinary circumstances, will not do; for the people must look to their own defence. I have no fear but that the people will settle this thing for themselves. They will take this *salus populi* into their own hands. Election or no election they will take Harpers Ferry; they will take the Gosport Navy Yard; and if you do not give them an opportunity to do so now, they will take them when

5. Especially sharp-eyed readers will have noticed that where Henry Wise claimed that the Gosport Navy Yard harbored 3,000 barrels of federal gunpowder, George Wythe Randolph had alleged a day earlier that the yard contained 30,000 barrels (see above, p. 170). Wise, who lived nearer to Gosport, knew better. Major General William B. Taliaferro, who directed the state's seizure of Gosport, reported that 2,800 barrels of federal gunpowder had been captured. Taliaferro to Governor John Letcher, April 23, 1861, *Official Records of the Union and Confederate Navies in the War of Rebellion*, ser. 1, vol. 4 (Washington, DC, 1896), 306–9. Thanks to Nelson Lankford for this citation.

6. In ancient times Thermopylæ was a narrow mountain pass, only fifty feet across, that provided invaders' best path toward Athens. Just as Greek defenders massed at Thermopylæ against Persian invaders, so Wise wanted his Virginia militia units to mass at Harpers Ferry and Norfolk, against federal invaders.

the enterprise will involve imminent dangers, and it may be, a sacrifice which we cannot now contemplate.

Let the people have an opportunity to protect their homes. . . . The arms . . . to protect them . . . are now within their reach, and they ought to have them, so that when an election is fairly held they may be able to act efficiently in defence of their homes and their liberties. . . .

Mr. BALDWIN: . . . By what authority is war upon us? Who has declared war? Who has authorized it? The President of the United States, it is true, has threatened a war against the Confederate States, and a war in which I am perfectly disposed to make common cause with the Confederate States. But it is not yet our war until we adopt it. It is not a war threatened or declared against us; but against those States which had seceded before the President's proclamation was issued. . . . There was and is no military necessity in the way of an intended attack upon the State of Virginia, unless that military necessity has been created without authority or law.

I understood from the gentleman from Princess Anne [Mr. WISE], today that an unauthorized expedition has been instructed to seize upon the armory at Harpers Ferry. If that be true, and that act is ratified and adopted by the Governor of the State, those persons engaged in it are acting in violation of law and in violation of the rights of the people of this State; and the Governor, in ratifying and adopting this act, is acting in violation of the Constitution of the State . . . [and] the rights of the people. . . . If this Convention adopts that unauthorized act, . . . the people of this State . . . [cannot decide] a question which they have reserved for their own decision. . . .

Sir, what right have we, when the people have said, that our action shall go back before them, to bring about a state of things that would prevent them from having the right to pass upon it? . . . They say revolutions never go backwards, and if we start at the outset without regard to the proper limitations of power, cautious as we may hereafter be, I tell you we are in danger of emerging from this revolution anything but a free people. It may be that we will make this war at a disadvantage, as a people governed by constitutional law; it may be that constitutional law may be unfavorable to the success in the State; but I would rather go into a war with all the disadvantages resulting from constitutional power than to throw off the reserves . . . necessary for the safety of the people.

For one, I never can consent to leave the principle of constitutional law, of limited government and of representative responsibility and restraint, to launch out upon any principle so vague, so ominous of evil as the principle announced in the maxim of *salus populi*. In the name of my constituency; in the name of constitutional law; in the name of constitutional liberty; in the name of representative responsibility, I protest against this act.

27

The Clarks-
burg Call,
April 22

John Baldwin predicted that most of Virginia's citizens would resist Henry Wise's strike. Although wrong about most Virginians, Baldwin was right about most northwesterners. Angry nonslaveholders in locales with scarcely a slave found disunion even more intolerable because troops had preempted voters' sole right to withdraw consent to be governed. So said many of the northern Trans-Allegheny delegates as they rushed from the convention after the April 17 secession vote, determined to rally their constituents against everything that Wise's horse pistol epitomized.

Upon reaching home, John Carlile wrote the first document in the second Virginia revolution of the week. At a hastily called meeting in Clarksburg on April 22, more than a thousand western Virginians massed behind Carlile's so-called Clarksburg Call. This newest preliminary declaration of independence summoned like-minded folk to a convention in Wheeling on May 13 aimed at initiating western Virginians' withdrawal of consent to be governed by Virginia.

At a large and enthusiastic meeting of from 1,000 to 1,200 of the citizens of Harrison county, assembled at the [Clarksburg] Court House upon a notice of forty-eight hours, on Monday, April 22, 1861, the following preamble and resolutions were adopted without one dissenting voice.

PREAMBLE.

WHEREAS—The Convention now in session in this State . . . adopted an ordinance withdrawing Virginia from the Federal Union: and whereas, by the law calling said Convention, it is expressly declared that no such ordinance shall have force or effect, or be of binding obligation upon the people of this State, until the same shall be ratified by the voters at the polls: and whereas . . . the Federal Government . . . is Virginia's Govern-

The Clarksburg Call, originally published in the *Wheeling Intelligencer,* April 25, 1861, can be accessed at www.wvculture.org/history/statehood/clarksburgconvention.html.

ment, and must in law and of right continue so to be, until the people of Virginia shall, by their votes, and through the ballot-box, that great conservator of a free people's liberties, decide otherwise: and whereas, the peculiar situation of Northwestern Virginia, separated as it is by natural barriers from the rest of the State, precludes all hope of timely succor in the hour of danger from other portions of the State, and demands that we should look to and provide for our own safety in the fearful emergency in which we now find ourselves placed by the action of our State authorities, who have disregarded the great fundamental principle upon which our beautiful system of Government is based, to wit: "That all governmental power is derived from the consent of the governed," and have without consulting the people placed this State in hostility to the Government by seizing upon its ships and obstructing the channel at the mouth of Elizabeth river, by wresting from the Federal officers at Norfolk and Richmond the custom houses, by tearing from the Nation's property the Nation's flag, and putting in its place a bunting, the emblem of rebellion, and by marching upon the National Armory at Harpers Ferry; thus inaugurating a war without consulting those in whose name they profess to act; and whereas, the exposed condition of Northwestern Virginia requires that her people should be united in action, and unanimous in purpose—there being a perfect identity of interests in times of war as well as in peace—therefore, be it

Resolved, That it be and is hereby recommended to the people in each and all of the counties composing Northwestern Virginia to appoint delegates, not less than five in number, of their wisest, best, and discreetest men, to meet in Convention at Wheeling, on the 13th day of May next, to consult and determine upon such action as the people of Northwestern Virginia should take in the present fearful emergency. . . .

28

The Convention's Ad Valorem Taxation Ordinance Adopted, April 26

The Clarksburg Call put a new perspective on the old campaign for ad valorem taxation and its underlying demand: that slaveholders must not compromise white egalitarianism, to solidify the inequality of blacks. Henry Wise's military strike arguably had violated one element of white republicanism: the people's right to withdraw their consent to be governed, before the guns of war determined the matter. In compensation, secessionists could remove a previous violation of republican equality: the unequal taxation of slaveholders' and nonslaveholders' property. Then less-offended western yeomen might better accept the loss of the Union, in effect achieved before the required majority had voted to secede.

So reasoned the first secessionist speaker in this book, Jeremiah Morton, as he asked the convention on April 26 to approve yet another ordinance. Morton proposed that ad valorem taxation of all property, including and especially property in slaves, commence on July 1 if the Virginia voters approved this supplementary ordinance at their referendum on May 23. Benjamin Wilson, one of the western Virginia Unionists who had not fled home, added that the revolution brewing in his own town, Clarksburg, made Morton's ordinance mandatory. The convention agreed, 66–26.

Mr. Morton: . . . In a crisis like this, when we are threatened with invasion, when we ought to have every heart in the Commonwealth of Virginia beating in unison, we ought to . . . give satisfaction to every portion of the Commonwealth.

The question of taxation . . . was not mooted during the last canvass, at least among my people. I don't know what their opinions are, but I take the responsibility, as their representative, of giving my vote in favor of that [ad valorem taxation] ordinance. I am confident . . . that my action in this matter will not only meet with their approval, but their gratification.

It is unquestionably a fact, that we are in a state of war, and that our

From Reese, *Proceedings* 4:532–34, 538–39.

revenue must be increased. We shall have to tax all the property that has not been taxed, and bring the whole of it under its due share of taxation. . . . The operation of that ordinance will, probably, be heavier upon me than upon any of my constituents. . . . I have an undue portion [of slaves] under 12 years of age now free from taxation, and I will cheerfully submit to their being subject to tax like any other property. The principle, sir, is . . . just. . . . A slave under 12 years of age is . . . increasing in value every year, . . . probably beyond any other description of property in the Commonwealth. A colt that is but one year old is not fit for service, and yet it is a taxable piece of property; and upon the same principle should slaves under twelve years be made subject to taxation.

But, Mr. President, . . . [whatever] the principle involved, . . . I press this question now upon this ground: . . . It is unquestionably our interest that . . . every portion of the Commonwealth should be united. We have passed an ordinance of secession. We have gone, I may say, out of one Confederacy and into another. Our friends from the West who . . . [have not departed] have stood up and acted manfully with us. . . . I ask, then— I appeal to the Eastern men, after what has occurred—I appeal to them as one man to come up and graciously grant . . . this ordinance. . . .

How triumphantly will our friends from the West who have voted with us for the ordinance of secession . . . return to their constituents, if by their fidelity in remaining at their posts this ordinance should pass. Instead of being censured by their constituents, they will stand higher than ever, while those who have deserted their posts will be remembered only with scorn and infamy. . . .

Mr. WILSON: It is very desirable in this crisis that we should have unity of action. . . . To produce that unity, . . . I most anxiously hope that this Convention will now pass this ordinance. Every mail from the Northwest brings me accounts of more and more dissatisfaction. . . . A paper I hold in my hand . . . shows that a meeting was held the other day in the North-west, . . . [seeking] to throw off allegiance to Virginia. That proceeding was based upon the passage of the ordinance of secession and a refusal . . . to pass the ordinance in relation to the tax question. . . .

I heard to day that personal conflicts are expected in my county, and that an influential gentleman there was threatened with personal violence because of his advocacy of secession. I have heard it stated that threats of personal violence were made towards me. . . . I heard it said that the ladies of our town [Clarksburg] have to go armed, and when that is the case, we may easily imagine . . . the condition of things. . . . Every letter which I receive from home satisfies me of the great necessity of passing this ordinance. . . . [Otherwise, no] hope of harmony and unity can exist. I hope, therefore, that the East will concede this act of justice, and defeat the purposes of those who are seeking to make this question the basis of discord and division in the North-west.

29

Popular Decisions in May

The May 13 Wheeling Convention, resulting from the Clarksburg Call, decided to await Virginia voters' verdict on the convention's secession and ad valorem taxation ordinances. On May 23 Virginia citizens approved the taxation ordinance by a nine-to-one margin and the secession ordinance by a four-to-one margin, with western Virginians disapproving of disunion by almost two-to-one. Then in June a second Wheeling Convention began the process of northwestern Virginia's secession from Virginia, despite eastern Virginians' concession of ad valorem taxation and despite some Trans-Allegheny counties' opposition to West Virginia statehood.

Lincoln's April 15 military proclamation and Wise's April 17 announcement of an imminent preemptive strike thus dissolved not only the Virginia convention's indecision, Virginia's ties to the Union, and western Virginians' ties to Virginia but also Trans-Allegheny Virginians' ties to each other. The Virginia secession convention, called to avert a civil war, had given way to multiple civil wars among whites, along with intensifying tension between blacks and whites as the Civil War commenced.

Suggestions for Further Reading

Abrahamson, James L. *The Men of Secession and Civil War, 1859–1861.* Wilmington, DE, 2000.

Ayers, Edward L. *In the Presence of Mine Enemies: War in the Heart of America, 1861–1863.* New York, 2003.

Bowman, Shearer Davis. "Conditional Unionism and Slavery in Virginia, 1860–1861: The Case of Dr. Richard Eppes." *Virginia Magazine of Biography and History* 96 (1988): 31–54.

Carmichael, Peter S. *The Last Generation: Young Virginians in Peace, War, and Reunion.* Chapel Hill, NC, 2005.

Crofts, Daniel W. *Reluctant Confederates: Upper South Unionists in the Secession Crisis.* Chapel Hill, NC, 1989.

Curry, Richard Orr. *A House Divided: A Study of Statehood Politics and the Copperhead Movement in West Virginia.* Pittsburgh, 1964.

Freehling, Alison Goodyear. *Drift toward Dissolution: The Virginia Slavery Debates of 1832.* Baton Rouge, LA, 1982.

Freehling, William W. "The Editorial Revolution, Virginia, and the Coming of the Civil War: A Review Essay." Pp. 3–11 in William W. Freehling. *The Reintegration of American History: Slavery and the Civil War.* New York, 1994.

———. *The Road to Disunion.* 2 vols. New York, 1990–2007.

Freehling, William W., and Simpson, Craig M., eds. *Secession Debated: Georgia's Showdown in 1860.* New York, 1992.

Gaines, William H., Jr. *Biographical Register of Members [of the] Virginia State Convention of 1861 First Session.* Richmond, 1969.

Gunderson, Robert G. *Old Gentleman's Convention: The Washington Peace Conference of 1861.* Madison, WI, 1961.

Holt, Michael F. *The Political Crisis of the 1850s.* New York, 1978.

Kimball, Gregg D. *American City, American Place: A Cultural History of Richmond.* Athens, GA, 2000.

Lankford, Nelson D. *Cry Havoc: The Crooked Road to Civil War, 1861.* New York, 2007.

Link, William A. *Roots of Secession: Slavery and Politics in Antebellum Virginia*. Chapel Hill, NC, 2003.

McGregor, James. *The Disruption of Virginia*. New York, 1922.

McPherson, James. *Battle Cry of Freedom: The Era of the Civil War*. New York, 1988.

Potter, David M. *The Impending Crisis, 1848–1861*. New York, 1976.

———. *Lincoln and His Party in the Secession Crisis*. New Haven, CT, 1942. Paperback ed. with a useful introduction by Daniel W. Crofts. Baton Rouge, LA, 1995.

Shade, William G. *Democratizing the Old Dominion: Virginia and the Second Party System, 1824–1861*. Charlottesville, VA, 1996.

Shanks, Henry T. *The Secession Movement in Virginia, 1847–1861*. Richmond, 1934.

Simpson, Craig M. *A Good Southerner: The Life of Henry A. Wise of Virginia*. Chapel Hill, NC, 1985.

Stampp, Kenneth M. *And the War Came: The North and the Secession Crisis, 1860–1861*. Baton Rouge, LA, 1950.

Varon, Elizabeth R. *Disunion! The Coming of the American Civil War, 1789–1859*. Chapel Hill, NC, 2008.

———. *We Mean to Be Counted: White Women and Politics in Antebellum Virginia*. Chapel Hill, NC, 1998.

Walther, Eric H. *The Shattering of the Union: America in the 1850s*. Wilmington, DE, 2004.

Wolf, Eva Sheppard. *Race and Liberty in the New Nation: Emancipation in Virginia from the Revolution to Nat Turner's Rebellion*. Baton Rouge, LA, 2006.

Wooster, Ralph A. *The Secession Conventions of the South*. Princeton, NJ, 1962.

Wyatt-Brown, Bertram. *Southern Honor: Ethics and Behavior in the Old South*. New York, 1982.